MONEY FOR EV

Why we need a Citi

Malcolm Torry

First published in Great Britain in 2013 by

Policy Press
University of Bristol
6th Floor
Howard House
Queen's Avenue
Clifton
Bristol BS8 1SD
UK
t: +44 (0)117 331 4054
f: +44 (0)117 331 4093
tpp-info@bristol.ac.uk
www.policypress.co.uk

North America office:
Policy Press
c/o The University of Chicago Press
1427 East 60th Street
Chicago, IL 60637, USA
t: +1 773 702 7700
f: +1 773-702-9756
sales@press.uchicago.edu
www.press.uchicago.edu

© Policy Press 2013

British Library Cataloguing in Publication Data
A catalogue record for this book is available from the British Library

Library of Congress Cataloging-in-Publication Data
A catalog record for this book has been requested

ISBN 978 1 44731 125 6 paperback
ISBN 978 1 44731 124 9 hardcover

Cover design by Andrew Corbett
Front cover: image kindly supplied by www.alamy,com
Printed and bound in Great Britain by Hobbs, Southampton
Policy Press uses environmentally responsible print partners.

Contents

List of figures

Abbreviations

BI	Basic Income
BIEN	Basic Income European Network (now the Basic Income Earth Network)
BIRG	Basic Income Research Group
BSP	Basic State Pension
CASE	Centre for Analysis of Social Exclusion
CI	Citizen's Income
DWP	Department for Work and Pensions
HMRC	Her Majesty's Revenue and Customs
LSE	London School of Economics and Political Science
NHS	National Health Service
OECD	Organisation for Economic Co-operation and Development
PAYE	Pay As You Earn
SEWA	Self Employed Women's Association (India)
STP	Single-tier State Pension[1]

[1] This terminology, and this abbreviation, are employed in: Department for Work and Pensions, *The Single-tier State Pension: Part 1 of the draft Pensions Bill – Work and Pensions Committee*, 4 April 2013, www.publications.parliament.uk/pa/cm201213/cmselect/cmworpen/1000/100004.htm. The Draft Bill itself: Department for Work and Pensions, *Draft Pensions Bill*, Cm 8529, January 2013, uses the terminology 'state pension'. To distinguish the new single-tier pension from the current Basic State Pension, we shall here use the 'STP: Single-tier State Pension' terminology.

Structure of the book

We start with some notes on terminology and on graphs. Chapter 1 then sets the scene by asking you to imagine yourself trying to solve the financial crisis, to imagine some representative people trying to cope with our tax and benefits systems, and to imagine yourself creating tax and benefits systems in a country without them. Chapter 2 offers a historical sketch, because it is helpful to know where we have been before we set off into the future; Chapter 3 studies that history, and also some reform proposals never implemented, in order to work out why some proposals succeed and others fail; and Chapter 4 asks how a Citizen's Income might be implemented in practice. Chapter 5 studies existing Citizen's Income schemes and pilot projects. Chapter 6 lists criteria for an ideal benefits system, and that and subsequent chapters then evaluate both the current benefits system and a Citizen's Income against those criteria: coherence and administrative simplicity in Chapter 6, the changing family in Chapter 7, incentives, efficiency and dignity in Chapter 8, and the changing labour market in Chapter 9. Chapter 10 pursues the discussion begun in Chapter 9 by asking whether a Citizen's Income would make it more or less likely that working age adults would seek employment. Chapter 11 asks whether a Citizen's Income would be an answer to poverty, inequality and injustice; Chapter 12, who should receive a Citizen's Income; Chapter 13, whether a Citizen's Income would be politically feasible; and Chapter 14, whether we can afford a Citizen's Income. Chapter 15 studies some alternative reform proposals, Chapter 16 discusses some social policy problems to which a Citizen's Income would not be the answer, and Chapter 17 offers a brief summary of a Citizen's Income and its characteristics.

A note about the related website

One relatively unusual characteristic of this book is that material that might normally have been found in appendices can instead be found on the Citizen's Income Trust's website. This material is of two kinds: first, more detailed developments of arguments contained in outline in the book; and second, costings, simulations and other calculations, which can quickly go out of date and will therefore need to be regularly updated.

All of this material will be found at www.citizensincome.org

A note on terminology

Terminology can be quite specific to its context, so the same word might mean quite different things in different countries. I base the following discussion on English as spoken in the UK, and where appropriate I discuss variations.

Universal benefits I take 'universal benefits' to mean 'unconditional and non-withdrawable cash payments made to every individual citizen as a right of citizenship'. In the UK, Child Benefit is restricted to children up to the age of 16 (older if still in education or training), so it is not strictly universal, and it is paid at different rates to the first and to subsequent children, so it is not strictly unconditional, but otherwise it fits the definition because equal amounts are paid to every main carer of the same number of children regardless of those carers' incomes, employment status, household structure or any other factor. I call Child Benefit 'universal' because it is paid for every member of an age-defined demographic group without condition, and no change of circumstances can cause its withdrawal.

Citizen's Income and Basic Income By 'Citizen's Income' I mean a genuinely universal, unconditional, and non-withdrawable income paid to every individual citizen simply by virtue of their status as a citizen. (We come to the meaning of 'citizen' in Chapter 12.) Another name for 'Citizen's Income' is 'Basic Income'. In English as spoken in the UK the word 'basic' can have derogatory overtones, so I choose not to use it. Similar words in other Germanic languages do not carry such overtones, and the same word in non-UK English might not, so in some countries 'Basic Income' can be a useful alternative to 'Citizen's Income'. I stick to 'Citizen's Income'. It describes what the benefit is: it is for every citizen, unconditionally.

Guarantee Some authors incorporate the word 'guarantee' into the name, as in 'Basic Income Guarantee'. I avoid 'guarantee' language for two reasons:

- The previous Labour government established a 'Minimum Income Guarantee', later called a 'Guarantee Credit', for pensioners, a means-tested payment to bring their household income up to a prescribed level. This is as far from a universal benefit as it is possible to get.
- The academic literature uses the term 'minimum income guarantee' for a prescribed level of net income to which a household is raised

by a payment dependent on the level of earned income. For instance, James Meade formulated his Modified Social Dividend proposal in terms of a universal benefit (a 'Social Dividend') and an additional means-tested payment to bring an individual up to a 'minimum income guarantee'.[2] While the Social Dividend might be a Citizen's Income, the means-tested supplement certainly is not.

We need to take care over several other terms.

Allowance 'Child allowance', 'family allowance' or simply 'allowance' refers to payments made to an individual or household (in the case of child allowances, on behalf of the child to the main carer). 'Income Tax allowance' or 'tax allowance' refers to an amount of earned income on which tax is not charged, tax only being charged on income above the 'tax threshold'.

Tax Credit A Tax Credit is an amount of money ascribed to an individual, usually weekly. It is paid in full if an individual has no other income, and it is withdrawn at a specified rate as earned income rises. As earned income continues to rise, the Tax Credit ceases to be paid, and the worker starts to pay Income Tax. If the individual is working and receiving a Tax Credit rather than paying Income Tax then the employer manages the Tax Credit. The 'Tax Credits' implemented by the last UK Labour government are not Tax Credits: they are a means-tested benefit.[3] Until 2005, Working Tax Credits were paid through the employer-administered PAYE (pay as you earn) Income Tax system, but were calculated separately from Income Tax. It could not have been otherwise, because, in the UK, Income Tax is calculated in an individual basis, whereas for 'Tax Credits' the household is the claimant unit. Since 2005, all 'Tax Credits' have been paid into people's bank accounts. They are not in any way integrated with the payment of wages or Income Tax, and they are withdrawn if a spouse's earned income rises. Genuine Tax Credits are not withdrawn in this way. In order to distinguish between the two very different uses of the same term, I place quotation marks around 'Tax Credit' when the term is

---

[2]   Meade, J.E. (1978) *The structure and reform of direct taxation,* A report of a committee chaired by Professor J.E. Meade, London: George Allen & Unwin, for the Institute for Fiscal Studies, pp 269-79

[3]   Godwin, M. and Lawson, C. (2009) 'The Working Tax Credit and Child Tax Credit 2003-08: a critical analysis', *Journal of Poverty and Social Justice,* vol 17, no 1, pp 3-14, p 12

used with the meaning of 'means-tested benefit', and not when the term means a Tax Credit.

Marginal deduction rate An important term employed throughout the book is 'marginal deduction rate'. If someone already earning above the Income Tax threshold earns an extra £1 then they are not better off by £1. First of all, Income Tax and National Insurance Contributions will be deducted. If the household is on Housing Benefit, then the Housing Benefit will be reduced if earnings rise. If they are on 'Tax Credits' then those will be reduced because earnings have risen. Let us suppose that after all of these deductions the worker finds him or herself 30p better off. This means that 70p has been deducted, a marginal deduction rate of 70 per cent. It is a 'marginal' deduction rate because it relates to *additional* earnings. The marginal deduction rate is important because it affects incentives to earn additional income. If the marginal deduction rate is low – that is, if not much of one's additional earnings is lost through the tax and benefits systems – then it is more worthwhile to earn additional income than if the marginal deduction rate is high.[4]

'Contributory' or 'social insurance' benefits, and the very different 'means-tested' benefits Two kinds of social security benefit will be encountered quite frequently:

• 'Contributory benefits' or 'social insurance benefits' are paid to individuals on the basis of contributions records. In the UK, records of contributions deducted by employers and paid to Her Majesty's Revenue and Customs (HMRC) along with Income Tax payments, or paid direct to HMRC by the self-employed, entitle the worker to National Insurance benefits during periods of illness and unemployment and after retirement. While the contributions

---

4   Brewer, M., Dias, M.C. and Shaw, J. (2012) *A dynamic perspective on how the UK personal tax and benefit system affects work incentives and redistributes income*, IFS Briefing Note BN132, London: Institute for Fiscal Studies, p 7, uses the terms 'marginal effective tax rate' and 'participation tax rate'. The former describes the 'fraction of an incremental change to gross family earnings … lost by the family through increased tax liabilities and reduced benefit entitlements', and the latter the 'fraction of the change in gross family earnings caused by one individual moving into work … lost by the family in terms of increased tax liability and reduced benefit entitlements'. Both describe the same phenomenon (the loss of additional income due to tax being deducted and benefits withdrawn), and because of this, and because 'marginal effective tax rate' is less complete a description than 'marginal deduction rate', I prefer 'marginal deduction rate'.

record determines the amounts of benefit paid, there is no direct link between the amount of benefit paid and the contributions made. 'National Insurance' is therefore a misnomer, because a genuinely 'insurance' benefit would be based directly on premiums paid and on an insurer's risk calculation. 'Social insurance', the term used elsewhere in the world, would be a less inaccurate term. (In the UK, during periods of sickness or unemployment, and in some other situations, contribution records are 'credited' with contributions. This is why 'contribution/credit records' is a more accurate designation than simply 'contribution record'.)

- A 'means-tested' benefit is one calculated on the basis of means available, that is, as other income rises, the amount of benefit falls. Means-tested benefits are often 'tested' in other ways too. They might suffer from work tests, that is, they will only be paid out if someone is available for work, and sometimes only if they can prove that they are trying to obtain it. Means-tested benefits can also be subject to relationship tests. Governments often assume that it is cheaper for two people to live together than for both of them to live separately, so the benefit paid to a couple will be less than twice the benefit paid to an individual. Claimants therefore have to declare their household arrangements so that their means-tested benefits can be correctly calculated.

Universal Credit You should never take the name of a social security benefit at face value unless you have studied its regulations to find out whether the reality matches the name. In the UK, from 2013 onwards, in-work and out-of-work means-tested benefits (for instance, Jobseeker's Allowance, Income Support and 'Tax Credits') will be combined into 'Universal Credit'. Unfortunately, 'Universal Credit' will not be universal. It will be withdrawn as earned income rises, so for every set of household circumstances there will be an earnings level above which Universal Credit will not be received. I therefore treat the term in the same way as 'Tax Credit'. Where 'Universal Credit' means the UK government's new means-tested benefit, I add quotation marks. A Universal Credit without quotation marks would, of course, be a Citizen's Income, but we already have a perfectly good name for that. Perhaps we should not complain too much. 'National Insurance' benefits have never been properly insurance payouts because total benefits paid out have never borne anything other than an oblique relationship to the total of 'National Insurance Contributions' collected. 'Supplementary benefit' was rarely supplementary to anything. 'Universal Credit' not being universal, and 'Tax Credits' not being Tax Credits, thus conforms to a pattern. No doubt such misnaming has been well intentioned: to reduce the stigma attached to claiming a benefit by giving the benefit a non-stigmatising name. Unfortunately, the benefits themselves have been stigmatising, so it is beside the point that their names have expressed non-stigmatising aspirations.

'System' and 'structure' In the UK, and, as far as I understand the situation, in other developed and developing countries, the tax system and the benefits system have developed independently of each other, the former designed to collect revenue for the government, and the latter to distribute income to members of the population on the basis of a variety of criteria. It therefore seems sensible to denote the tax system as 'the tax system' and the benefits system as 'the benefits system'. I do not use the term 'the tax and benefits system' because the two systems developed separately and continue to do so. However, the two systems together determine an individual's or a household's net income, and whenever we discuss reform options we need to discuss how the two systems relate to each other today, and how they will relate to each other in the context of the proposed reform. I use the term 'tax and benefits structure' to denote the combination of the tax system, the benefits system, and how the two relate to each other in today's context and in the context of any reform proposal. I recognise that this distinction between, on the one hand, 'the tax system' and 'the benefits system', and, on the other, 'the tax and benefits structure', is my own invention and is a somewhat arbitrary use of words, but as I have written this book it has become clear to me that some such collection of terms is required, and I have discovered no author who has developed and used a systematic terminology that expresses the necessary distinctions.

A note on graphical representation[5]

For those who like to look at graphs, the following simple graphs represent different systems. (Further graphs, describing alternative reform options, can be found in Chapter 15.)

---

5   For some important three-dimensional graphs, see Duclos, Jean-Yves (1992) 'Freeing up the labour market?' *BIRG Bulletin*, no 14, February 1992, pp 17–19.

Figure 0.1 describes a simple means–tested benefits system. The horizontal axis shows earned income, and the vertical axis net or disposable income, that is, what the person or household has left to spend after tax has been deducted and benefits have been added.

Figure 0.1: Graphical representation of a means-tested benefit withdrawn at 100% of earned income

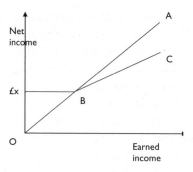

The line OA shows what net income would be if no tax were deducted and no benefits were paid. If a means–tested benefit of £x is paid, and is withdrawn £1 for £1 as earned income rises, then net income remains at £x until the benefit is exhausted. If from the level of earnings at which this happens tax is deducted, then the line BC shows net income above that point, that is, earnings reduced by a proportion of earnings. A variant is shown in Figure 0.2. Here the means–tested benefit is withdrawn at less than 100 per cent of earnings as earnings rise.

(Both graphs assume that tax starts to be paid on earned income above the point at which benefits are exhausted. Things are rarely as simple as this.)

Figure 0.2: Graphical representation of a means-tested benefit withdrawn at less than 100% of earned income

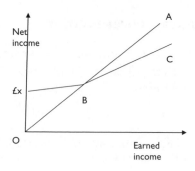

As the graphs make clear, until the individual or household has reached point B, no or little improvement to their economic position is possible.

Figure 0.3 describes a Citizen's Income scheme. A Citizen's Income of £x is paid and all earnings are taxed. The line EF describes the individual's or household's net income.

Figure 0.3: Graphical representation of a Citizen's Income

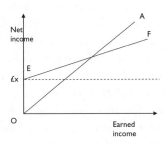

Here we can see that at any earnings level the individual and household can improve their economic position at the same rate.

Figure 0.4 shows the difference between Figures 0.2 and 0.3.
The gap between the lines EF and EBC describes the extent of the difference that a Citizen's Income would make to an individual's or household's net income. But that is only to look at the static effect.

Figure 0.4: Graphical representation of both a means-tested benefit and a Citizen's Income

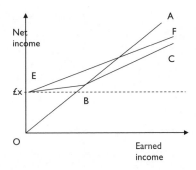

The graph shows that at low earnings a Citizen's Income would enable an individual or household to improve their economic position more rapidly as earnings rose than could an individual or household on means-tested benefits. It is this effect that provides a greater incentive to enter employment or to increase one's earnings, and it is this effect that means that a Citizen's Income could eliminate poverty in ways in which means-tested benefits never could.

Additional net income has to be paid for, of course, so the gap between the lines also represents a cost in public expenditure. We have therefore drawn line EF at a shallower angle than line BC, representing a slightly higher rate of Income Tax. If the lines EF and BC continue in their current directions then they will cross. At earned incomes above the point at which the lines cross, the gap between the two lines will represent the loss of net income that would be suffered by individuals or households on higher incomes if the Citizen's Income were to be implemented. There will always be a higher rate of Income Tax at which the Citizen's Income scheme will be revenue-neutral, that is, at which there will be no additional public expenditure. Whether a revenue-neutral scheme is required, or whether additional public money will be spent (whether through quantitative easing, reducing other public expenditure budgets, or increasing other taxation) will be a decision that the government of the day would need to make.

About the author

Dr Malcolm Torry is Vicar of Holy Trinity, Greenwich Peninsula, in the Church of England Parish of East Greenwich. He is Director of the Citizen's Income Trust, and was a visiting research fellow at the London School of Economics and Political Science from May 2011 to April 2012.

Acknowledgements

My gratitude must go back a long way. In 1976 the manager of Brixton's Supplementary Benefits office employed me to work as a clerical officer on the public counter. I worked there for two years. Thus began my interest in the tax and benefits systems, and my belief that it did not have to be the way that it is. Paul Spicker has written that his 'head is cluttered with old rules and regulations dating back through the last thirty-five years'.[6] I can sympathise.

In 1982 I was a curate at the Elephant and Castle in South London – the parish containing Alexander Fleming House, the headquarters of the Department of Health and Social Security – and Sir Geoffrey Utting, the Permanent Secretary, invited me to attend the Department's summer school. The Rev'd Angus Galbraith, my training vicar, allowed me to go. There I met Hermione (Mimi) Parker, and numerous other people seriously discussing a Citizen's Income as a viable way of reforming the benefits system.

In 1985, Mimi invited me to join a group recently convened by Peter Ashby at the National Council for Voluntary Organisations. This group became the Basic Income Research Group, and then the Citizen's Income Trust, and its trustees and many others related to it have been a constant source of inspiration.

Between 1994 and 1996 I studied part-time for a Master of Science degree in social policy and administration at the London School of Economics and Political Science (LSE). I learnt academic rigour and much else from my teachers, and particularly from Professor David Piachaud. In 2001 I was asked by the trustees of the Citizen's Income Trust to become its honorary Director for a second time (I had been Secretary and then Director between 1988 and 1992), and the Bishop of Woolwich at the time, the Rt. Rev'd Colin Buchanan, gave me permission to take up the post. When in 2011 Professor Hartley Dean invited me to take up a visiting research fellowship for a year at the LSE, the Bishop of Southwark, the Rt. Rev'd Christopher Chessun, kindly granted me permission to do so. I am grateful to all of them. I am grateful to my colleagues in the Parish of East Greenwich for taking on additional responsibilities while I undertook the research fellowship and then wrote this book, and especially to the Rev'd Jeremy Fraser for taking on the coordinating role in the Greenwich Peninsula

---

6   Spicker, Paul (2011) *How social security works: An introduction to benefits in Britain*, Bristol: Policy Press, p xi.

Chaplaincy, and to a generous financial donor for paying for additional assistance in the parish.

I am grateful to Professor Holly Sutherland of the Institute for Economic and Social Research at the University of Essex. In 2003 she taught me how to use POLIMOD, a computer programme that employed family expenditure survey data to calculate the disposable income effects of making changes to the tax and benefits systems; and more recently she and her colleagues have given me access to EUROMOD, a new version of the software, and invited me to participate in a training course at the university.

In relation to this book I am grateful to all of those who have commented on early drafts, and particularly to Dr Alex Cobham and Professors Hartley Dean, Jay Ginn and Bill Jordan, who have read an entire draft and offered most useful comments. As always, any remaining mistakes and infelicities are entirely my responsibility. I am most grateful to Emily Watt and her colleagues at Policy Press for their help and encouragement, and to Policy Press's referees, whose suggestions I have found most helpful. My thanks to Deborah Dukes for help with the index.

I am grateful to all of the above for enabling me to pursue my interest in the Citizen's Income debate, and to those many people who during the past twenty-five years have contributed to my knowledge of the field. Above all, I am grateful to my wife Rebecca for putting up with spells of overwork; and to our sons Christopher, Nicholas and Jonathan for help and advice.

I am grateful to the trustees of the Citizen's Income Trust for permission to quote from material previously published by the Trust.

All royalties from this book will be donated to the Citizen's Income Trust.

Foreword

Guy Standing[7]

For those with a troubled conscience about the direction of our social policies and the gross inequalities in our society, please read this book. As someone who has advocated a Citizen's Income – an unconditional, non-withdrawable income for every individual – for rather longer than I would wish to admit, I welcome it with enthusiasm.

It is written by someone with a sense of compassion, by a 'man of the cloth', as British people used to say with a sense of respect. One does not need to be a Christian or to belong to any religion to recognise the value and appeal of real compassion. And we should remember the difference between compassion and pity, just as we should between rights and charity. Compassion derives from treating people as equals; pity derives from treating people as inferior, as fallen. Social policy should be about strengthening compassion and rights, leaving pity and charity to individual consciences.

Compassion emphasises our commonality, our human similarity, recognition that while today we may need help and may be in a position to help others, tomorrow it might be the other way round. Pity, by contrast, as David Hume taught us, is akin to contempt. At best it is paternalistic and patronising. Worse, it easily leads lazy minds to think they are superior and are being magnanimous in giving a little to help the 'deserving poor'. That is not a worthy sentiment, because it does not exercise our will to do something to change the situation that produces wretchedness among affluence. It is compassion that reinforces our sense of social solidarity, so that we see ourselves in each other.

This book is about an idea that has a long heritage. Some of the greatest minds through history have supported it. Today, there are reasons to believe that its time is coming. Across the world, suddenly we find numerous thoughtful people responding to the call for a Citizen's Income with a 'Why not?' when only a few years ago we heard 'What utopian folly!'

The international network we established in 1986, named BIEN (Basic Income Earth Network), has drawn thousands of members from

---

7   Guy Standing is Professor of Economic Security, University of Bath, and Professor in Development Studies, School of Oriental and African Studies. He is the author of *The precariat* (Bloomsbury, 2011).

across the world, so that there are now national networks in countries as different as Germany, Italy, Japan, South Korea, Brazil, Argentina, the US and the Netherlands. The UK has its network member in the Citizens' Income Trust, which has been ably led by Malcolm Torry. I urge readers to join BIEN and the Citizens' Income Trust. The BIEN Congress is held every two years, when dozens of papers are presented and discussed avidly, as they were in the Munich Congress in September 2012.

The growing interest in an unconditional basic income as a right for all stems from many ethical and social rationales. It is also a pragmatic reaction to the reality that during three decades of economic growth inequalities have grown remorselessly, while millions of people in the UK have wallowed in impoverishment. Governments have tinkered, but have found all sorts of excuses for leaving inequality to grow to historically unprecedented levels. As this is being written, there is still no prospect that the main political parties in the UK will do anything other than tinker with the situation. The socioeconomic fragmentation of our society will drag on. Instead, we have had a steady drift to political utilitarianism that does nobody any credit. Make the 'middle class' happy. That is where the votes are! Give the deserving poor conditional benefits, in pity. Give all those undeserving 'scroungers' some harsh medicine, to be kind to them in the longer term. How smug and prejudiced.

Those who claim there are numerous 'scroungers' across the country – some alien breed who are 'not like You and Me' – and that swathes of people are 'dependent', should be confronted by a simple question: how do you know? And are we not all dependent on others, just as some are dependent on us? Anecdotal evidence of a few people makes for prejudicial and moralistic policy, which is invariably bad policy.

Recently, a much-cited opinion poll found that a majority of British people agreed with the proposition that benefits should be cut. This has been the claim made by newspapers and mainstream politicians, none of them relying on benefits for subsistence. Now, suppose those polled had been asked first, 'What is the weekly amount an unemployed person receives? What is the average amount someone with disability receives?' How many of them would have known the correct answers, or the conditions in which the vast majority seeking benefits have to live? And yet those who responded to the poll were persuaded that the level should be cut. It is a mentality that stems from decades of moving away from solidaristic systems based on principles of compassion to one based on targeting, probing, and stigmatising, through means tests and behaviour tests.

There is something else happening that may turn the tide in favour of a Citizen's Income. Today, millions of people, in Britain and globally, are entering the precariat, which I have depicted in a recent book as the new dangerous class because they see their need for basic security wilfully ignored by the mainstream political parties described as 'centre right' and 'centre left'. Most of those in the precariat are just trying to create a meaningful life for themselves. And yet so far they have been factored out of political calculations. It would be dishonest of politicians to pretend that a combination of means tests and behaviour-tests could overcome the poverty traps – whereby the precariat often pay a marginal tax rate of over 80 per cent, twice what the 'middle class' is expected to pay – let alone what I have called the precarity traps, which make it the fact that many end up paying more than 100 per cent 'tax' on income gained in some precarious short-term job. Those in the precariat know that, and are beginning to growl about the inequity and inequality in which they have to live. Their anger is justifiable, and it will not go away.

Malcolm Torry is a voice of reasonableness. He can see that providing every one of us – sinners as well as saints – with a Citizen's Income is affordable and would actually help make people more productive, not lazier, and make more people more likely to be responsible citizens, with a greater sense of altruism and tolerance.

Like most of us who support moving towards a Citizen's Income – and it is the direction that counts – he is realistic enough to know that it will only come about when those who believe in it have the courage and energy to struggle for its realisation. Sadly, we have just been through a period of political timidity and opportunism, tinged with amorality. I hope Malcolm Torry's book helps redress the balance.

Preface

We should give money to everyone: to every resident, unconditionally. The same amount to every working age adult, the same amount to every older person, and the same amount for every child. The wealthiest working age adult in the country would receive the same as the poorest. The wealthiest older person would receive the same as the poorest. Whatever someone's earnings or savings, and whatever someone's household arrangements, this Citizen's Income would never be taken away or reduced. It would always be there: a rock to build on.

Ridiculous? No, it's not. It is a perfectly sensible and feasible idea; and, as this book shows, it is a necessary idea, because it would fit with how we live and work today in ways in which our current tax and benefits structure really does not.

This book is about this one single idea: a Citizen's Income – an unconditional and non-withdrawable income paid to every individual as a right of citizenship

It is a remarkably simple idea, with the potential to make our economy and our labour market more efficient, to encourage training and enterprise, to enable people to benefit financially from their labour, to make our society more cohesive, to reduce poverty and inequality, and to set people free from bureaucratic intrusion

Many of the arguments that I present, for and against a Citizen's Income, will apply anywhere in the world. Sometimes I compare a benefits system based on a Citizen's Income with the UK's current benefits system, simply because that is the system that I know best. In particular, I compare a Citizen's Income to Child Benefit, the UK's currently universal, unconditional and non-withdrawable benefit for children; and I contrast it with the UK's means-tested benefits, and with the future 'Universal Credit', in order to reveal many of the advantages of a Citizen's Income. But I also look elsewhere in the world, and give a whole chapter to Citizen's Incomes paid or piloted in other countries

This is the right time for this book:

- It is more than 10 years since the last general treatment in English of arguments for a Citizen's Income.[8]

---

[8]   Parker, H. (1989) *Instead of the dole: An enquiry into integration of the tax and benefit systems*, London: Routledge; Walter, T. (1989) *Basic Income: Freedom from poverty, freedom to work*, London: Marion Boyars; Fitzpatrick, T. (1999) *Freedom and security: An introduction to the Basic Income debate*, Basingstoke: Macmillan, was published in 1999.

- Richard Wilkinson and Kate Pickett's *The spirit level: Why more equal societies almost always do better*, has become a bestseller. This is particularly interesting because Wilkinson has been writing about inequality for 40 years, but only now has his work made such an impact on the public imagination. A book that has raised a similar level of public interest is Daniel Dorling's *Injustice*. These two books offer diagnosis, but little by way of prescription. They both mention a Citizen's Income as worth studying,[9] so it is essential to have available a thorough treatment of the idea.
- Inequality, poverty, a changing employment market, economic insecurity, and a lack of social cohesion, have generated unrest around the world. Our benefits system negatively affects all of these factors. We need solutions to the causes of unrest, so we need to reform our tax and benefits systems.
- Maybe the time is right. In Germany, the book *1.000 Euro für jeden* (*'A thousand euros for everyone'*),[10] by Götz W. Werner and Adrienne Goehler, has prompted a widespread debate about Citizen's Income. This debate needs to happen in every country, across Europe, and globally.

(A book that from its front cover might appear to be on the same theme as this book is in fact not. Daniel Ben-Ami's *Ferraris for all* is what the subtitle says it is: a *defence of economic progress*.[11] Whether or not we should seek economic progress is a question that might be of relevance to Chapter 14 of this book, but that question is very different from the question as to whether we should receive a Citizen's Income.)

We are all involved in the tax and benefits systems. They have profound effects on our society, our relationships, our life's work, and our welfare; and they circulate truly vast sums of money. We all need to understand the damage that the current systems inflict, and the alternatives on offer. And we all need to understand the good that a Citizen's Income could do for our society and for every one of us.

Malcolm Torry, 2013

---

[9] Wilkinson, R. and Pickett, K. (2009) *The spirit level: Why more equal societies almost always do better*, London: Allen Lane/Penguin Books, p 264; Dorling, D. (2010) *Injustice: Why social inequality persists*, Bristol: Policy Press, p 267

[10] Werner, G.W. and Goehler, A. (2010) *1.000 Euro für jeden*, Berlin: Econ, Ullstein Buchverlage

[11] Ben-Ami, D. (2010) *Ferraris for all: In defence of economic progress*, Bristol: Policy Press

CHAPTER 1

Imagine ...

Imagine this ...

The banking crisis has happened. The government – and this could be any government – has bailed out the banks, so there is less to spend on public services. Jobs are not as secure as they were. People without jobs are struggling to get back into work, and people with jobs are worrying that soon they might not have them. People are still spending, and they are getting into debt; or they are not spending, and they are just about getting by.

There is at least one good piece of news: inflation is low – so the government decides that it can print some extra money without creating the high inflation which that would cause in more normal times. Let us imagine that instead of giving the money to the banks, which created the crisis, the government gives an equal weekly income to every citizen: a Citizen's Income. Citizens might spend it on goods and services, thus creating employment; or they might save it, making lending and investment possible.

As the economy picks up, inflation starts to rise, and so the government decides that it can no longer print money. We have got used to receiving a Citizen's Income, so the government reduces personal tax allowances and most means-tested and National Insurance benefits so that it can continue to pay equal amounts of money to everyone. Because the universal payment is worth the same as the tax allowance used to be worth, and is similar to what means-tested and social insurance benefits used to be worth, few people's disposable incomes change very much. But now things are different. People who had been on means-tested benefits are now on lower amounts of them, so lots of them decide that they have had enough of bureaucratic interference in their lives and they come off benefits and look for work. Often a part-time job will be enough to top up their Citizen's Income; or perhaps part-time work and a bit of self-employment. Starting a business looks more attractive than it once did: after all, nobody is going to take away their Citizen's Income, so they will always have that to rely on. And families on means-tested in-work benefits now receive a Citizen's Income, and that is not taken away as their earnings rise: so they look for a better job, or they do a training course so that they can look for a better job, and their partner also looks for work or starts a small business – it was not worth them doing that before because so much of the household's benefits would be taken away if they did.

For many families life is now very different. They feel more secure, they are in control, and they can make choices that they could never make before. They no longer have to claim benefits by filling in long forms, and they no longer have to attend interviews to answer questions about their living arrangements. Nor do they have to prove that they are seeking employment: although most previously unemployed people are actively looking for jobs because it has become so much more worthwhile to work for a living: and if people cannot find jobs then they create their own.

Wealthy people are paying far more in tax than they receive in Citizen's Income, so it really is no problem that they receive a Citizen's Income along with everyone else.[12] Previous large inequalities of income and wealth are diminishing, while the simplicity and universality of the Citizen's Income ensures that everyone feels part of the same society. Now we really are all in it together.

In difficult times, a government might be tempted to reduce spending on the Citizen's Income: but its universality is now as politically important as that of the UK's National Health Service (NHS). Economists explain that if marginal deduction rates were to rise then people would be less likely to seek employment, seek training, or start their own businesses. The economy would suffer. At the next election, parties in government tell their electorates that 'the Citizen's Income is safe with us', and they mean it.

Imagine these people ...

In whichever country you are reading this book, you are likely to pay a variety of taxes: Income Tax, taxes when you purchase goods and services, capital gains taxes, and others. On the income side, you might receive wages, a personal pension, occupational pensions paid by previous employers, social security benefits, or several of these. Social insurance benefits[13] might be paid during sickness, disability,

---

[12] Spicker, Paul (2011) *How social security works: An introduction to benefits in Britain,* Bristol: Policy Press, pp 15, 117

[13] The International Social Security Association website contains useful country profiles at www.issa.int/Observatory/Country-Profiles. Unfortunately these do not include in-work means-tested benefits designed to supplement low wages.

unemployment, or on retirement. There might also be universal benefits, paid for children; and there might be means-tested benefits, paid when all else fails, or paid to top up low wages, or to top up social insurance benefits that are too low to live on. The means-tested benefits might be administered either nationally or locally, but in either case they will involve answering numerous questions about personal circumstances, either in writing or in interviews with officials.

Think of a mother with a young child in your own country. What happens to her income if the number of hours she works changes, or if her hourly wage rate changes, or if she moves in with someone and her new partner has fluctuating income? And then what happens if sometimes she lives with her partner, and sometimes they live apart?

Or think of a man with a young family. He loses his job. What happens to his net income while he is unemployed, what happens to it if he finds occasional employment, and what happens to it if his partner's[14] earnings change?

In both cases: How much form-filling will they have to do, and how many interviews with officials will they need to attend? How likely are they to conceal changes to their circumstances, and why? And how secure is their income? In particular: How likely are they to seek employment, or to seek additional employment?

The part of the system to study closely is the means-tested part: those benefits given to people in particular circumstances (for instance, if you are sick, unemployed, on low wages, or a full-time carer for children or a frail adult), conditionally (on submission of a medical certificate to say that you are unfit for work, or on the submission of proof that you have tried to find employment, or on the submission of evidence of low pay), and withdrawably (that is, if you earn additional income then the benefit is wholly or partly withdrawn). If you live with others, then the amount that you receive is usually reduced, because your partner's income is taken into account when yours is calculated, and because the regulations might assume that two people living together can live more cheaply than two individuals living separately. A change in any of these circumstances might trigger a recalculation of the means-tested benefit.

In countries with means-tested elements among their social security benefits, which includes most developed countries and some developing ones, the system will discourage people in a variety of different circumstances from seeking new skills or additional employment. For any increase in earned income, the increase in net income would be unpredictable, too small, or both; and reporting the change in

---

[14] 'Partner' implies spouse or partner.

circumstances, and ensuring that the right amount of benefit is paid at the right time, can be hard work. Anyone receiving means-tested benefits would have to surmount considerable challenges in order to improve their own and their household's economic position.

Imagine these people in the UK

A mother registers the birth of her child and completes the simple five page form to claim universal Child Benefit.[15] If the child continues to live with her then she will continue to receive Child Benefit until the child is sixteen years old, or for longer if the child remains in full-time education or training. She will need to notify any change of address, and she will receive extra Child Benefit for each additional child. If she earns nothing, she will receive Child Benefit. The amount is unaffected when she takes a part-time or a full-time job. If she works full-time then her Child Benefit will remain the same. If one week she earns nothing, the next week £500, and the week after that £50, her Child Benefit will remain at the same rate throughout.

The mother we have imagined was working before her child was born, but the shop she worked in has closed. She claims Income Support, a means-tested benefit. The form is 57 pages long.[16] The questions about her partner and his pay are complicated because he is a builder who sometimes lives with her and sometimes does not, depending on the location of his work; and sometimes he earns a good wage and sometimes he earns little or nothing. She does not know whether they are together or whether they are separated. She phones the local Department for Work and Pensions (DWP), and she asks her friends, and everyone is very helpful. She fills in the form and the payments begin. Her friend finds her a part-time job in another shop. It is mornings only, which is just right, as her mother can look after the child. She is working fifteen hours a week, and so can continue to receive Income Support. She tells the department about the earnings. The money stops, and then it starts again, at a lower rate. And then she is offered lunchtime work in the café next to the shop. After a couple of weeks she tells the department, and discovers that as she is now working more than 16 hours a week, she has to claim 'Tax Credits'[17] instead of Income Support. This claim form is only ten pages long, but the working sheets take quite a while to understand and fill in. Her

---

[15]   www.hmrc.gov.uk/childbenefit, 10/09/2011
[16]   www.dwp.gov.uk/advisers/claimforms/a1.pdf, 10/09/2011
[17]   www.hmrc.gov.uk/taxcredits, 10/09/2011

Income Support stops, her friends help her out for a few weeks, and then the 'Tax Credits' start. After a couple of months the café no longer needs her. They have decided to employ a full-timer instead. So now she is off 'Tax Credits' and back onto Income Support – though now she is a bit quicker at filling in the form. Her 'Tax Credits' stop, her Income Support starts. Not too much of a gap this time. Her employer asks her if she might be able to work Wednesday afternoons as well as the mornings. She says no.

While in other countries the situation will be different, and in the UK after 2013 Income Support and 'Tax Credits' will be combined into 'Universal Credit', the fundamental problems will remain. Means-tested benefits impose administrative burdens on both claimants and government departments, they discourage flexible employment patterns, and they can make it less than worthwhile for someone to seek employment or to increase the number of hours that they work.

Imagine a man with a young family. His wife has a part-time job. The firm he works for closes down, so he claims National Insurance benefits, but these are not enough to live on so he claims the means-tested Jobseeker's Allowance. It takes about an hour at his computer to fill in the form, but he gets there in the end: though his wife's missing payslips make a bit of guesswork necessary, as she earns different amounts each week. He cannot find a full-time job, but his friend's boss offers him labouring work on Saturdays. He accepts. He goes to the Jobcentre, and they make a note. His money stops. He phones them up. They say they will look into it. His money starts again, but at a lower rate. The Saturday work becomes more intermittent. He tells them that the Saturday work has stopped. After four weeks his money goes back up again. The next time he is offered weekend work, he tells them nothing.

He gets a job. He earns lower wages than he is used to, so he claims 'Tax Credits', Housing Benefit, and Council Tax Benefit. The family does not seem to be much better off, and it is still a struggle to pay the bills. He is offered overtime, and he takes it so that he can pay for a holiday, and for bikes for the children. A year later, he gets a letter telling him to pay back £500 of 'Tax Credits', but he no longer has the money. The next week he is made redundant, and he claims Jobseeker's Allowance again. Next time he is offered an interview, he goes, because he has to, but he is not trying to get the job. He gets depressed, he hits his wife, and she tells him to leave. She claims 'Tax Credits', and then Housing Benefit and Council Tax Benefit. Her employer, knowing that she could do with the money, asks her if she wants to increase her hours. She declines.

These stories might fit people you have known, and one of them might fit you. They are based on several real people whom I have known. None of them are lazy people. They all want to support their families and to contribute to society. But the only income they could rely on was Child Benefit because it continued to be paid, and the amount received only changed if they had a new child or a child reached sixteen or the end of their education or training. For none of them did the NHS cease to treat their illnesses, or schools cease to educate their children. But taking a job, or increasing the number of hours they worked, put their income at risk.[18] Quite understandably we avoid risk. So people in the situations that we have imagined will often choose not to seek employment, or they might refuse employment, or they might not declare employment income; and when they do these things they are doing them for the best of motives: to have secure incomes with which to feed, clothe and house their families.

The UK government knows that there is a problem, and it will soon combine Income Support, Jobseeker's Allowance, Housing Benefit, various other benefits, and 'Tax Credits', into a single 'Universal Credit'.[19] This will avoid the need to claim different benefits for different numbers of hours of employment, and it will reduce marginal deduction rates. But the people we have met will still need to fill in long forms; they will still need to inform the DWP when their partner moves in or out, or they receive casual earnings, or someone new joins the household, or the rent changes; they will still have their 'Universal Credit' reduced if their partner's earnings rise;[20] and they might still receive repayment demands that they cannot afford to pay.

'Universal Credit' is a step in the right direction.[21] But a much better way would be a Citizen's Income. This would never change, whatever our household arrangements, however many hours we were employed, and however flexible our employment pattern became. Some families would still need means-tested benefits, but there would be a substantial incentive to get off them, and often the opportunity to do so. The Citizen's Income would be a secure ground on which to build, in the way that Child Benefit is now; and it would come to define

---

[18] See Simon Collyer's narrative at www.corporatewatch.org.uk/?lid=4478

[19] www.dwp.gov.uk/docs/universal-credit-full-document.pdf, 10/09/2011

[20] Miller, Anne (2011) 'Universal Credit: welfare that works', *Citizen's Income Newsletter*, issue 1, pp 4–10

[21] Citizen's Income Trust, 'A response by the Citizen's Income Trust to *21st Century Welfare*', *Citizen's Income Newsletter*, issue 3, pp 3–9

what 'social security' means in the same way that the NHS defines what healthcare means.

In whatever country, and whatever the current benefits system, a Citizen's Income would improve the situation. It would reduce marginal deduction rates, create security in an increasingly insecure employment market, and provide a rock on which everyone can build, whatever their family and household arrangements, and however insecure their other income.

Imagine the difference that a Citizen's Income would make to the households that we have imagined in this chapter. They are not untypical. We lead complex lives in which circumstances can change rapidly. In the future our households, relationships, wages, hours of employment, and kinds of employment, are likely to change even faster than they do now. Our Citizen's Income would be the one thing that would never change, and it would give us the security we need to enable us to plan for our own and our families' futures, and to welcome some of the changes that a changing world will bring

Imagine a country ...

Imagine that you live in a country in which everyone belongs to a household earning enough money to provide a good standard of living; and let us assume that in every household everything is shared so that everyone has everything they need. This imagined country does not need a benefits system. It will need taxes to provide for other things, but not to provide an income for anyone.

But now let us be realistic and recognise that in this country there are people who do *not* have enough to live on: older people without children to support them; households in which no-one receives a wage because their members are too disabled or ill, or because the companies they worked for have closed down; and households in which earned incomes are too low to provide a decent standard of living. The country's government might decide to give money to those who need it, which will mean setting up tax and benefits systems to collect in and pay out the money. That is the easy bit. Rather more difficult is deciding how the money should be collected and how it should be distributed.

There are two ways of distributing money: 1. the same amount for everyone, and 2. different amounts for different people.

    1. We simply give everyone of the same age the same amount of money. Children might get less than working

age adults, and retired people more, but administration
of that is easy enough.

2. We decide to give different amounts to different people,
   or to give money to some and not to others. Then we
   have some awkward questions to answer: How do we
   decide who should receive the money? And how do we
   calculate what different people should get?

If we take the second route, then we might give money to those who
are not working and not to those who are, so we shall need to know
who is working and who is not; or we might give money to those
without enough to live on and not to those who do have enough, in
which case we shall need to decide how much is enough, and we shall
need to know people's incomes. We might also decide that people who
have more children need more to live on, so we shall need to know
how many children people have; and we might decide that if there are
two families with children, one with nobody earning, and one with a
wage coming in, then the money we collect would be better spent if
more went to the family earning less money: so we shall need to know
who is living with whom, and how much money is coming into the
household, rather than just who is earning what.

This is all beginning to look rather complicated.

So now let us ask another question: How are we going to collect the
money that we are going to distribute? What is the fairest way to do
that? Presumably by doing what we do now: we shall ask those who
have more to pay more.

The decision we were trying to make about how to organise an ideal
benefits system is now starting to look a bit different:

1. If we give everyone the same to start with – a Citizen's
   Income – and we then take more from the rich than we
   take from the poor, then, in total, poorer families will
   receive more from public funds than wealthier families,
   and many wealthier families will be paying in more than
   they take out.

2. If we give more to the poor and less to the rich, then we
   shall be doing the same job twice: first working out who
   should pay more tax, and then working out who should
   receive little or no means-tested benefit – and some of
   them might be the same people. Such duplication of
   systems is wasteful.

In our imagined country with no benefits system, the decision is an easy one: We should give to every individual a Citizen's Income: without conditions (unconditional), always the same, whatever else is going on (non-withdrawable), and paid to individuals (not to households or couples); and we should take more tax from those who earn more, and less tax from those who earn less. But because we are familiar with our existing complicated benefits system, we find it hard to imagine that the world might be different and much simpler. It can take a thought experiment, like the one that we have just been through, to reveal the truth: that means-testing people, and assessing people for Income Tax, is to do the same job twice. The duplication is entirely unnecessary.

Putting it together

In most countries, tax systems and benefits systems have developed entirely separately from each other: tax systems in order to collect revenue for the government, and benefits systems to provide resources when individuals and households need them. Symptomatic of this approach in the UK is the report of the recent Institute for Fiscal Studies review of taxation. The report is about tax, and it treats Income Tax as if it is the only government system relating to a household's net income.[22]

This is strange, as both the benefits and tax systems are doing such similar things: one working out how to pay more to those who do not have enough, and the other working out how to take less from those who do not earn as much as other people do. They are the mirror image of each other. In the UK, both Income Tax and 'Tax Credits' are administered by the same government department. It is something of a surprise that nobody has suggested saving money by abandoning the means-testing of in-work benefits.

This book has a simple message: that we need a Citizen's Income: a universal, unconditional, non-withdrawable income – that is, an income

---

[22]   Adam, Stuart et al (eds) (2010) *Dimensions of tax design: The Mirrlees Review*, Oxford: Oxford University Press for the Institute for Fiscal Studies; Adam, Stuart et al, (2011) *Tax by design: The Mirrlees Review*, Oxford: Oxford University Press for the Institute for Fiscal Studies; *Fiscal Studies*, vol 32, no 3, September 2011: a special issue on the Mirrlees Review. Cf. Albi, Emilio and Martinez-Vazquez, Jorge (eds) (2011) *The Elgar Guide to tax systems*, London: Edward Elgar; and Alm, James (ed.) (2011) *The economics of taxation: The International Library of Critical Writings in Economics 251*, London: Edward Elgar, both of which study the tax system largely in isolation from the benefits system. See also Jones, Owen (ed.) (2012) *Why equality matters*, London: Centre for Labour and Social Studies, p 27, where reforms of the tax system are listed as means to greater income equality, but the benefits system is ignored.

that every individual receives, at the same rate, and never reduced or taken away by any change in circumstances. Older adults would get a larger unconditional income (a Citizen's Pension) to compensate for the costs of increasing frailty and disability. In the UK, children already have an unconditional and non-withdrawable benefit, and all we need to do is to keep Child Benefit universal, unconditional, and non-withdrawable, and at the same time increase its value. In other countries we would need to establish a new Children's Citizen's Income alongside Citizen's Incomes for working age adults and Citizen's Pensions for older people. How we should pay for a Citizen's Income I discuss later, and there is of course legitimate debate over the level at which a Citizen's Income should be paid: but in the meantime it is worth saying again: *It would be no problem that the rich would receive a Citizen's Income, because they pay far more in Income Tax than the amount of Citizen's Income that they would receive.*[23]

A Citizen's income would be as simple to administer as the UK's Child Benefit. The administrative costs would be less than 0.5 per cent of the total Citizen's Income budget.[24] We would all have far more choice over hours of employment, over how we combine different kinds of employment, over how we divide employment between household members, and over how we form relationships. Because each household would have more control over its employment pattern, we would see more part-time employment and therefore more voluntary activity. Above all, everyone would have a secure income floor and would be

---

[23]   Walker, Carol (2011) 'For universalism and against the means test', pp 133–52 in Walker, Alan, Sinfield, Adrian and Walker, Carol (eds) *Fighting poverty, inequality and injustice: A manifesto inspired by Peter Townsend*, Cambridge: Polity Press, pp 149–50

[24]   HMRC, 'Business Plan Indicators: Quarterly Performance: Q3 – Oct-Dec 2012': www.gov.uk/government/publications/business-plan-indicators. The cost of administering Child Benefit is 0.68 x 12 bn = £81.6 million. There are probably 11.6 million under-16s in the UK, and 51.1 million over-16s (Office for National Statistics (2008) *National population projections, 2006-based*, Basingstoke: Palgrave Macmillan, p 1). The Citizen's Income scheme published in evidence by the House of Commons Work and Pensions Committee's Benefits Simplification Inquiry (House of Commons Work and Pensions Committee (2007) *Benefits simplification: Seventh report for the sessions 2006–7*, vol II, London: The Stationery Office, pp Ev 84–90, www.publications. parliament.uk/pa/cm200607/cmselect/cmworpen/463/463ii.pdf, 10/09/2011) envisages £189 billion being paid out in Citizen's Income to a total population of 62.7 million people. Making a conservative assumption that Citizen's Income will cost twice as much per claim as Child Benefit, the total administrative cost will be £882 million (81.6m x 62.7m x 2 ÷ 11.6m). The cost of administering a Citizen's Income would therefore be 0.46p per £1 of benefit (882m ÷ 189bn) and could be lower if we were to make a less conservative assumption about cost per claim.

able to take risks that at the moment they cannot take. Society as a whole would benefit because we would all receive a Citizen's Income, and a new social solidarity would be the result.

Some problems would remain. The Citizen's Income would be unlikely to be high enough to enable all means-tested benefits to be abolished, so a residual means-tested scheme might be required. In any country, housing costs are different in different places, so there might still need to be a means-tested benefit to help with housing costs. There will always be people with disabilities who need extra income. These are problems facing any benefits system, they are not generated by the Citizen's Income proposal, and they should not interfere with discussion as to whether we should establish a Citizen's Income.

How should we debate the possibility of a Citizen's Income?

There are two ways in which the discussion might proceed. As in the thought experiment about the imagined country, we could invent tax and benefits systems, and we could then compare our current complicated systems with the systems that we have invented; or we could ask how we can solve the problems that the current systems have given to us. We might legitimately mix the two methods, of course, as the same points can be made by asking about the benefits of a Citizen's Income and by asking how a Citizen's Income might improve on the current system. I prefer to argue from the 'ideal country' thought experiment. This avoids the common problem that when we are presented with new ideas we tend to compare them with what we do now, as if somehow what we do now is normal and right, and what we might do instead needs to pass the tests that the current system passes: tests that might be irrational, irrelevant, or both. For instance: means-tested benefits pass this test: Are we only giving money to people who need it most? A Citizen's Income does not pass that test: but, as we have seen, it is not a sensible test in the first place. As the tax system takes from those with higher incomes more money than they would receive in a Citizen's Income, it is irrelevant that those who could manage without a Citizen's Income would receive one along with everyone else.

We should not be asking whether a Citizen's Income passes the test that the current system passes. We should instead study any new idea on its merits. Then, if the new system looks useful, we should ask how the current system compares with that. Perhaps the new system should decide on the tests, and then we should see whether the old system passes them. A Citizen's Income passes this test: Do the rich end up paying more to the government than they receive from the government? This is in fact the same question as the one we discussed earlier, but differently phrased. Worded like this, both a Citizen's Income and the current system pass the test. Take another test: Is it as simple as possible to administer? A Citizen's Income passes the test, but the current system does not. Another question is this: Does the system encourage households to take risks with their employment patterns? A Citizen's Income will pass that test more convincingly than the current system ever could. It rather looks as if we must always ask ourselves whether we need to reframe a question. Take the question: Is it right to take more money from the wealthier members of society in order to provide a universal benefit? Maybe the right question to ask is this: Is it right to extract a higher proportion of any additional earnings from the low paid than we do from the higher paid? – because that is what happens now.

If the new idea generates the questions, and the new idea passes the tests and the current system does not, then we might need to stop using the current system as a yardstick against which to judge other systems.

Similarly, if we replace one system with another, then some people will end up with more money, and some with less. We tend to assume that this means that there is a problem with the new system. It could equally well mean that there is a problem with the present system, and that the new system would offer a fairer distribution than the current system. Where there might be gainers and losers, we need to ask three questions: Is the new system fairer than the old one? Can every individual and every household end up in a better position in the end? And can we create transitional arrangements to protect those who would lose the most on the day on which the change to the new system occurred? If we can answer Yes to all of those questions, then it really does not matter that there will be gainers and losers.

In answer to the first question: Later on we shall be studying the distribution of net incomes that a Citizen's Income might give to us, but it is worth saying here that if we find that the incomes of the wealthiest reduce by four per cent, and the incomes of the poorest rise by twenty per cent, then we might regard the new distribution as fairer than the current one; and, as we shall see later, increasing income equality could have a variety of beneficial effects both on our society and on our economy.

The second question is this: Can every individual and every household end up in a better position in the end? Take two individuals. A has an income of £16,000, but for every extra £1 she earns she loses

76p in Income Tax and reduced benefits. B has an income of £15,000, but for every extra £1 he earns he loses just 35p because he receives a non-withdrawable Citizen's Income and not the means-tested benefits under which A is suffering. Which of them is better off? In the short term, the answer has to be A. In the longer term, the answer could easily be B, by a long way, because if he obtains higher earnings then he will keep more of them, so he will have more incentive to seek additional earnings, and to seek the training that would make that possible. A will keep less of any additional earnings, and so will have less of an incentive to earn more, and less incentive to train or retrain. In the longer term, B is likely to be better off than A.

Can we create transitional arrangements to protect those who would lose the most on the day the change to the new system occurs? We might need transitional arrangements, because the complexity of the current system is bound to mean that some low earners will experience reductions in disposable income if a Citizen's Income were to be implemented. However, we would not need such arrangements for long. The changes that a Citizen's Income would generate in the economy at large, and in people's household economies, would soon rectify any initial disparities between a household's net income before and after the change.

When considering any change in policy, another question that we need to ask is this: If we were running the new system, would we be better off if we changed to what we are doing now? Birnbaum offers an interesting example of this type of argument: If we all had a Citizen's Income, then 'John' might have a part-time job, coach a children's football team, go fishing, and play the guitar. If the Citizen's Income were to be removed then he might have to accept a full-time job and not have the time or the energy for other activities. The new situation would be beneficial neither for John nor for his community.[25] Similarly: someone on a Citizen's Income might be undertaking a training course in order to seek a better job so that she can fund a better lifestyle for her family. If her Citizen's Income were to be replaced by a means-tested benefit, then if she got a better-paying job her disposable income would increase by less, she might decide not to look for increased earnings, and she might not undertake a training course. Such detrimental individual effects added up across our society would constitute a substantial social and economic loss.

---

[25]   Birnbaum, Simon (2012), *Basic Income reconsidered: Social justice, liberalism, and the demands of equality*, New York: Palgrave Macmillan, p 59

So if everyone received a Citizen's Income, would we vote for a government that planned to abolish it in favour of means-tested benefits? The answer to that question is: Possibly, yes. However good the arguments for universal benefits, however beneficial their effects, and however efficient they are for the government, for individuals, and for households, there will always be people who will want to means-test them. At the time of writing, in the UK Iain Duncan Smith, Secretary of State for Work and Pensions, has proposed means-testing pensioners' currently universal winter heating allowance. As Gaby Hinsliff suggests, means testing the allowance might 'make it harder for the genuinely needy to claim, as well as pushing up administration costs'.[26] It would make far more sense to retain the universal winter heating allowance and to lower the age-related Income Tax allowances. The most vulnerable would continue to be able to pay their heating bills because the money would arrive automatically and they would not need to complete a complicated claim form; no additional administrative costs would be incurred; the wealthy are already paying more in Income Tax than they receive in the form of heating allowance; and the wealthy would be paying a little more in Income Tax as well, so the effect on the public finances and on the net incomes of the wealthy would be the same as if the heating allowance were to be means-tested. It is difficult to identify any advantages at all to means-testing the heating allowance.

But that does not change the fact that in the minds of policy makers, and of the general public, means-testing is the default position. We seem to possess an innate desire to means-test, even though it is unnecessary, expensive, inefficient, and has a variety of unfortunate social and economic effects. There are usually far simpler ways of saving public money than means-testing benefits, and there are few more effective ways of wasting money than spending it on administering means tests. It is unfortunate that, even if we had a Citizen's Income, we might need to argue for retaining it. So, if you are reading this book in a few years' time, in the midst of a debate as to whether your country should retain an existing Citizen's Income, then I hope that you will find it as useful as those who used its arguments to establish the Citizen's Income in the first place.

If you already think that a Citizen's Income would be a good idea, then I hope that this book will confirm you in your belief. If you think that a Citizen's Income would be a bad idea, or if you are not sure,

---

[26] Hinsliff, Gaby (2012) 'This "granny bashing" is only fair', *Guardian Weekly*, 15 June. p 21

then I hope that I have already persuaded you to keep an open mind until you reach the end of the book.

In our subsequent chapters we shall pursue in more depth some of the questions raised in this introduction. To start with we shall tackle two questions, the answers to which should provide essential background for the subsequent discussion: How did we get to where we are now? and: Why do some reform proposals succeed, and some fail?

CHAPTER 2

How did we get to where we are now?[27]

In our first chapter we found ourselves arguing for a Citizen's Income from two different directions: from criteria for an ideal benefits system, and from the problems experienced by our present system. In order to understand the present system we need to see how it evolved in all of its complexity (this chapter) and then focus on previous attempts at radical reform of the tax and benefits structure (Chapter 3). Readers from countries other than the UK might wish to study the histories of their own benefits systems, and particularly the history of any current universal benefits.

A means-tested past and a means-tested future?

In the UK, we have got to where we are now by evolutionary change rather than by radical reform, and by the swing of a pendulum, moving back and forth between universality and selectivity, between providing for everybody and providing for people who fit into particular categories. The pendulum has rarely reached either end of the spectrum. It has more often been near to the selectivity end, but it has taken an occasional lunge towards universality, only to be dragged swiftly back towards the other end.

The 1601 Poor Law set up local administrations to provide for people unable to provide for themselves, and to establish 'houses of correction' for able-bodied men who could not find work: suggesting that those physically able to work but not working, for whatever reason, were in need of 'correction'. By the end of the eighteenth century, unemployment was increasing and wages were not keeping up with living costs. The administration of the Poor Law being local, experiment was inevitable, and in 1795 at Speenhamland the Poor Law Guardians

---

27 Parts of this chapter are drawn from Torry, Malcolm (1996) 'The Labour Market, the Family, and Social Security Reform: A dissertation for the Master of Science degree in social policy and planning at the London School of Economics'. See also Barr, Nicholas (1987) *The economics of the welfare state*, London: Weidenfeld and Nicholson; Hill, Michael (1990) *Social security policy in Britain*, Aldershot: Edward Elgar

began to subsidise low wages as a means of relieving poverty. Amidst fears that this policy would lead to a general reduction in wages, and a belief that a man who cannot provide for his family loses his dignity, a review was held. The ensuing debate led to the Poor Law Amendment Act 1834, which enshrined the idea of 'less eligibility': that is, that the unemployed man or woman should not be paid as much as they would get if they were employed. Before 1834, 'out relief' had provided food for families that could not afford to feed themselves. After 1834, those who could not support themselves were admitted to the workhouse and isolated from the rest of society: a system meant to deter people from voluntary poverty and to propel the rural poor into the urban labour market required to power the industrial revolution.

By the beginning of the twentieth century, the poverty in which many older people found themselves was causing concern, partly because Charles Booth's and Seebohm Rowntree's surveys in London and York had revealed the extent of poverty. The government implemented a flat-rate noncontributory pension for older people who had not received Poor Relief and whose incomes were below £31 per annum. Central government administered the pension, and since then there has been a constant movement away from the local management of benefits payments and towards centralised administration.[28] The next development was contributory Unemployment Benefit in certain industries in 1911, paid for out of employee and employer contributions, and payable for twenty-six weeks;[29] and during the 1920s social insurance benefits were extended to more industries and were paid beyond the period for which they could be funded by contributions. During the subsequent depression the financial cost of contributory benefits could no longer be sustained, so assistance when Unemployment Benefit had expired was given via a rather draconian household means test.[30]

During the Second World War, the government extended its influence into many areas of people's lives, and the scene was set for substantial government intervention in healthcare, education, and income maintenance. In the midst of the war, a population looking forward to a better life welcomed William Beveridge's 1942 report,

---

[28] While Housing Benefit is administered locally, the scheme is a national one. Council Tax Benefit is to be largely locally managed from 2013.

[29] Thane, Pat (2011) 'The making of National Insurance, 1911', *Journal of Poverty and Social Justice*, vol 19, no 3, pp 211–19

[30] Lynes, Tony (2011) 'From Unemployment Insurance to Assistance in interwar Britain', *Journal of Poverty and Social Justice*, vol 19, no 3, pp 221–33

which proposed a system of National Insurance benefits and a centrally administered National Assistance to maintain the incomes of people without sufficient income.[31] An Act of Parliament in 1945 led to Family Allowances (the forerunner of Child Benefit); an Act in 1946 led to National Insurance, (contributory) Retirement Pensions, Unemployment Benefit, and Sickness Benefit; and an Act in 1948 to means-tested National Assistance. Beveridge intended contributory benefits to be the heart of the system and National Assistance to be a safety net for the few; but because National Assistance covered housing costs, and the levels at which contributory benefits were set were never sufficient to cover the cost of housing, far more people than Beveridge had intended ended up on means-tested benefits.[32] An adequate contributory system could have enhanced social cohesion. The largely means-tested system[33] which emerged has had the opposite effect.[34]

Few changes were made during the 1950s and 1960s, although one change that we shall later see to be significant is that in 1957 Child Tax Allowances were reintroduced (having first been introduced in 1909), enabling workers with children to pay less Income Tax.[35] Low wages continued to cause poverty. A Negative Income Tax was discussed, but the Inland Revenue did not want the tax system to be used for anything other than revenue collection. In 1971 the government decided to supplement low wages and so implemented the previous Labour government's plan for a means-tested benefit, Family Income Supplement,[36] which in 1985 became the more generous 'Family Credit'. While this reduced some households' marginal deduction rates to below 100 per cent, the simultaneous freezing of Child Benefit[37] meant that 'Family Credit' increased the means-tested proportions

---

31 Beveridge, Sir William (1942) *Social insurance and allied services*, Cmd 6404, London: Stationery Office

32 Atkinson, A. B. (1969) *Poverty in Britain and the reform of social security*, Cambridge: Cambridge University Press, p 24

33 Bradshaw, Jonathan and Bennett, Fran (2011) 'National Insurance: past, present, and future?' *Journal of Poverty and Social Justice*, vol 19, no 3, pp 207–209

34 Thane, Pat (2011) 'The making of National Insurance, 1911', *Journal of Poverty and Social Justice*, vol 19, no 3, pp 211–219

35 Creedy, John and Disney, Richard (1985) *Social insurance in transition*, Oxford: Clarendon Press, p 41

36 Banting, Keith G. (1979) *Poverty, politics and policy: Britain in the 1960s*, London: Macmillan, p 89

37 Barr, Nicholas and Coulter, Fiona (1991) 'Social security: solution or problem', pp 274–337 in Hills, John (ed.) *The state of welfare: The welfare state in Britain since 1974*, Oxford: Clarendon Press, p 282

of many people's incomes and therefore imposed higher marginal deduction rates higher up the earnings range.

Apart from renaming benefits, and tinkering with regulations, nothing has changed since then. 'Working Families Tax Credit' replaced Family Credit, and this in turn was replaced by 'Working Tax Credits' and 'Child Tax Credits' in 2003. This was an attempt to establish a wage subsidy distinguishable from a family benefit so as to remove from it the stigma generally attached to means-tested benefits. The 'Working Tax Credit' was available to single adults without children, which the 'Working Families Tax Credit' had not been; but because the benefit's calculation still took into account a spouse's or partner's earnings, and because 'Working Tax Credit' was paid along with 'Child Tax Credit', there was still plenty of stigma attached to it.[38]

When they were established, the various 'Tax Credits' were more generous than Family Credit, and so provided a means-tested in-work benefit further up the earnings range. This provided many families with one-off incentives to seek employment: but in welfare 'it is the long-term impact of policies which is of key importance', and, with 'Tax Credits', 'once a person is into the Tax Credit system, few will be able by their own efforts to escape'.[39] As Frank Field goes on to say, a new welfare dependency has been created by a government that said that it intended to end such dependency. 'Tax Credits' have created a ceiling, and not a floor on which people can build.

'Universal Credit' will reduce the effects of the unemployment and poverty traps by reducing the amount of benefit withdrawn for every extra £1 of earnings:[40] but it will not change the structure, which will still be a mixture of National Insurance (contributory) benefits, means-tested benefits for people who do not have enough to live on, and universal Child Benefit. Neither will it change the presuppositions underlying the system: that benefits should be paid to households; that the man is the head of the household; that households are stable and constituted by permanent relationships; and that permanent

---

[38]   Dean, Hartley and Mitchell, Gerry (2011) *Wage top-ups and work incentives: The implications of the UK's Working Tax Credit scheme: A preliminary report*, London: LSE; Dean, Hartley (2012) 'The ethical deficit of the UK's proposed Universal Credit: pimping the precariat?' *Political Quarterly*, vol 83, no 2, pp 353–9

[39]   Field, Frank (2002) *Welfare Titans: How Lloyd George and Gordon Brown compare, and other essays on welfare reform*, London: Civitas, pp 54, 57

[40]   Centre for Social Justice (2009) *Dynamic benefits: Towards welfare that works*, London: Centre for Social Justice, p 265; DWP (2010) *21st Century welfare*, Cm 7913, London: The Stationery Office, p 21; DWP (2011) *Universal Credit: Welfare that works*, Cm 7957, London: The Stationery Office, p 13

---

employment is the norm, and diverse employment patterns therefore an aberration.

The minor changes that have occurred have, as we have seen, been the result of circumstance: a greater awareness of poverty among older people, the depression of the 1930s, and a major war inspiring a desire for a better world after it. Even the Beveridge Report, trumpeted as a major new start, was largely a tidying up of existing national, local, and voluntary provision. Beveridge's new contributory benefits were modelled on the contributory schemes that voluntary societies and trade unions were already running.

Why has there been so little change to the tax and benefits systems? The reason is that 'the UK social security system is a large, complex juggernaut that has grown in a largely incremental way over at least the last century',[41] government ministers' relative inexperience means that they find it easier to tinker than to risk coordinated change across the system as a whole, and the seventeenth century idea that the poor need 'correction' lives on in work and cohabitation tests. Social cohesion is as far from being realised now as it was then. We are still awaiting a genuine paradigm shift.

We shall be studying later the changes that families and the labour market have undergone. Households are now fluid, the labour market is global and increasingly fluid,[42] and household employment patterns need to be fluid. There will always be some constants: individuals and households need a home and sufficient income to enable them to provide for their needs and to participate in society; children need a stable home; and vulnerable people need to be cared for: but in a changing world those constants will require a changing income maintenance system. To keep running the structure that served the world of seventy years ago, without asking whether a better alternative might be available, ought not to be an option.

---

[41]   McKay, Stephen and Rowlingson, Karen (2008) 'Social security and welfare reform', pp 53-71 in Powell, Martin (ed.) *Modernising the welfare state,* Bristol: Policy Press, p 53

[42]   Bauman, Zygmunt (2000) *Liquid modernity*, Cambridge: Polity Press

Universal benefits in the UK[43]

The UK already has a variety of universal benefits. The three most important are the National Health Service (in which consultations with a general practitioner and treatment in hospital have been free at the point of use for over sixty years), education up to the age of eighteen, and Child Benefit (paid for every child until they are sixteen, or for longer if they remain in full-time education or training). There are others, such as winter fuel payments for every pensioner, free dental care for those under 19, free prescriptions for children and pensioners, and free television licences for those over 75.

Family Allowance

Before the First World War, Seebohm Rowntree, on the basis of his survey of poverty in York, had called for wages sufficient for families with three children, and allowances from the state for the fourth and further children. After the war, Eleanor Rathbone argued that a worker's wage could never be expected to support a large family, and suggested that mothers therefore needed an income from the state to enable them to care for their children.[44] In 1924, Rathbone's *The disinherited family* made the same point.[45] William Beveridge suffered 'instant and total conversion'.[46] He was then Director of the London School of Economics and Political Science (LSE), and when in 1925 he chaired a Royal Commission on the mining industry, he recommended that employers should pay child allowances as a way of keeping wages down at the same time as providing a subsistence income for every family. The General Strike intervened and miners' child allowances never happened, but at the LSE child allowances were soon being paid in addition to wages. When Beveridge was asked to chair a committee

---

[43] For a more detailed study see Torry, Malcolm (2012) 'The United Kingdom: only for children?' pp 235–63 in Caputo, Richard (ed.) *Basic Income guarantee and politics: International experiences and perspectives on the viability of Income Guarantee,* New York: Palgrave Macmillan

[44] Macnicol, John (1980) *The Movement for Family Allowances, 1918–1945: A study in social policy development,* London: Heinemann, pp 5–10, 20–23; Thane, Pat (1996) *Foundations of the welfare state,* 2nd edn, London: Longman, pp 63–4, 202

[45] Rathbone, Eleanor (1924/1986) *The disinherited family,* Bristol: Falling Wall Press, pp 139, 167, 353

[46] Beveridge, William (1949) in Rathbone, Eleanor, *Family allowances,* London: George Allen & Unwin (new edition of *The disinherited family* with an epilogue by William Beveridge) p 270

---

on the future of social insurance, and found that child allowances were not on the agenda, he simply wrote them into the presuppositions at the beginning of his report.[47] Child allowances were already being paid with Unemployment Benefit, so when unemployed men with large families found paid employment, they often found that the wage on offer, unsupplemented by child allowances, could be lower than the benefits that they had been receiving. The solution was to pay child allowances to everyone. Beveridge chose not to means-test the allowances because 'little money can be saved by any reasonable income test'.[48]

In 1945 the Family Allowance Act was passed with all party support, and the first Family Allowances were paid in 1946. Unfortunately, in order to achieve the level of child allowance that he wanted, Beveridge had had to compromise and agree not to pay an allowance for the first child. The Treasury had achieved another victory, too: 'Family Allowance' rather than 'Child Allowance'.

Among the reasons for Rathbone's and Beveridge's success were the argument that wages would never provide sufficient income for large families, the labour market disincentives that had so disturbed Beveridge, the unhealthy state of young adults, fear of inflation (Family Allowances would reduce the pressure for higher wages[49]), that by the time of the Second World War more women were members of trade unions (women were more likely to support child allowances, men more likely to support child tax allowances), and, for a few, the enhanced status for women that child allowances would promote. Above all, the war had raised expectations of a better Britain, and no political party wanted to vote against the popular new child allowances because they might have lost votes if they had. One of Rathbone's major achievements was that she was able to persuade MPs of the benefits of child allowances in relation to their own diverse interests, and in particular that she was able to persuade both William Beveridge (on the basis of reduced disincentives in the labour market) and John Maynard Keynes (for whom reducing inflation was a priority).[50]

---

[47] Another of the presuppositions on which Beveridge based his report was another proposed universal benefit: the National Health Service.

[48] Beveridge, Sir William (1942) *Social insurance and allied services*, Cmd 6404, London: Stationery Office, p 154, 157, 163, 177

[49] Harris, J. (1981) 'Some aspects of social policy in Britain during the Second World War', pp 247–62 in Mommsen, W. J., *The emergence of the welfare state in Britain and Germany, 1850–1950*, London: Croom Helm, p 249

[50] Land, Hilary (1975) 'The introduction of family allowances: an act of historic justice?' pp 157–230 in Hall, Phoebe, Land, Hilary, Parker, Roy, and Webb, Adrian, *Change, choice and conflict in social policy*, London: Heinemann, pp 169, 173–9, 195–6, 205, 221, 227

Family Allowance becomes Child Benefit

Just for once, a name change was not just that. Child Benefit really was an improvement on Family Allowance.

By the mid-1960s, fourteen per cent of families with someone in full-time employment, and with six children or more, were living below National Assistance levels.[51] Child Tax Allowances were still being paid, but these were of little use to families near to the tax threshold because they paid little or no tax anyway. In 1965, the Child Poverty Action Group showed that high-earning families obtained three times the benefit from Child Tax Allowances than did low-earning families.[52] Research by Richard Titmuss, Brian Abel-Smith and Peter Townsend had revealed that almost one in five families were on incomes below half the average;[53] and in 1966 the play *Cathy come home,* which recounted a family's slide from unemployment into homelessness and disintegration, brought home the realities of poverty to a broad spectrum of the population. The new Child Poverty Action Group argued for higher Family Allowances, for Family Allowance to be paid for every child, including the first,[54] and for the abolition of Child Tax Allowances. By 1968 the idea of paying 'Child Benefit' for every child[55] had gained substantial support in the Cabinet, largely because this would increase labour market incentives.[56] The Labour Party returned to power in 1974 after a few years of Conservative government, and parliament passed a Bill to establish Child Benefit. No start date was set. In 1976, Frank Field, Director of the Child Poverty Action Group, published leaked Cabinet minutes that revealed government concern that to abolish Child Tax Allowances would reduce net incomes for men and would therefore cause higher wage demands and higher inflation. The Child

---

[51]   Atkinson, A. B. (1969) *Poverty in Britain and the reform of social security,* Cambridge: Cambridge University Press, p 24

[52]   Banting, Keith G. (1979) *Poverty, politics and policy: Britain in the 1960s,* London: Macmillan, pp 66, 95; Townsend, Peter (1979) *Poverty in the United Kingdom,* Harmondsworth: Penguin, p 151

[53]   Abel-Smith, Brian and Townsend, Peter (1965) *The poor and the poorest: A new analysis of the Ministry of Labour's Family Expenditure Surveys of 1953–54 and 1960,* London: Bell; Titmuss, Richard (1962) *Income distribution and social change,* London: Allen and Unwin

[54]   Hill, Michael (1990) *Social security policy in britain,* London: Edward Elgar, p 41

[55]   Atkinson, Tony (2011) 'The case for universal child benefit', pp 79–90 in Walker, Alan, Sinfield, Adrian and Walker, Carol (eds) (2011) *Fighting poverty, inequality and injustice: A manifesto inspired by Peter Townsend,* Cambridge: Polity Press, p 83

[56]   Atkinson, A. B. (1969) *Poverty in Britain and the reform of social security,* Cambridge: Cambridge University Press, p 141

Poverty Action Group's 'Child Benefit Now' campaign, along with Barbara Castle MP's parliamentary support, resulted in Child Benefit being established: for every child, and at a level higher than the previous Family Allowance, but at a level lower than originally intended.[57]

Why was Child Benefit introduced?

Child Benefit was achieved through the efforts of such individuals as Margaret Herbison MP (a former Minister of Social Security), Barbara Castle, Frank Field, and the Cabinet mole; because the balance within the Cabinet had shifted against the means-testing of benefits for children;[58] because trade unions now contained more women members; and because enough MPs could find reasons to support Child Benefit. Twenty years of positive experience of Family Allowance also counted for a lot. It was simple to claim and administer, very little of it went unclaimed, and it did not attract the stigma that means-tested benefits attracted. It was popular with women because the main carer of children received it personally, and it reduced child poverty because mothers were more likely to spend the Family Allowance on their children than fathers were to spend the value of their Child Tax Allowances on them. Above all, Family Allowance did not change with the family's circumstances, and so did not discourage household members from seeking additional earnings.[59]

Will it last?

From 1979 Child Benefit was uprated in line with prices rather than wages; and in 1985 it was frozen.[60] At the same time, Family Income Supplement became the more generous but still means-tested Family Credit, so Child Benefit became a relatively less significant element of a family's income. The slogan was 'targeting'. What few ministers and MPs understood was that Child Benefit, in the context of a tax system in which the tax rate rises as income rises, is a highly efficient targeting of resources.

---

[57] Walley, John (1986) 'Public support for families with children: A study of British politics', *BIRG Bulletin*, no 5, Spring, pp 8–11

[58] Banting, Keith G. (1979) *Poverty, politics and policy: Britain in the 1960s*, London: Macmillan, pp 102–103

[59] Barr, Nicholas and Coulter, Fiona (1991) 'Social security: solution or problem?', pp 274–337 in Hills, John (ed.) *The state of welfare: The welfare state in Britain since 1974*, Oxford: Clarendon Press, p 291

[60] Hill, Michael (1990) *Social security policy in Britain*, Aldershot: Edward Elgar, p 57

In 1989, Frank Field (by then an MP, and no longer with the Child Poverty Action Group) proposed the reintroduction of Child Tax Allowances. This sparked a debate that, just for once, was about the relationship between cash benefits and tax allowances. Hermione Parker and Holly Sutherland put the different options to the test. They concluded that to replace Child Benefit with Child Tax Allowances (their option 1) would redistribute from the poor to the rich, that a dual system (option 2) would still redistribute from the poor to the rich, that increased Child Benefit (option 3) would redistribute from rich to poor, and that a small Citizen's Income (option 4) would redistribute from rich to poor.[61] When John Major became Prime Minister he unfroze Child Benefit.

Given the efficiency and beneficial effects of universal Child Benefit, it is somewhat strange that at the 2010 Conservative Party Conference the Chancellor of the Exchequer announced that he intended to withdraw Child Benefit from every household containing at least one higher rate taxpayer. Television interviewers asked members of his audience what they thought of the idea. They approved. As they said: Why give the money to people who don't need it? The government has now recognised how difficult it would be to match up Child Benefit recipients with higher rate taxpayers in order to means-test Child Benefit, so the current plan is to withdraw the value of Child Benefit through the tax system. For the first time we shall have a tax on children, but we can at least be grateful that we shall retain the highly efficient Child Benefit: efficient for the government, because of its low administrative cost, and efficient for families, because after the initial few minutes of form-filling, no time has to be spent on claiming Child Benefit – unlike most other benefits, for which hours can be spent visiting offices, phoning offices, and filling in forms to send to offices.[62] Child Benefit is also efficient in the sense that it does not interfere with decisions about how much employment to take, how much to earn, or the number of hours each partner should work. This means that it is efficient for people's employers, too. In the economist's language: Child Benefit does not compromise the efficiency of the labour market, or the efficiency of the household's economy. It is easy

[61]   Parker, Hermione and Sutherland, Holly (no date) *Child tax allowances? A comparison of child benefit, child tax reliefs, and basic incomes as instruments of family policy*, London: Suntory-Toyota International Centre for Economics and Related Disciplines, LSE, p 133

[62]   Bennett, Fran, Brewer, Mike and Shaw, Jonathan (2009) *Understanding the compliance costs of benefits and tax credits*, London: Institute for Fiscal Studies

and efficient to give Child Benefit to everyone, and because the rich pay more tax than the poor, *there is no reason not to give Child Benefit to every family with children.*

Conclusion

We have explored the UK's benefits landscape, made up of a diverse collection of means-tested, contributory and universal elements, and we have found the historical process to be evolutionary, with political, social and economic considerations generating minor changes which have moved the system as a whole in one direction or another. There have been occasional major new departures, such as Family Allowance, but these have been few and far between, and they have not affected to any major degree the means-tested direction of the system.

The result is a highly complex tax and benefits structure which at first sight might appear to be too complicated to reform radically by introducing a Citizen's Income. If the world around us was changing slowly then it might not be too much of a problem to retain the current system, but the world is in fact changing sufficiently fast to make reform of the increasingly anachronistic tax and benefits structure urgent.

While the UK might have one of the more complicated structures, the systems of other developed countries are not dissimilar, and some, because nongovernmental players are more prominent, are institutionally more complex than the UK's. Developing countries' systems are heading in the direction of complexity and will soon be facing the same problems as the UK's.

This all suggests that we are overdue for major reform in the direction of greater simplicity, and that at national, regional and global levels study of the future possible directions of our societies and economies, and of the kinds of tax and benefits regimes that might be appropriate, is an urgent requirement. If it is simplicity that is required, then a benefits system based on universal benefits has to be the way to go. They are simple to administer, require no intrusive investigation of personal circumstances, and do not interfere with labour markets or any other kind of market. They attract no stigma, and take-up is almost one hundred per cent.[63]

---

[63] Spicker, Paul (2011) *How social security works: An introduction to benefits in Britain,* Bristol: Policy Press, pp 119, 14

CHAPTER 3

Why do some reform proposals succeed, and some fail?

We have already studied two related successful reform proposals: the UK's Family Allowance and Child Benefit. We shall begin this chapter with some proposals that did not succeed, and then discuss some current proposals likely to reform the UK's benefits system. I invite readers from other countries to seek comparisons and contrasts in their own past and present social policy histories.

Proposals that failed

Child Benefit happened, and it is still with us: but other attempts at major reform of the tax and benefits systems have not reached the statute book. Why not?

Tax Credits

In the early 1970s a Conservative government proposed a genuine Tax Credit scheme. These Tax Credits would have replaced tax allowances, would have been paid in full if an individual had no other income, and would have been withdrawn at a specified rate as earned income rose. As earned income continued to rise, the Tax Credits would have ceased to be paid out and the worker would have started to pay tax:

> The Tax Credit system is a reform which embodies the socially valuable device of paying tax credits, to the extent that they are not used against tax due, positively as a benefit … [so as to] bring together what people pay and what they receive … Fewer people will be means-tested and others means-tested less often, and for the community there will be a large saving in administrative staff.[64]

---

[64] Her Majesty's Government (1972) *Proposals for a tax-credit system*, Cmnd 5116, London: Stationery Office, p iii

The scheme would have been encumbered with a number of complexities, but eventually most individuals and most households would have found themselves covered by it.[65] Tax Credits were to be withdrawn at 30 per cent as earned income rose: that is, for every extra £1 of earnings below the tax threshold, the employer would have deducted 30p of the Tax Credit, meaning that the individual would have been 70p better off; and for every £1 of extra earnings above the threshold, tax would have been deducted at 30 per cent, again meaning an additional 70p of net income. As we shall see later, this would have gone a long way to creating a genuine free market in labour, and would have reduced considerably the labour market disincentives that many people experienced.

Do tax credits redistribute resources? Yes. Consider three different people receiving a tax allowance: Someone paying only lower rate tax will have their total tax bill reduced by the tax allowance multiplied by that lower rate. Someone paying higher rate tax will have the amount of income taxed at the higher rate reduced, and not the amount of income taxed at the lower rate. Their tax bill will therefore be reduced by the tax allowance multiplied by the higher tax rate. Someone earning below the tax threshold will be paying no tax, but the amount of tax they escape will be less than the tax escaped by the other two people who are earning more than they are. Tax Credits would have been paid out to the taxpayer if their income fell below the threshold, so everyone would have been in the same position: having every extra £1 of earnings reduced by 30p (or by more than that if they were paying higher rate tax).[66] (How particular households' net incomes would have changed would have depended on individual circumstances.)[67]

The original report on Tax Credits allocated Child Tax Credits to children's fathers. The parliamentary select committee recommended that they be paid to the mother as cash payments at the Post Office, thus effectively increasing Child Benefit rather than being part of the

---

[65] Her Majesty's Government (1972) *Proposals for a tax-credit system*, Cmnd 5116, London: Stationery Office, pp 5, 18

[66] House of Commons Select Committee on Tax-Credit (1973) *Report and proceedings of the Committee*, Session 1972–73, vol I, report no 341–I, London: Stationery Office, pp 3, 28

[67] Atkinson, A.B. (1973) *The Tax Credit scheme and the redistribution of income*, London: Institute for Fiscal Studies, pp 54–5. cf Atkinson, A.B. and Sutherland, H. (1984) *A Tax Credit scheme and families in work*, Tax, Incentives and the Distribution of Income no 54, London: LSE; a discussion of a tax credits scheme proposed by Philip Vince in Vince, Philip (1983) *Tax credit – the Liberal plan for tax and social security*, London: Women's Liberal Federation

Tax Credits system. This was an interesting recognition of the efficiency and effectiveness of Child Benefit, and of universal unconditional benefits generally.[68]

The select committee recommended acceptance of the Tax Credits scheme because it appeared 'to offer the possibility of improving the amount of income retained from increased earnings ...':[69] but the general election of 1974 delivered a Labour administration that preferred Family Income Supplement to Tax Credits. If the Conservative Party had won the general election in 1974 then we might by now have had nearly forty years' experience of Tax Credits: real ones. We would also have learnt that revenue foregone in the form of tax allowances, and revenue paid out in the form of benefits, have the same effect on the public sector borrowing requirement: an obvious fact, though not obvious enough to encourage the government to include the revenue foregone through tax allowances in the public expenditure figures.

In 1979, Philip Vince developed for the Liberal Party a scheme of 'tax-free credits, some of them universal and some withdrawn as other income rises.' In 1983, Richard Wainwright, a Liberal Party MP, presented an uprated version of the scheme to the Treasury and Civil Service Committee's enquiry into 'The Structure of Personal Income Taxation and Income Support'.[70] Tax Credits were party policy. In 1988, the Liberal Party merged with the Social Democratic Party to become the Liberal Democratic Party, and during the early 1990s a Citizen's Income was party policy.[71] Unfortunately, the Liberal Party had few MPs and little influence. Neither a Citizen's Income nor Tax

---

[68] House of Commons Select Committee on Tax-Credit (1973) *Report and proceedings of the Committee*, Session 1972–73, vol I, report no 341–I, London: Stationery Office, pp 5, 20–24

[69] House of Commons Select Committee on Tax-Credit (1973) *Report and proceedings of the Committee*, Session 1972–73, vol I, report no 341–I, London: Stationery Office, p 7

[70] Vince, Philip (1986) 'Basic Incomes: some practical considerations', pp 5–8 in *BIRG Bulletin*, Spring. p 5; Parker, Hermione (1989) *Instead of the dole: An enquiry into integration of the tax and benefit systems*, London: Routledge, pp 168–89; Philip Vince, correspondence with the author, dated 6 April 2011; Creedy, John and Disney, Richard (1985) *Social insurance in transition*, Oxford: Clarendon Press, pp 38–46, 198

[71] Vince, Philip (1990) 'Citizen's Income', *BIRG Bulletin*, no 11, July, pp 20–1

Credits remain party policy,[72] though a Citizen's Pension became party policy in 2005.[73]

Attempts at a Citizen's Income

In the eighteenth century, Thomas Paine believed all citizens to be 'of one degree ... all men are born equal and with equal natural rights', and he wanted to see the state provide incomes for the poorest.[74] His ideas then moved on, for if

> the earth, in its natural, uncultivated state was, and ever would have continued to be, the common property of the human race, ... every proprietor ... of cultivated lands owes to the community a ground-rent ... for the land which he holds; and it is from this ground-rent that ... there shall be paid to every person, when arrived at the age of twenty-one years, the sum of fifteen pounds sterling, as a compensation in part, for the loss of his or her natural inheritance, by the introduction of the system of landed property. And also, the sum of ten pounds per annum, during life, to every person now living, of the age of fifty years, and to all others as they shall arrive at that age ... to every person, rich or poor, ... because it is in lieu of the natural inheritance, which, as a right, belongs to every man, over and above the property he may have created, or inherited from that who did.[75]

---

[72] Goodhart, William and Parker, Hermione (1994) 'To BI or not to BI? An exchange of letters between Sir William Goodhart QC and Hermione Parker', *Citizen's Income Bulletin*, no 18, July, pp 9–12; Goodwin, Stephen (1994) 'Liberal Democrats' Conference: Citizen's Income plan dropped', *The Independent*, 22 September, www.independent.co.uk/news/uk/liberal-democrats-conference-citizens-income-plan-dropped-1450315.html

[73] Correspondence with Philip Vince, 12 August 2012. See the section on Citizen's Pension later in this chapter.

[74] Paine, Thomas (1992) *The rights of man,* Indianapolis: Hackett, first published 1791–2, pp 273–6; Claeys, Gregory (1989) *Thomas Paine: Social and political thought,* Boston: Unwin Hyman, p 125; Quilley, Stephen (1994) 'What's left? Citizen's Income and Thomas Paine (1737–1809)', *Citizen's Income Bulletin*, no 17, January, pp 2–4. John Locke also believed that a level of common ownership meant that every household had the right to sufficient income to enable it to work and maintain itself: Layman, Daniel (2011) 'Locke on Basic Income', *Basic Income Studies*, vol 6, no 2, pp 1–12

[75] Paine, Thomas (1796/2004) 'Agrarian Justice' (first published 1796) in Cunliffe, John and Erreygers, Guido (eds) *The origins of universal grants: An anthology of historical writings on basic capital and Basic Income*, Basingstoke: Palgrave Macmillan, pp 4–7

During the following century, Joseph Charlier argued for a 'territorial dividend' paid to every citizen on the basis of their equal rights over the land; and John Stuart Mill recommended an equal payment 'for the subsistence of every member of the community, whether capable or not of labour'.[76]

By the early twentieth century, the adverse consequences of augmenting income for the poor through means-tested benefits were hard to ignore, and Mabel and Dennis Milner and Bertram Pickard, all Quakers, established the State Bonus League to campaign for a Citizen's Income, or 'state bonus', of 9/- [nine shillings = 45p] for each citizen.[77] In 1921, the Labour Party Executive Committee discussed the idea, and rejected it.

Not everyone agreed with the conclusions to which William Beveridge came in his 1942 report *Social insurance and allied services*. Lady Juliet Rhys Williams, Secretary of the Women's Liberal Federation,[78] issued a minority report, which she then expanded and published as *Something to look forward to*. Her objection to Beveridge's plan was that the combination of time-limited National Insurance benefits and means-tested National Assistance benefits would mean that many families would receive too little of any additional earnings, and that there would be too little incentive to seek paid employment. This would mean that to get people to accept employment would require coercion, which was anathema to Liberal politicians.[79]

---

[76] Charlier, Joseph (1848) *Solution du problème social ou constitution humanitaire*, Bruxelles: Chez tous les libraries du Royaume; Mill, John Stuart (1987) *Principles of political economy*, New York: Augustus Kelley (first published 1849), both quoted in Van Parijs, Philippe (2001), 'A Basic Income for All', pp 3–26 in Cohen, Joshua and Rogers, Joel, *What's wrong with a free lunch?* Boston: Beacon Press, pp 6–7

[77] Excerpts from Milner, E. Mabel and Milner, Dennis (1918) *Scheme for a state bonus*, in Cunliffe, John and Erreygers, Guido (eds) (2004) *The origins of universal grants: An anthology of historical writings on basic capital and basic income*, Basingstoke: Palgrave Macmillan, pp 121–133; Pickard, Bertram (1919) *A reasonable revolution, being a discussion of the state bonus scheme – a proposal for a National Minimum Income*, in Cunliffe, John and Erreygers, Guido (eds) (2004) *The origins of universal grants: An anthology of historical writings on basic capital and Basic Income*, Basingstoke: Palgrave Macmillan, pp 134–140; Van Trier, Walter (1995) *Every one a king*, Leuven: Departement Sociologie, Katholieke Universiteit Leuven, pp 31–142

[78] Harris, J. (1981) 'Some aspects of social policy in Britain during the Second World War', pp 247–262 in Mommsen, W. J., *The emergence of the welfare state in Britain and Germany, 1850–1950*, London: Croom Helm, p 258

[79] Rhys Williams, Juliet (1943) *Something to look forward to*, London: MacDonald and Co., pp 13, 45, 139–47

Rhys Williams' concern was both for the worker and for the economy. She wanted to see every worker receiving 'the whole benefit of wages (less taxation)',[80] and she also wanted to see part-time labour available to industries for which that was appropriate. The problem was that a main breadwinner who accepted part-time employment was unavailable for other work, and so could not claim unemployment benefit, and was therefore unlikely to achieve a subsistence income. It was therefore for practical economic reasons that Rhys Williams wanted to see a Citizen's Income, but there was also a principle involved:

> The State owes precisely the same benefits to all of its citizens, and should in no circumstances pay more to one than to another of the same sex and age, except in return for services rendered . . . Therefore the same benefits [should be paid] to the employed and healthy as to the idle and sick. . . . The prevention of want must be regarded as being the duty of the State to all its citizens and not merely to a favoured few.[81]

While the scheme would have been universal, and would have provided the same benefit to every adult, it would not have been entirely unconditional, so it does not strictly count as a Citizen's Income. Rhys Williams would have required workers to visit the Labour Exchange and to accept any employment offered, though she clearly expected the reduced marginal deduction rates to provide sufficient incentive to seek employment.[82]

As she herself later suggested, Rhys Williams' scheme would have resulted in greater administrative simplicity, would have raised employment incentives, would have reduced means-testing, would have increased possibilities for useful activity during periods of unemployment, and would have seen an improvement in married women's status.[83]

Juliet Rhys Williams was a Liberal. Her son, Sir Brandon Rhys Williams, was a Conservative MP, but that did not stop him from

---

[80] Rhys Williams, Juliet (1943) *Something to look forward to,* London: MacDonald and Co., p 147
[81] Rhys Williams, Juliet (1943) *Something to look forward to,* London: MacDonald and Co., pp 139, 145
[82] Rhys Williams, Juliet (1943) *Something to look forward to,* London: MacDonald and Co., p 167
[83] Rhys Williams, Juliet (1953) *Taxation and incentives,* London: William Hodge and Co., p 138

sharing his mother's enthusiasm for reforming the tax and benefits systems. In March 1973 he was a witness during the select committee hearings on Sir Arthur Cockfield's Tax Credits proposal,[84] and in 1982 he recommended a 'Basic Income Guarantee' – a Citizen's Income – to another select committee:[85, 86]

> Every British Citizen should be awarded a personal allowance of a value related to personal status, not to resources.

As Hermione Parker's synopsis of the scheme explained:

> Every citizen would be entitled to a personal basic income or PBI. These guaranteed basic incomes would replace virtually all existing benefits and allowances.[87]

The final exchange between Sir Brandon and the subcommittee Chair is instructive:

> *Chair:* There seem to me to be many benefits of this system.

> *BRW:* There are.

> *C:* Clearly you are expressing them very eloquently. Clearly they would go a long way toward easing the unemployment and poverty traps.

> *BRW:* There would not be any unemployment under these schemes. You would not need to register as unemployed. There would be people who were not in full-time work

---

[84] House of Commons Select Committee on Tax-Credit (1973) *Report and Proceedings of the Committee*, Session 1972–73, vol I, London: Stationery Office, 341–I

[85] 'Guarantee' here means that the citizen is guaranteed to receive an unconditional income. This was before the use of 'guarantee' for a guaranteed net income level, so its use didn't cause any confusion.

[86] This was the same subcommittee that considered Richard Wainwright's Tax Credit proposals.

[87] House of Commons Treasury and Civil Service Committee Sub-Committee (1982) *The structure of personal income taxation and Income Support: Minutes of evidence*, HC 331–ix, London: Stationery Office, p 423; cf. Rhys Williams, Brandon, *Stepping stones to independence: National Insurance after 1990*, Aberdeen: Aberdeen University Press, 1989; Parker, Hermione (1989) *Instead of the dole: An enquiry into integration of the tax and benefit systems,* London: Routledge, pp 224–53

but they would not need to have themselves labeled as unemployed. If they got an opportunity of work or casual work they could take it and nobody would have to know.

C: Are you saying that the unemployment benefit trap would be virtually eradicated by this?

BRW: Certainly.

C: Also it would be administratively much simpler.

BRW: Yes, it would.

C: I wonder what degree of redistribution of resources there would be or is that one of the matters that could be flexible within the system?

BRW: This is optional. This is why I have not put figures in my paper because you could make the scheme do what you liked. If you want to help people on low wages or low incomes you can tilt the tax and benefit structure in such a way that it is redistributive in certain directions.[88]

The committee recommended that the government should consider a Citizen's Income as a serious option for reform, that more work should be done, and that

> the Government should put such work in hand. ... Meanwhile, it is desirable that changes to the present system should be compatible with an eventual move to an integrated structure of tax and social security.[89]

In 1983 a general election was called and the proposals were taken no further.

---

[88] House of Commons Treasury and Civil Service Committee Sub-Committee (1982) *The structure of personal income taxation and Income Support: Minutes of evidence*, HC 331–ix, London: Stationery Office, p 459

[89] House of Commons Treasury and Civil Service Committee (1983) *Enquiry into the structure of personal income taxation and Income Support*, Third Special Report, Session 1982–3, section 13.35, quoted in Parker, Hermione (1989) *Instead of the dole: An enquiry into integration of the tax and benefit systems*, London: Routledge, p 100

In 1984, a group of individuals interested in the Citizen's Income approach to tax and benefits reform established the Basic Income Research Group (BIRG) (renamed the 'Citizen's Income Trust' in 1994). Since then, the Trust has promoted debate on Citizen's Income, published a regular newsletter (originally the *BIRG Bulletin*, now the *Citizen's Income Newsletter*), organised meetings, maintained a library and website, responded to requests for information, and submitted evidence to parliamentary committees. In 2007 the Trust submitted to the House of Commons Work and Pensions Committee's enquiry into benefits simplification a fully costed and revenue neutral Citizen's Income scheme;[90] since Iain Duncan Smith established his Centre for Social Justice, the Citizen's Income Trust has contributed to the Centre's exploration of tax and benefits reform; and it has also contributed evidence at each stage of the government's discussion of the 'Universal Credit' proposals that came out of the Centre for Social Justice. The Trust's message has been consistent: 'Universal Credit' is a useful few steps along the road to a Citizen's Income. A few more steps in a more universal direction would create a Citizen's Income and secure the benefits which that would offer in terms of income security, employment incentives, poverty reduction, and social cohesion.[91]

In 1994, the Labour Party's Commission on Social Justice issued its report, *Social justice: Strategies for national renewal*:

> It would be unwise ... to rule out a move towards Citizen's Income in future: if it turns out to be the case that earnings simply cannot provide a stable income for a growing proportion of people, then the notion of some guaranteed income, outside the labour market, could become increasingly attractive.[92]

When it came to power in 1997, the Labour Party introduced a National Minimum Wage, and then the misnamed 'Tax Credits'. We now have 'Universal Credit' on the way. The Liberal Democrats have given up Citizen's Income as party policy. Is the situation hopeless for a Citizen's Income in the UK?

---

[90] House of Commons Work and Pensions Committee (2007) *Benefit simplification*, the Seventh Report of Session 2006–7, HC 463, London: The Stationery Office, pp Ev.84–90

[91] Citizen's Income Trust (2010) 'A response to *21st century welfare*', *Citizen's Income Newsletter*, Issue 3, pp 3–9

[92] Commission on Social Justice (1994) *Social justice: Strategies for national renewal*, London: Vintage, p 264

A Citizen's Pension?

In April 2011 the Department for Work and Pensions (DWP) published a consultation paper, *A state pension for the 21st century*. One of the options floated in the paper is a Single-tier State Pension (STP) of £140 per week (at 2010 prices) for every individual with thirty years of National Insurance Contributions or credits.[93] This is not exactly a Citizen's Pension, because it is not entirely universal and it is not unconditional, but if a residency requirement were to replace the contribution record then it would become one.

Currently, the state pension is made up of two contributory components: a flat rate Basic State Pension (BSP) dependent on the number of years of National Insurance Contributions or credits, and an additional pension dependent on both the contribution/credit record and on earnings levels during the working life (though employers and employees can contract out of contributing to this second pension if their own occupational schemes are at least as adequate). The full BSP provides an income of below 16 per cent of average earnings, and most pensioner women receive a reduced amount and also a lower additional pension than men do. For those households with insufficient total income, means-tested Pension Credit can be claimed. This consists of a Guarantee Credit (worth about 25 per cent of the national average wage) and a Savings Credit that tapers the reduction in Guarantee Credit for those with more than a certain level of savings. (This last element is the most recent, and was added because the 100 per cent withdrawal of Guarantee Credit as savings rose was discouraging low earners from saving for their retirement.) In addition, pensioners can claim Housing Benefit and Council Tax Benefit. In 2009, a report by the Institute of Actuaries expressed concern that 40 per cent of current pensioners could qualify for the means-tested Guarantee Credit, that this percentage could increase, and that up to 1.8 million pensioners who could claim Pension Credit failed to do so because of 'the complexity of the claiming process and the stigma associated with being dependent on state benefit'. The report's authors were also disturbed by the increasing income gap between pensioners with private pensions funded by contributions on which tax relief had been granted, and pensioners reliant on means-tested Pension Credit. The

---

[93]   DWP (2011) *A state pension for the 21st century*, Cm 8053, London: The Stationery Office, pp 10, 29–35. Statements since the publication suggest that the Single-tier State Pension would be paid only to those reaching state pension age after the date of implementation.

Institute pointed out that to provide a universal pension at the same rate as the threshold for means-testing would cost only one third of the cost of tax relief on private pension contributions.[94]

Means-testing of Pension Credit, along with the complexity of the different elements, makes it difficult for anyone to predict the income that they are likely to receive from the state when they reach statutory retirement age. The younger someone is, the more difficult it is to predict their working life in terms of employment, earnings, and marital and parental status, what the state pension age will be when they reach the end of their working life, or what they will receive in state pensions when they reach that age. People on low incomes therefore have little incentive to save for their retirements, because savings might merely reduce their eligibility for means-tested Pension Credit.

The Single-tier State Pension (STP) discussed in the government's consultation document would be a big step in the right direction for future pensioners (– it is envisaged that it will only be paid to those reaching state pension age after 2015, thus excluding existing pensioners). It would largely remove means-testing (apart from the means-testing related to Housing Benefit and Council Tax Benefit), and it would not be conditional on the amount that people had saved through pensions or in other forms. Everyone would know where they stood.

The proposal is to reduce the pension pro rata if someone has less than thirty years of contributions/credits, and to exclude those with under seven years' worth of contributions. This means that some people, such as recent migrants or ethnic minority women whose culture discourages their employment, will still need means-tested Pension Credit, which will take them up to, or close to, the level of the STP (although the future indexation of Pension Credit is uncertain). This does seem to be rather a waste of effort. Why not simply give the Single-tier State Pension to everybody? – that is, why not pay a Citizen's Pension? A genuine Citizen's Pension would take no account of savings, or of private or occupational pensions, or of National Insurance Contributions records, and so would encourage everyone to take out private pensions, and to save in other ways.[95] John Creedy has shown that a Citizen's Pension would make less optimal the kind

---

94 Salter, Tony, Bryans, Andrew, Redman, Colin and Hewitt, Martin (2009) *100 Years of state pension: Learning from the past*, London: Institute of Actuaries, p 178
95 Salter, Tony (1997), 'Being realistic about pensions reform', *Citizen's Income Bulletin*, no 24, July, pp 9–11

of labour market behaviour that results in low incomes in later life.[96] A Citizen's Pension would also go a long way to equalise state pension provision for men and women.[97] As things stand, for everyone with a thirty year contribution/credit record who reaches state pension age after 2015, the proposed STP would have the same effect as a Citizen's Pension because it would already be above the level of the current Guarantee Credit. All that would be needed in the future would be to remove the contribution record condition and substitute a suitable residency requirement. Ideally, existing pensioners with less than the full BSP (mainly women who had lost out through non-employment or part-time employment during years of unpaid domestic work and caring) would all be brought up to the STP level. The government's consultation paper on the STP envisaged that accrued entitlements to the current second state pension which take pensioners above the level of the STP would be honoured by paying additional amounts that would result in total state pension payments equal to those that the pensioner would have received under the current system. The additional pension would then be phased out in favour of occupational and private pension schemes.[98] We would envisage a similar solution for those with accrued rights to the additional pension if a Citizen's Pension were to be implemented.

Steven Webb, the Minister of State for Pensions, and therefore responsible for formulating the options in the consultation paper, is no newcomer to the Citizen's Income idea. In 1990 he published a book on the subject with Samuel Brittan, *Beyond the welfare state: An examination of basic incomes in a market economy*:

> A Basic Income is a payment received by every person or household adequate to provide a minimum income, based only on age and family status, but otherwise unconditional.[99]

In the book, Webb proposes to calculate the Citizen's Income on a household basis, and not on an individual basis. Therefore what he proposes is not a Citizen's Income, and it would suffer from the same problems suffered by every benefit based on households rather than

---

[96] Creedy, John (1998), *Pensions and population ageing*, London: Edward Elgar

[97] Ginn, Jay (1996), 'Citizens' pensions and women', *Citizen's Income Bulletin*, no 21, February, pp 10–12

[98] DWP (2011) *A state pension for the 21st century*, Cm 8053, London: The Stationery Office, p 31

[99] Brittan, Samuel and Webb, Steven (1990) *Beyond the welfare state: An examination of Basic Incomes in a market economy*, Aberdeen: Aberdeen University Press, p 1

individuals: it would interfere with decisions about relationships, it would complicate household formation, and it would require the government to investigate people's intimate relationships. It would only take a minor change to turn the book's proposal into a genuine Citizen's Income, with all of the advantages that its simplicity would offer; and, in a similar way, it would only require a small change to the STP to turn it into a Citizen's Pension, which would again offer all of the advantages of simplicity.

In 1986, a working party drawn together by the Citizen's Income Trust (then the Basic Income Research Group) concluded that a Citizen's Pension would solve a wide variety of anomalies and would remove the savings trap;[100] in 2002, the National Association of Pension Funds recommended a Citizen's Pension of £100 per week for each individual citizen;[101] in 2004 the Pensions Policy Institute studied New Zealand's Citizen's Pension,[102] and the Citizen's Income Trust again joined in the debate.[103]

The Citizen's Pension idea has a history; the Minister for Pensions, Steven Webb, understands the issues and is consulting on a Single-tier State Pension (STP); and Webb's Secretary of State is Iain Duncan Smith, one of the few ministers who understands the disincentive effects of means-tested benefits and is trying to do something about them.

The Citizen's Income Trust has, of course, made a submission to the consultation on the options for pension reform, outlining the considerable advantages of the STP, suggesting that a Citizen's Pension

---

100 Basic Income Research Group (1986) 'Basic Incomes and elderly people', *BIRG Bulletin*, no 6, Autumn, pp 5–10

101 National Association of Pension Funds (2002) *Pensions – plain and simple*, London: National Association of Pension Funds; O'Connell, Alison (2004) *Citizen's pension: Lessons from New Zealand*, London: Pensions Policy Institute; National Association of Pension Funds (2004) *Towards a citizen's pension: Interim report*, London: National Association of Pension Funds. This latter report discusses options for recognising accrued rights in existing contributory state pensions. cf. Salter, T.A. (1990) 'Pensions, taxes and welfare', *BIRG Bulletin*, no 10, Autumn/Winter, pp 17–20

102 O'Connell, Alison (2004) *Citizen's pension: An introduction*, London: Pensions Policy Institute; James, Sean and Curry, Chris (2010) *A foundation pension: A PPI evaluation of NAPF* [National Association of Pension Funds] *proposals*, London: Pensions Policy Institute; Spicker, Paul (2011) *How social security works: An introduction to benefits in Britain*, Bristol: Policy Press, p 121

103 Citizen's Income Trust (2004) 'Further Support for a citizen's pension,' *Citizen's Income Newsletter*, issue 2, pp 1–2

would have even more advantages, and pointing out that it would take only a small change to turn an STP into a Citizen's Pension.[104]

Could a Citizen's Income happen?

We have discussed some proposals that remained proposals:

- Juliet Rhys Williams' minority report contained some good arguments, and it appeared during a period of debate on the future of the benefits system; but instead of a simple unconditional payment for everyone, we got National Insurance benefits and means-tested National Assistance.
- The Labour government that followed the general elections of 1974 decided not to replace a means-tested wages supplement with the Tax Credit scheme formulated by the previous Conservative government.
- Brandon Rhys Williams proposed a perfectly feasible scheme that would have offered many advantages; but the parliamentary subcommittee meeting considering it became inquorate, and the government took no notice of the committee's recommendation that the idea should be considered.

We have also discussed some proposals that have resulted in the reform of the tax and benefits systems or which are likely to do so:

- Eleanor Rathbone's proposal for a child allowance resulted in Family Allowance.
- The Child Poverty Action Group's proposal to increase the level of Family Allowance, and to extend it to the first child in every family, resulted in Child Benefit.
- William Beveridge's proposals for National Insurance and National Assistance benefits shaped the post-war welfare state.
- The 'Universal Credit' proposal has a ministerial champion, it is designed to tackle an identifiable problem (lack of incentive to increase earnings because of the high rate at which existing benefits are withdrawn as earnings rise), and it is backed by thorough research. It is likely to be introduced.

---

[104] Citizen's Income Trust (2011) 'The Citizen's Income Trust's response to the Department for Work and Pensions' consultation paper *A state pension for the 21st century*, April, Cm 8053', *Citizen's Income Newsletter*, issue 3, pp 1–6

- Similarly, the proposal for an STP has a ministerial champion, it is designed to tackle an identifiable problem (disincentives to save for retirement), and it is backed by research. It too is likely to happen.

It is possible to identify three patterns here:

1. The proposals that have changed the system, or that are likely to do so, have been for identifiable groups of people: Family Allowance and Child Benefit for children, National Insurance benefits for those with contribution records and facing particular situations (unemployment, sickness, old age), National Assistance for the same groups of people but only for those with insufficient income, 'Universal Credit' for households without sufficient income, and the STP for future pensioners. Failed proposals have been for everyone (Citizen's Income) or for all working age adults (the Heath government's Tax Credits). Do we therefore conclude that only those reforms that relate to definable groups of people, other than working-age adults, are likely to become reality?

While it was made up of a variety of elements for different groups of people, Beveridge's reforms affected everyone. It is therefore arguable that his reforms ought to be in the list of proposals that benefit everyone. If so, it is the only such set of proposals to have succeeded. Beveridge formulated his plan after a serious economic depression and during a major war. Do we conclude that only during a major crisis do the difficulties faced by major reform pale sufficiently into insignificance to make it possible for major reform to succeed?

2. Those proposals that have changed the system have benefited from longstanding and widespread debate and a reasonable level of public understanding of what was intended. Do we conclude that only publicly debated and understood proposals are likely to be legislated? Given the level of public ignorance of the tax and benefits systems, this would be a high bar to jump.

Research by D.V.L. Smith Associates in 1991 showed that 'few respondents had a clear understanding of the UK system of pensions and benefits', and that many people could not comprehend reform options when they were explained to them.[105] Debate among apparently intelligent members of the Conservative Party about the government's current proposals for depriving some families of Child

---

[105] D.V.L. Smith and Associates (1991) *Basic Income: A research report*, Prepared for Age Concern England, London: D.V.L. Smith and Associates, pp 5, 29

Benefit ('They don't need it') showed a woeful ignorance of the efficiency and incentives advantages of universal benefits, of the context of a progressive tax system (which withdraws from wealthy families far more than they receive in Child Benefit), and of the disadvantages of means-testing. When people's pay rises and they realise that they are no better off, because their 'Tax Credits' and Housing Benefit have been reduced and they are paying more tax, or, even worse, they are now off 'Tax Credits' and Housing Benefit and they have lost free school meals for their children: they might moan that it is a terrible system, but they take no positive steps to change it. I suspect that there are two reasons for this: firstly, means-testing has been with us for so long, and its incidence has risen to such an extent during the past thirty years,[106] that it is experienced as a fact of life and not as a mechanism that we might be able to abandon; and secondly, if we do not understand something then we do not press for change because we have no wish to risk being shown up for not understanding it.

If a prerequisite for change in the benefits system is substantial public debate and understanding, it looks as if there is little chance of a Citizen's Income being implemented, or, indeed, of any major change in the system. The level of public debate in Finland and Denmark has been far higher than in the UK,[107] and there have been periods when debate in the Netherlands[108] and in Ireland has been lively.[109] Debates

---

[106] Evans, Martin and Williams, Lewis (2009) *A generation of change, a lifetime of difference? Social policy in Britain since 1979*, Bristol: Policy Press, p 140. cf. Evans, Martin and Eyre, Jill (2004) *The opportunities of a lifetime: Model lifetime analysis of current British social policy*, Bristol: Policy Press

[107] Andersson, Jan Otto (2001) 'Why does Basic Income thrill the Finns, but not the Swedes?' *Citizen's Income Newsletter*, issue 2, pp 2–4; Christensen, Erik (2008) *The heretical political discourse: A discourse analysis of the Danish debate on Basic Income*, Aalborg: Aalborg University Press

[108] van der Veen, Robert J. (1997) 'Basic Income in the Netherlands?' *Citizen's Income Bulletin*, no 23, February, pp 11–13

[109] Callender, Rosheen (1989) 'Basic Income in Ireland: the debate so far', *BIRG Bulletin*, no 9, Spring/Summer, pp 10–13; O'Malley, Chris (1989) 'Proposal for a Basic Income in the Republic of Ireland', *BIRG Bulletin*, no 9, Spring/Summer, pp 13–16; Baker, John (1995) 'Basic Income in Ireland: recent developments', *Citizen's Income Bulletin*, no 20, July, pp 10–11; McManus, Anne (1997) 'Is Basic Income the answer? Some findings from Ireland', *Citizen's Income Bulletin*, no 23, February, pp 4–6; FitzGerald, Garret (1997) 'Basic Income system has merit for Ireland', *Citizen's Income Bulletin*, no 24, July, p 4–6; Lee, Joe (1997) 'Social security in the computer age', *Citizen's Income Bulletin*, no 24, July, pp 7–8; Clark, Charles M.A. (2002) *The Basic Income guarantee: Ensuring progress and prosperity in the 21st century*, Dublin: The Liffey Press; Miller, Anne (2003) 'The Irish situation', *Citizen's Income Newsletter*, issue 2, pp 1–5

to watch are those in East Timor, Catalonia, South Africa, Germany, and New Zealand.[110] Perhaps the size of a country's population is a factor in the level of debate that we can expect: which leads me to wonder whether an independent Scotland might implement a Citizen's Income well before the rest of the UK.

A possible counterexample is this: When Gordon Brown was Chancellor of the Exchequer, he replaced the means-tested Family Credit, run by the Department for Work and Pensions, with the means-tested 'Tax Credits', run by his own department. There was no meaningful public debate. 'Universal Credit' is likely to happen, and so is the STP, even though there has been little public understanding or debate about either of them. So while public understanding and debate might once have been a prerequisite for success, they would appear not to be so now.

3. Those proposals that have become Acts of Parliament are those that have not reduced the number of civil servants, and those that have not become Acts of Parliament would have done so.

Family Allowance was a new benefit and so added to the total number of civil servants. Child Benefit displaced Child Tax Allowances, but the overall effect would have been little change in the number of tax inspectors. The 1970s Tax Credits might or might not have reduced the number of civil servants, so it might have happened; and Steven Webb's STP retains contribution/credit records and so is unlikely to reduce the number of public servants by very many: though there should be some loss of posts related to fewer pensioners claiming means-tested benefits.

As Harris has suggested in relation to an early attempt at something like a Citizen's Income: 'Like most schemes for abolishing bureaucrats, Lady Juliet's proposals met with an official wall of silence.'[111] Juliet Rhys Williams' and Brandon Rhys Williams' proposals would have reduced the number of civil servants administering existing benefits. Permanent Secretaries have an interest in maintaining the size of their departments, and in retaining departmental functions. It is Permanent Secretaries who brief ministers. Public servants might exhibit a certain level of altruism in the exercise of their professional tasks, but it would be asking for a

---

110 Murray, Matthew C. and Pateman, Carole (eds) (2012) *Basic Income worldwide: Horizons of reform*, New York: Palgrave Macmillan
111 Harris, J. (1981) 'Some aspects of social policy in Britain during the Second World War,' pp 247–262 in Mommsen, W. J., *The emergence of the welfare state in Britain and Germany, 1850–1950*, London: Croom Helm, p 258

miracle not to expect them to brief in such a way as to preserve the size and functions of their departments. Schemes that would reduce the size and functions of their own departments are therefore unlikely to happen unless a Secretary of State is so convinced of the benefits of a scheme that they can achieve sufficient institutional momentum, in the Cabinet, in Parliament, and in their own department, to propel the scheme onto the statute book.

Sadly, withdrawing the value of Child Benefit through the tax system for households containing a higher rate taxpayer will increase the number of public servants. It is therefore likely that the relevant departmental heads will be briefing in favour of this change, and for obvious reasons.

Conclusion

At first glance, things do not look good for a Citizen's Income. A Citizen's Income of any size, if funded by reducing tax allowances, means-tested benefits, and most contributory benefits, would take few civil servants to administer and would take people off means-tested benefits; and a sizeable Citizen's Income could result in the abolition of means tested benefits and thus in a substantial drop in the number of civil servants (though on a continuing Housing Benefit see Chapter 16). Iain Duncan Smith has persuaded the Chancellor of the Exchequer to allow the Department for Work and Pensions (DWP) to run 'Universal Credit', which will mean the Treasury no longer running 'Tax Credits'. The DWP will presumably take in the Her Majesty's Revenue and Customs staff currently running Child Benefit and 'Tax Credits', and will increase in size. The Secretary of State and his Department will have been entirely agreed on the implementation of 'Universal Credit'. For a Secretary of State to advocate a Citizen's Income would be a lot more difficult, unless, of course, it was initially a very small one which would not displace too many households from means-tested benefits and might therefore add slightly to the number of civil servants required. Similarly, if a Citizen's Income were to be funded by another means, such as a tax on carbon-based fuels, or a tax on financial transactions, or if a Citizen's Income were to be implemented on a European rather than on a national basis, then there would be no reason for departmental heads to resist the idea and they might actually welcome it.

Civil servants would find it fairly easy to argue against a Citizen's Income as well as having an interest in doing so. To replace tax allowances with cash benefits would look as if it would increase public expenditure. This objection was actually made by the Treasury when Margaret Thatcher's policy unit proposed a Citizen's Income.[112] It is an irrational objection, because, as Atkinson and Sutherland have pointed out: 'In terms of cash, there is no difference between paying less tax and receiving a benefit, as was recognised when child tax allowance and family allowance were fused into a single child benefit.'[113] If revenue foregone by the Treasury through tax allowances is replaced by an income paid out to citizens, and the revenue foregone is equal to the money paid out, then the Treasury will suffer no loss and public expenditure will not have increased. We should surely regard as public expenditure all revenue foregone through the effect of tax allowances, and we should regard the personal tax allowance as a benefit that tends to redistribute from poor to rich. We might then be able to have a more rational discussion about the benefits of a Citizen's Income because we would be regarding tax allowances as a social policy issue alongside cash benefits. As things stand, any proposal to shift income maintenance from tax allowances to cash payments will suffer from an irrational disadvantage, and any proposal to shift policy from cash payments to tax allowances will experience an irrational positive advantage.

At first glance, it looks as if it might be difficult for a UK government to implement a Citizen's Income: but many of us still hope that if a policy proposal would benefit individuals, households, society, and the economy, then the government would implement it – and that the government might therefore be willing to implement a Citizen's Income. The next chapter will study two ways in which it might do that.

---

[112] Monckton, Christopher (1993) 'Universal benefit', *Citizen's Income Bulletin*, no 16, July, pp 4–6, p 6

[113] Atkinson, A.B. and Sutherland, Holly (1988a) *Integrating incomes taxation and social security: Analysis of a partial Basic Income*, Tax, Incentives and the Distribution of Income paper no 123, London: LSE, p 1; Atkinson, Tony and Sutherland, Holly (1988b) 'Analysis of a partial Basic Income', *BIRG Bulletin*, no 8, Autumn, pp 12–14

CHAPTER 4

How might we implement a Citizen's Income?

I have drawn the following lessons from the history of the UK's tax and benefits systems:

- The proposals that have changed the system have been for identifiable groups of people.
- Those proposals that have changed the system have benefited from longstanding and widespread debate and a reasonable level of public understanding of what was intended.
- Those proposals that have become Acts of Parliament are those that have not reduced the number of civil servants, and those that have not become Acts of Parliament would have reduced the number of civil servants.

If you have drawn different conclusions from your own context then you will need to draw your own conclusions as to the best way to implement a Citizen's Income. If you have drawn similar conclusions to mine then you might agree that there could be two possible ways of implementing a Citizen's Income:

1. **One demographic group at a time**. The fact that it is the proposed changes to the system that would benefit particular groups that have become law suggests that implementing a Citizen's Income one demographic group at a time might be the approach most likely to succeed.
2. **Start with a small Citizen's Income for everyone**. Proposals that do not reduce the number of civil servants are more likely to succeed. A small Citizen's Income would not reduce the number of civil servants because many households would still need means-tested and other existing benefits, and a new administrative mechanism would be needed to implement the Citizen's Income. The small Citizen's Income could then grow.

We shall look at each option in turn.

1. Universal benefits for different demographic groups

The UK already has a Citizen's Income for children. It will probably not be long before we see a Single-tier State Pension (STP), and it might not be much longer before that becomes a Citizen's Pension. Some other countries have universal benefits for children, or have implemented benefits for children which they intend to universalise. Some countries already have Citizen's Pensions. To establish universal benefits for children and a Citizen's Pension could be the best way for any country to begin the process of establishing a Citizen's Income.

A 'Third Age' income for the over 55s could come next. The twenty years between 55 and 75 constitute a time of transition for many people, and also a time of opportunity, in which many would prefer a mixture of paid, caring and voluntary activity. A 'Third Age income', a Citizen's Income for this age group, would reduce the stigma experienced by those no longer in full-time employment and who have little chance of finding another full-time job. It would also make part-time employment more viable, it would make it easier for people to care for older parents or for grandchildren, it would encourage the kind of sustained community involvement to which people in their third age have so much to contribute, and it would value all of this as socially useful work. Charles Handy suggests that the Third Age 'provides an opportunity for pilot testing. It is a discrete section of society but one that will increasingly set norms and fashions for the rest. ... We could experiment with them, at moderate cost, and so make the idea [of a Citizen's Income] workable and practicable to the rest.'[114]

Next could come a young adult's income, for the under 25s, to facilitate the training and education that our economy will increasingly need them to have. (The provision of a coherent income structure for 16 to 25 year olds has for a quarter of a century been a primary motive for pursuing a Citizen's Income agenda, though more clearly during the 1980s than today.[115])

Once these unconditional incomes had been established, it would not be too difficult to raise 25 to 30, and reduce 55 to 50, and then to fill the twenty-year gap between them.

---

[114] Handy, Charles (1990) 'The Third Age', *BIRG Bulletin*, no 11, July, pp 3–4, p 4
[115] Smith, Douglas (1985) 'Going, going ... gone: the vanishing rights of young people to supplementary benefit', *BIRG Bulletin*, no 3, Spring, p 16; Morley, Robert E. (1985) 'Out of touch: the Flower reforms of social security', *BIRG Bulletin*, no 4, Autumn, pp 3–4; The BIRG youth group (1985) 'Basic Incomes and young people', *BIRG Bulletin*, no 4, Autumn, pp 8–11; Lewis, Paul (1986) 'A Basic Income for youth', *BIRG Bulletin*, no 6, Autumn, pp 3–5

2. A small Citizen's Income for everyone

Now we shall consider the possibility of establishing a small Citizen's Income for every adult and then allowing it to grow, with tax allowances and means-tested and social insurance benefits reducing as the Citizen's Income rises.[116] There would be good reasons for doing it in this way:

- A gradual introduction would enable individuals and households to adapt slowly to the new labour market incentives, to additional options for household employment patterns, and to new options for household structure.
- It would enable adjustments to net income, and to the higher net incomes that lower deduction rates would make possible, to be handled more easily.
- It would enable the labour market to become more flexible gradually. None of us have ever known a labour market without rigidities imposed by the tax and benefits systems. Such a major new experience might be best tackled slowly.

A small Citizen's Income would not create major changes in people's marginal deduction rates, it would not increase labour market options in a major way, it would not redistribute very much, and it would not reduce poverty very much: so would the implementation of a small universal payment give us genuine experience of a Citizen's Income? The answer to that question is 'Yes'. However small it is, the Citizen's Income would reduce the marginal deduction rates that people suffer and would thus reduce disincentives in the labour market. If a household were to receive a Citizen's Income of just half the value of any means-tested benefits which they currently receive, then they would find themselves suffering from high marginal deduction rates across just half of the earnings range across which they suffer them now. As earnings rose, they would much more quickly reach a position from which net income could increase rapidly as earnings rose. This could have a major effect on a household's employment pattern and net income.

Research at the LSE has suggested that a partial Citizen's Income 'represents a definite and practicable scheme ... and the results ...

---

[116] Parker, Hermione (1989) *Instead of the dole: An enquiry into integration of the tax and benefit system*, London: Routledge, pp 333–80; Gray, Anne (1993) 'Citizen's Income, minimum wages, and work sharing', *Citizen's Income Bulletin*, no 16, July, pp 14–18; Murphy, Jason B. (2010) 'Baby steps: Basic Income and the need for incremental organizational development', *Basic Income Studies*, vol 5, no 1, pp 1–13

indicate that it could be introduced without having major distributional consequences'.[117] This absence of redistributional effects would enable a Citizen's Income to be introduced without major transitional arrangements being required; and a partial Citizen's Income, even a small one,[118] would reduce disincentives, would reduce the effects of the unemployment and poverty traps, and would bind us together as a society because everybody would receive it.

While all that we require for debate about a Citizen's Income to be realistic is one viable route from the current situation to the payment of a Citizen's Income, we are in the fortunate position of being able to choose between two possibilities.[119] Each route coheres with one of the conclusions that we have drawn from studying the history of the UK's benefits system, but one of them – starting with a small Citizen's Income for everyone and letting it grow – offers the additional reason that we would be able to evaluate the effects of the Citizen's Income as they occurred.

A further implementation method would be to follow Samuel Brittan's suggestion and slowly remove the tapers relating to 'Tax Credits' and at the same time pay 'Tax Credits' to people not currently receiving them.[120] This is an implementation method that might have some merit, and on which a small amount of research is now available.[121] Another implementation method would be slowly to universalise social insurance benefits, in much the same way as Steven Webb's STP would extend the coverage of the UK's Basic State Pension.[122]

Implementation in practice

The implementation methods that we have discussed are themselves ideal types, for, as Bill Jordan has pointed out, social policy reform is rarely so orderly. It is more a 'winding country lane' than a 'majestic

---

[117] Atkinson, A.B. (1989) *Poverty and social security*, London: Harvester/Wheatsheaf, p 334

[118] Parker, Hermione and Sutherland, Holly (1995) 'Why a £20 CI is better than lowering Income Tax to 20%', *Citizen's Income Bulletin*, no 19, February p 15–18

[119] Ronald Dore (1996) 'A feasible Jerusalem?' *The Political Quarterly*, vol 67, no 1, pp 58–63

[120] Brittan, Samuel (2001) 'An attraction for Gladstonian Liberals', *Citizen's Income Newsletter*, issue 1, p 2

[121] See an appendix for this chapter at www.citizensincome.org

[122] Bennett, Fran and Sutherland, Holly (2011) *The importance of independent income: Understanding the role of non-means-tested earnings replacement benefits*, ISER working paper no 2011–09, Colchester: Institute for Social and Economic Research, University of Essex

highway'. Taking the UK as an example, and employing a slightly different metaphor, Jordan compares the 'high road', represented by a Citizen's Income, and inspired by an equality and libertarian agenda, to the 'low road', motivated by the need to fix the current benefits system: a road well represented by 'Universal Credit'.[123] The problem is that

> if progress towards a true basic income (more generous, with individual rather than household eligibility, and without work enforcement) stalled at this point, the other gains associated with it, in terms of liberty and equality, would remain out of reach;[124]

and a small Citizen's Income, designed to make labour markets more flexible, might remain small and fulfil only its initial purpose rather than growing and therefore reaping the wider benefits of a Citizen's Income.

The first steps towards a Citizen's Income may become politically feasible for a variety of reasons, at a number of different developmental stages, all of which will also be perilous for the principle in various ways – but those steps should not for that reason be rejected:

> Social policy can seldom deal in pure principles or utopian solutions, and basic income is no exception. It cannot resolve all the challenges of globalization … in a single reform, but these measures may be a step in the right direction.[125]

We can now recognise the current coalition government's 'Universal Credit' as a step in the direction of a Citizen's Income. We shall discover later, in Chapter 13, that every mainstream political ideology can generate arguments for a Citizen's Income, and that any ideology's arguments against a Citizen's Income relate to more general anxieties rather than to the political ideology itself. Here we have discovered that the last and present governments' actual policy directions are steps along the 'winding country lane' towards a Citizen's Income. What would be helpful would be more political recognition of this fact, an all party commitment to continue in this direction, and in

---

123 Jordan, Bill (2012) 'The low road to Basic Income? Tax-benefit integration in the UK', *Journal of Social Policy*, vol 41, no 1, pp 1–17

124 Jordan, Bill (2012) 'The low road to Basic Income? Tax-benefit integration in the UK', *Journal of Social Policy*, vol 41, no 1, pp 1–17, p 3

125 Jordan, Bill (2011) 'The perils of basic income: ambiguous opportunities for the implementation of a utopian proposal', *Policy & Politics*, vol 39, no 1, pp 101–14, p 112

particular a commitment to lower marginal deduction rates and the individualisation of the benefits system: both worthwhile objectives in their own right, as well as steps along the lane towards a Citizen's Income. Gradual convergence of benefit rates and the cash values of personal tax allowances would also contribute towards ease of transition when tax allowances are turned into cash payments in order to establish a Citizen's Income.[126] At the moment, the Personal Allowance is moving in the right direction.

At each step along the way we shall need to be sure not only that individual households' gains or losses are not too great, but also that the administrative steps required are easy to achieve;[127] and we shall also need to ensure that the direction in which we are travelling is in fact towards a Citizen's Income: an unconditional and non-withdrawable income for every individual as a right of citizenship. While it is true that the details of a Citizen's Income will be context-specific (for instance, in terms of the frequency of payment, or in terms of precisely how the regular sum is paid to each individual), what we must never do is declare that a Citizen's Income has been implemented if its universality, unconditionality, or nonwithdrawability, have in any way been compromised.[128]

Before we leave unchallenged the idea that 'pure principles or utopian solutions'[129] are not a realistic way to do social policy, we ought at least to consider Eleanor Rathbone's explicit attempt to create a utopia in which child poverty had been abolished in the UK. That was the intention behind the Family Allowance, and she got her way. Ruth Levitas suggests that we might do more useful social policy if we had in our minds the kind of society that we want, rather than identify problems in today's society and then try to fix them. The world that Levitas wants to see is Rathbone's utopia, a world without child poverty;

---

[126] Jordan, Bill, Agulnik, Phil, Burbidge, Duncan and Duffin, Stuart (2000) *Stumbling towards Basic Incomes: The prospects for tax-benefit integration*, London: Citizen's Income Trust, pp 11, 28, 42, 56

[127] A Citizen's Income scheme that could be achieved in one step from the current system with a handful of simple changes to regulations can be found on the website, and also an unconditional benefit for adults in employment which would be a step towards a Citizen's Income.

[128] De Wispelaere, Jürgen and Stirton, Lindsay (2005) 'The many faces of Universal Basic Income', *Citizen's Income Newsletter*, issue 1, pp 1–8. In my view, De Wispelaere and Stirton allow too much potential conditionality into their definition of 'Universal Basic Income'.

[129] Jordan, Bill (2011) 'The perils of basic income: ambiguous opportunities for the implementation of a utopian proposal', *Policy & Politics*, vol 39, no 1, pp 101–14, p 112

and her methods for achieving it are Child Benefit paid at a higher rate, and a Citizen's Income for adults.[130]

Anatomy of a debate

We have shown that implementation of a Citizen's Income is a practical possibility. In Chapter 13 we shall ask whether a Citizen's Income might be politically feasible. In the context of this chapter on implementation it is important to ask a related question: Can we conceive of a process of debate that might lead to the implementation of a Citizen's Income?

We have seen that the essential debate to win is the one with ministers and civil servants, but that public debate and understanding might also be helpful. In the UK, we shall need that public debate in order to persuade the British public that there is a better way than means-testing, for only by doing that shall we be able to persuade Members of Parliament of the necessity of change. The same might be true in other countries too.

In the UK, there has been plenty of debate about Citizen's Income among academics and policy makers. For thirty years the volume of academic debate on income maintenance reform proposals – Negative Income Tax, Tax Credits, Citizen's Income and so on – has grown exponentially. Some of this growth has been because thirty years ago there was very little research literature on universal benefits, and the field therefore offered plenty of opportunity for theses, dissertations, books and articles. Think tanks such as the Centre for Social Justice, and the consultants who work for them, have found the field to be an underpopulated and therefore a productive and profitable one; and the Citizen's Income Trust has, of course, played its own part in promoting and publicising debate on Citizen's Income. Universal benefits can be studied from within a wide variety of disciplines – economics, social policy, sociology, moral philosophy, theology, and more – and so have attracted widespread academic interest. The extent to which academic and policy maker interest has translated into public interest and debate is an interesting question, to which the answer is 'probably very little'.

The same will be true of Members of Parliament. They will all be aware that many of their constituents report difficult experiences with the benefits system, and that the system really is not fit for purpose; but

---

[130] Levitas, Ruth (2012) 'Utopia calling: eradicating child poverty in the United Kingdom and beyond', pp 449–73 in Minujin, Alberto and Nandy, Shailen (eds) *Global child poverty and well-being: Measurement, concepts, policy and action*, Bristol: Policy Press

that does not mean that they have thought deeply about *why* there is a problem with the system, or about options for reform.

It is an unexpected pleasure to have at the Department for Work and Pensions two people who *do* understand something about tax and benefits: the Secretary of State, Iain Duncan Smith, who has studied the effects of the present system and is committed to making some useful changes; and the Minister for Pensions, Steven Webb, who has an intimate knowledge of the detail of the system, and understands the advantages of universal benefits. But this is rare. For the past thirty years we have had as Secretary of State for Social Security or for Work and Pensions Members of Parliament who never really wanted the job, but who accepted it in the hope that they would soon be moved to another department. Not since Norman Fowler have we had a Secretary of State with a vision for change. This is a pity. What we need is a series of long-term Secretaries of State willing to work at an all-party plan for reform, so that they can hold a thorough review of the tax and benefits systems, and of the ways in which they interact; develop a variety of options for reform, among which would be a Citizen's Income; look ahead to the kind of society and the kind of economy that we are likely to experience during the next fifty to a hundred years; and choose and implement the appropriate option. This will be a long-term task and it will require long-term people. It will also require MPs to understand both the current system, and the feasible reform options, so that they can participate in an intelligent debate.

The deeper understanding required would clearly benefit from widespread public debate, a widespread understanding of the need for change, an understanding of the range of options available, and engagement with the arguments for and against each one of them: but how is this to happen, given the widespread public ignorance of the present system, and widespread lack of understanding of the merits and demerits of different reform options? Can we do for the tax and benefits structure what Wilkinson and Pickett have done for an understanding of inequality and its effects?[131] Is it possible for a sufficient number of members of the public to realise that getting the structure right is as important as the level of benefits,[132] that the employment contract need not be the only normative route to an income,[133] that means-testing

---

[131] Wilkinson, Richard and Pickett, Kate (2009) *The spirit level: Why more equal societies almost always do better*, London: Allen Lane

[132] Horton, Tim and Gregory, James (2009) *The solidarity society: Why we can afford to end poverty, and how to do it with public support*, London: Fabian Society, p 98

[133] Offe, Claus (2001) 'Pathways from here', pp 111–18 in Cohen, Joshua and Rogers, Joel, *What's wrong with a free lunch?* Boston: Beacon Press, p 113

is no better at targeting money on the poor than is a universal benefit along with a progressive Income Tax, that means-testing benefits in the context of an Income Tax with a personal tax allowance is to do the same job twice, that to means-test some members of society and not others is socially divisive, that means-testing creates numerous traps[134] that imprison people in poverty, and that to abandon means-testing is perfectly feasible and would set millions of individuals and households free to earn their way out of poverty and to contribute to society in ways about which they can only dream at the moment? Is a widespread paradigm shift a possibility?[135] – that is, is it possible for a revolution to take place in the way in which people see the possibilities for organising our income maintenance system, in the same way that such shifts have taken place in our understanding of the universe and of human origins?

For a paradigm shift to occur, numerous individual conversions need to take place. Conversion occurs when a way of thought that explains our experience of life faces difficulties. Evidence mounts up against it, and mental conflict of one sort or another is the result. A new resolution is required. That is what our conscious minds know. What is not always clear to us is that our subconscious minds have been working through a variety of conceptual options: and then suddenly everything seems to fall into place, and we see things differently. A new way of thinking about things now makes sense of everything. What has happened is that a conceptual structure on which our subconscious mind has been working has broken through into our conscious mind to provide us with a new conceptual framework.

Sometimes the process really is a sudden one. We are offered an explanation or an idea that makes sense of the world of our experience better than our previous ideas did, and we find ourselves having 'changed our minds'. Our brains have worked fast to evaluate the new possibility, to test it against our experience, to find the new ideas a better explanation than ideas previously held, and our conceptual map is rapidly revised. Ideas, actions and commitments connected to a previous structure are quickly reconnected to the new one, often in quite unfamiliar configurations. The process can be both invigorating and deeply disturbing.

---

134 Esping-Andersen, Gøsta (1996) 'Positive sum solutions in a world of trade-offs?' pp 256–67 in Esping-Andersen, Gøsta (ed.) *Welfare states in transition: National adaptations*, London: Sage, p 262

135 On paradigm shifts and how they occur in the scientific community, see Kuhn, Thomas S. (1962) *The structure of scientific revolutions*, Chicago: Chicago University Press

During our discussion of the history of the UK's benefits system we noted Beveridge's and Keynes' conversions to universal Family Allowances. These appear to have been happy conversion experiences. However, Beveridge preferred contributory and means-tested benefits to Juliet Rhys Williams' suggestion of something like a Citizen's Income, however consistent such a universal benefit might have been with the structure of Family Allowances – which just goes to show that we can never assume consistency. One conversion does not necessarily lead to another, even if the logic suggests that it should.

So the question is this: Is it possible for sufficient numbers of people to be converted from a commitment to means-testing as the foundation of the benefits system to a commitment to universal benefits as the most efficient way of distributing incomes?

As Moscovici has suggested, agreement expressed publicly is more likely to side with majority opinion than agreement expressed privately:

> A minority, which by definition expresses a deviant judgment, a judgment contrary to the norms respected by the social group, convinces some members of the group, who may accept its judgment in private. They will be reluctant to do so publicly, however, either for fear of losing face or to avoid the risk of speaking or acting in a deviant fashion in the presence of others.[136]

I would add that they might also be afraid of being asked to explain their position when they know that the field is a complex one and that they might not be able to answer every possible question that they might be asked: a position which all of us are in when it comes to tax and benefits policy.

So in public we have 'compliance' behaviour, and in private 'conversion' behaviour; and when a whole group is behaving in this way, an act of courage by one member willing to express their conversion can reveal that large numbers have in fact been converted to a new way of thinking about the subject. Moscovici finds that

> a consistent minority can exert an influence to the same extent as a consistent majority, and ... the former will

---

[136] Moscovici, Serge (1980) 'Toward a theory of conversion behavior', pp 209-39 in Berkowitz, Leonard (ed.) *Advances in experimental social psychology*, vol 13, New York: Academic Press, p 211

generally have a greater effect on a deeper level, while the latter often has less, or none, at that level.[137]

This means that a minority that has understood the arguments for universal benefits might, just might, start the process towards a paradigm shift. It is encouraging that research published by the Joseph Rowntree Foundation suggests that public opinion can be changed:

> Public attitudes towards those experiencing poverty are harshly judgemental or view poverty and inequality as inevitable. But when people are better informed about inequality and life on a low income, they are more supportive of measures to reduce poverty and inequality.[138]

They are happy to support a welfare state and

> willing to contribute to the collective good as long as the distribution of burdens and benefits is regarded as just.[139]

There might still be rather less concern in the UK about overall income inequality than about the few who earn very large sums of money,[140] but Wilkinson and Pickett, and academics such as Daniel Dorling,[141] have contributed to a widespread shift in public opinion that we might now characterise as 'inequality matters'. The question for us is this: Is a similar shift possible in relation to universal benefits? And if such a shift did take place, would parliament be willing to approve major change? In fact, if ever a government were to publish a consultation paper on a radical overhaul of the benefits system in the direction of universal benefits, then ministers might be surprised at the extent to which parliament would welcome the idea. Research has revealed considerable support for a major review of income maintenance policy, and for

---

137 Moscovici, Serge (1980) 'Toward a theory of conversion behavior', pp 209–39 in Berkowitz, Leonard (ed.) *Advances in experimental social psychology*, vol 13, New York: Academic Press, pp 214–16
138 Hanley, Teresa (2009) *Engaging public support for eradicating UK poverty*, York: Joseph Rowntree Foundation
139 Mau, Steffen and Veghte, Benjamin (eds) (2007) *Social justice, legitimacy and the welfare state*, Aldershot: Ashgate, p 13
140 McKay, Stephen (2010) 'Where do we stand on inequality? Reflections on recent research and its implications', *Journal of Poverty and Social Justice*, vol 18, no 1, pp 19–33
141 Dorling, Daniel (2010) *Injustice: Why social inequality persists*, Bristol: Policy Press

serious consideration being given to a Citizen's Income.[142] Similarly, Bochel and Defty have found an interesting willingness among MPs to question previous policy positions.[143]

But would a Secretary of State for Work and Pensions be able and willing to bring to Parliament a Bill to establish a Citizen's Income? While we have recognised that a proposal that might reduce the number of civil servants might not have an easy ride, the present government's statements about policy-making suggest that such a Bill would be a possibility. Bochel and Duncan identify a group of policy-making principles in government literature: that policy should be

- forward looking
- outward looking (with cross national policy learning)
- innovative, flexible and creative
- evidence–based
- inclusive
- joined up
- constantly reviewed
- constantly evaluated
- always learning lessons from experience.[144]

A Citizen's Income would conform to all of these principles: it would serve well almost any conceivable future economic and social configuration; it would learn from experiments in Namibia and elsewhere, and from universal pensions in New Zealand,[145] Denmark,[146]

---

[142]   The Citizen's Income Trust (2007) 'Both the House of Commons and the House of Lords support a Citizen's Income approach to the reform of tax and benefits', *Citizen's Income Newsletter*, no 2, pp 1–2

[143]   Bochel, Hugh (2011) 'Conservative approaches to social policy since 1997,' pp 1–22 in Bochel, Hugh (ed.) *The Conservative Party and social policy*, Bristol: Policy Press, p 13; Bochel, Hugh and Defty, Andrew (2007) *Welfare policy under New Labour*, Bristol: Policy Press

[144]   Bochel, Hugh and Duncan, Sue (eds) (2007) *Making policy in theory and practice*, Bristol: Policy Press

[145]   O'Connell, Alison (2004) *Citizen's Pension: An introduction*, London: Pensions Policy Institute; James, Sean and Curry, Chris (2010) *A foundation pension: A PPI evaluation of NAPF* [National Association of Pension Funds] *proposals*, London: Pensions Policy Institute

[146]   Trier, Adam (1989) 'Denmark's basic pension', *BIRG Bulletin*, no 9, Spring/Summer, pp 7–9; Ginn, Jay (1996) 'Citizens' pensions and women', *Citizen's Income Bulletin*, no 21, February, pp 10–12

and Mexico City;[147] it would be innovative, flexible and creative, and it would enhance people's ability to innovate, to work flexibly, and to be creative; it would be evidence-based (Child Benefit is the evidence); it would be inclusive (by definition); it would join up the different stages of people's lives, would facilitate employment transitions, and would repair many of the fissures in our society; it would be simple to review and to evaluate; and it would learn lessons from past experience (and particularly from the disincentive effects of our current system).

National, regional, or global?[148]

We have assumed throughout this chapter, and throughout the book so far, that if a Citizen's Income were to be implemented then it would be implemented within a single country, or one country at a time.

Globalisation – the increasing connectedness of our economies, labour markets and cultures – means that the local, the regional, the national, the continental, and the global, all experience social and economic change, that they affect each other in unpredictable ways, that social policy needs to take account of social and economic realities at all of these levels, and that at all of these levels we need to take account of increasing unpredictability in relation to context, policy formation, and the effects of policy change (and here 'policy change' encompasses leaving policy as it is, because in a changed context the same policy will have new effects). No longer can social policy be discussed as if we lived on an island. The labour market, the economy, and social trends, are now as global as they are local, regional, and national. This makes life far more complicated for every country's government. A change in benefits regulations in one country will have effects that will be difficult to predict because the context will be not just the labour market in that country, but the labour market across its region and beyond; and so for the UK, the context will be not just our society, but European and global society as well; and the context will be not only our own economy, but the global economy too. The current banking and currency crises are global realities. No longer can a national government make plans that assume simply a national context.

---

147   Yanes, Pablo (2012) 'Mexico: The first steps toward Basic Income', pp 217–33 in Caputo, Richard (ed.) *Basic Income guarantee and politics: International experiences and perspectives on the viability of income guarantee,* New York: Palgrave Macmillan, pp 218–22
148   See the website appendix for this chapter at www.citizensincome.org for a longer discussion of globalisation.

For complex tax and benefits systems, this situation poses real difficulties. It would be difficult enough to predict the effects of policy or regulation change on a purely national basis. It is far more difficult to predict the effects of change when the wider context needs to be taken into account.

There are at least two implications:

- The simpler the system, the fewer will be the unpredictable effects at national, regional and global levels.
- We should no longer assume that tax and benefits policy is a purely national issue.

In relation to the second implication: in the European Union it is understandable that national governments want to maintain control over their tax and benefits policies; but if the economy and the labour market are increasingly both European and global then this might not be the most rational approach. Complete Europe-wide welfare state integration is not sustainable politically, and entirely national welfare states are no longer sustainable economically, so what we might need is a European benefits layer, composed of a Citizen's Income, to complement continuing national schemes.[149] A European Citizen's Income could start with a European universal child benefit,[150] then a European universal pension,[151] and finally a Citizen's Income for working age adults. A European Citizen's Income would be easy to administer,[152] a European carbon tax could pay for it, it would blend nicely with whatever national schemes national governments wished

---

[149] Van Parijs, Philippe (1996) 'Basic Income and the two dilemmas of the welfare state', *The Political Quarterly*, vol 67, no 1, pp 63–6, p 66; cf. Atkinson, A.B. (1992) *Towards a European social safety net?* Discussion paper WSP/78, London: The Welfare State Programme, STICERD, LSE, a booklet based on his 1992 Institute for Fiscal Studies lecture, but omitting the lecture's reference to a Citizen's Income. For a general discussion of Europe-wide and national benefits provision, see Kleinman, Mark and Piachaud, David (1993) 'European social policy: conceptions and choices', *Journal of European Social Policy*, vol 3, no 1, pp 1–19, p 7

[150] Hayward, Beresford (1993) 'Citizen capital: why children must come first', *Citizen's Income Bulletin*, no 16, July, pp 21–6; Atkinson, A.B. (1995) 'Interviews: Susan Raven talks to two members of the Borrie Commission', *Citizen's Income Bulletin*, no 19, February, p 11

[151] Goedemé, Tim and Van Lancker, Wim (2009) 'A Universal Basic Pension for Europe's elderly: options and pitfalls', *Basic Income Studies*, vol 4, no 1, pp 1–26

[152] van Dijk, N. (1988) 'A European guaranteed Basic Income system?' *BIRG Bulletin*, no 8, Autumn, pp 15–19

to retain or invent,[153] and in aggregate it could provide the kind of financial transfers between nation states in the Euro zone that might enable the Euro to survive.[154] A global Citizen's Income would in aggregate provide similar transfers between nations across the world, and so could provide the basis for development in poorer countries and thus make economic migration less necessary.[155]

Given the developmental and climate change challenges that we face globally, there is a case for a global tax regime alongside diverse national ones, and both financial transactions taxes ('the Tobin tax') and carbon taxes would be easy taxes to administer globally – and in fact might only work globally. If we want to see efficient global markets in labour, goods and services, then there is an equally good case for a global benefits layer, perhaps starting with global universal benefits for older people and for young people.[156] Could that happen sooner than we think?

Conclusion

A Citizen's Income is a good idea. As we shall see in subsequent chapters, it is more important than ever that we should have one, and that it should replace means-tested benefits. It will soon be essential that we should have one. In the meantime, a Citizen's Income needs to act as a 'regulative principle', establishing an ideal position against which benefit reforms can be measured. This will have two effects: It will prepare the ground for the debate on benefits system reform that needs to happen, and it will mean that changes to the tax and benefits systems might at least be consistent with the implementation of a Citizen's Income later on.

However, a Citizen's Income must never remain just a regulative principle. It is both a whole new way of seeing the way we live together, and at the same time it is a relatively minor useful change in the way in which we redistribute income[157] (and in this respect it is surely a

---

153   Genet, Michel and Van Parijs, Philippe (1992) 'Eurogrant', *BIRG Bulletin*, no 15, July, pp 4–7
154   Philippe Van Parijs (2012), 'No Eurozone without Euro dividend', presentation, 14 September, 14th BIEN Congress, Munich, www.uclouvain.be/8609.html
155   Philippe Van Parijs (2012), presentation, 15 September, 14th BIEN Congress, Munich
156   Blackburn, Robin (2011) 'The case for a global pension and youth grant', *Basic Income Studies*, vol 6, no 1, pp 1–12
157   Roebroek, Joop M. and Hogenboom, Erik (1990) 'Basic Income: alternative benefit or new paradigm?' *BIRG Bulletin*, no 11, July, pp 8–11

rather unusual social policy). We need a Citizen's Income for both of these reasons. Change in our economy, our labour market, and our society, means that we shall need a Citizen's Income, not just the idea of one; and the benefits systems that we operate today are increasingly unsustainable. One day radical change will occur, and its direction will be determined by the factors that we have discussed and by the government's ideological position:[158] and as we shall see, there is no reason why a decision to establish a Citizen's Income should not be made by any foreseeable government on that basis.

---

[158] Farnsworth, Kevin (2011) 'From economic crisis to a new age of austerity: the UK', pp 251–70 in Farnsworth, Kevin and Irving, Zoe M. (eds) *Social Policy in challenging times: Economic crisis and welfare systems*, Bristol: Policy Press

CHAPTER 5

Has it ever happened?

In the UK, we already have Child Benefit, which functions as a universal benefit for children. The UK's NHS is a universal, unconditional and non-withdrawable benefit, and it is highly efficient, but because it is not a cash benefit it is discussed in the website appendices rather than in the body of this chapter.[159] In this chapter I shall discuss the social dividend (a form of Citizen's Income) distributed in Alaska, a recent Citizen's Income experiment conducted in Namibia, Iran's new cash benefit, and a current experiment in India.

Alaska[160]

Since 1977, the State of Alaska has been receiving royalties from oil extraction on state owned land at Prudhoe Bay, and about 20 per cent of the royalties have been saved in the Alaska Permanent Fund. When the fund was established in 1976, the state legislature decided that the principal of the fund should accumulate, so that future generations could benefit from what was bound to be a temporary income stream. No decision was made about how income from the fund's investments should be used, except that sufficient was to be added to the capital to inflation proof the fund. When in 1979 Governor Jay Hammond[161] proposed that some of the surplus interest might be distributed to Alaska's citizens, the idea was warmly received. The initial proposal was that the dividend received by each citizen should be proportional to the number of years that they had lived there, but a legal challenge on the basis that this would discriminate against recent arrivals succeeded, and the outcome was an equal annual payment to every citizen of Alaska who had lived in the state for at least a year.[162] (In 2011, the

---

159 www.citizensincome.org

160 Citizen's Income Trust (2000) 'Alaska Permanent Fund', *Citizen's Income Newsletter*, issue 3, pp 6–7; Widerquist, Karl (2010) 'Lessons of the Alaska dividend', *Citizen's Income Newsletter*, issue 3 pp 13–15; Widerquist, Karl and Howard, Michael (2012) *Alaska's Permanent Fund dividend: Examining its suitability as a model*, New York: Palgrave Macmillan

161 Hammond, Jay S. (1994) *Tales of Alaska's bush rat governor*, Kenmore, WA: Epicenter Press

162 O'Brien, J. Patrick and Olson, Dennis O. (1991) 'The Alaska Permanent Fund and dividend distribution program', *BIRG Bulletin*, no 12, February, pp 3–6

Alaska Permanent Fund had a total value of $37.5 bn,[163] and the annual dividend paid was $1,174 to each eligible resident[164]) The world had its first Citizen's Income: though in some ways it has not behaved like one because the amount fluctuates with the profits generated by the Permanent Fund, meaning that the dividend cannot be relied upon to provide a firm income floor.[165]

When he had been Mayor of Bristol Bay Borough, Jay Hammond had tried unsuccessfully to establish a social dividend on the basis of fishing revenues. When he became Governor of Alaska in 1974, he decided to try again, on a larger scale, and for the same reasons: to prevent resources being squandered on public projects driven by interest groups, to help the poor, and to reflect the common ownership of the state's natural resources. This time he succeeded. The Alaska Permanent Fund owes its existence to the right person being in the right place at the right time.

It also owes its existence to public opinion. In 1966, Alaska sold oil drilling rights, and spent all of the money. Public perception was that the proceeds had been wasted. Suggesting that a proportion of oil revenues should be saved for future generations was therefore a popular move. But the distribution of some of the fund's interest as a dividend was rather more difficult to achieve.[166] The fund itself had been relatively easy to establish, because legislators of a variety of political views could support it. It remained popular, partly because it was prudently managed, particularly by the first Director of the Alaska Permanent Fund Corporation, David Rose. The dividend, however, divided opinion, and was eventually achieved only slowly, by making compromises, and by building a coalition of policy makers. Unlike the Fund, the dividend is not protected by a constitutional amendment. It is protected by the fact that every resident receives it, and none of them would wish to lose it.

The dividend has increased personal income, and therefore consumption, and has therefore increased employment. In 1990 it was estimated that for every $1 million distributed, 13 Alaskan jobs, mainly in the service and trade sectors, were created. The dividend has had

---

[163] www.apfc.org/home/Content/home/index.cfm, 22/09/11

[164] www.pfd.state.ak.us, 22/09/2011

[165] Zelleke, Almaz (2012) 'Basic Income and the Alaska model: Limits of the resource dividend model for the implementation of an Unconditional Basic Income', pp 141–68 in Widerquist, Karl and Howard, Michael, *Alaska's Permanent Fund dividend: Examining its suitability as a model*, New York: Palgrave Macmillan, p 150

[166] Rose, Dave and Wohlforth, Charles (2008) *Saving for the future: My life and the Alaska Permanent Fund*, Kenmore, WA: Epicenter Press

an anti-inflationary effect,[167] and it has helped the poor. Alaska is the only state in the US in which inequality has decreased during the past twenty years.[168] Whereas in 1980 Alaska's net income inequality was the highest in the United States, now it is the lowest.[169]

Can the model be exported? Such dividends are popular once they are in place. Even with its oil revenues, Alaska is not among the states with the highest per capita income, and it uses only a small proportion of the interest generated by the Alaska Permanent Fund to pay the dividend. If 'resources' were to be sufficiently broadly defined to include land values, then most countries could establish resource dividends if they wished to do so. Therefore the Alaska model can and should be tried elsewhere: and dividends established elsewhere would be at least as secure as Alaska's. A change of government can easily lead to the abolition of targeted programmes, but a change of political ethos cannot damage the Alaska Permanent Fund or the Dividend. The Dividend has no enemies, so there is no opposition movement in which a politician can make a home.[170] Remember: Sarah Palin was Governor of Alaska.

Iran[171]

Iran now has a cash transfer programme that looks remarkably like a Citizen's Income. Ninety-six per cent of the population[172] are now receiving 810,000 rials (about £43 or US$66) per person once every two months. There is no means test. The Iranian government is paying

---

[167] Goldsmith, Scott (2012) 'The economic and social impacts of the Permanent Fund dividend on Alaska', pp 49–63 in Widerquist, Karl and Howard, Michael W. (eds) *Alaska's Permanent Fund dividend*, New York: Palgrave Macmillan

[168] Widerquist, Karl (2010) 'Lessons of the Alaska dividend', *Citizen's Income Newsletter*, issue 3, pp 13–15

[169] Goldsmith, Scott (2012) 'The Economic and social impacts of the Permanent Fund dividend on Alaska', pp 49–63 in Widerquist, Karl and Howard, Michael W. (eds) *Alaska's Permanent Fund dividend*, New York: Palgrave Macmillan, p 53

[170] Widerquist, Karl (2010) 'Lessons of the Alaska Dividend', *Citizen's Income Newsletter*, issue 3, pp 13–15; Widerquist, Karl and Howard, Michael (2012) 'Conclusion: lessons from the Alaska model', pp 121–7 in Widerquist, Karl and Howard, Michael W. (eds) *Alaska's Permanent Fund dividend*, New York: Palgrave Macmillan

[171] Tabatabai, Hamid (2011) 'Iran's economic reforms usher in a de facto Citizen's Income', *Citizen's Income Newsletter*, issue 1, pp 1–2; Tabatabai, Hamid (2011) 'The Basic Income road to reforming Iran's price subsidies', *Basic Income Studies*, vol 6, no 1, pp 1–24

[172] Tabatabai, Hamid (2012) 'Iran: a bumpy road toward Basic Income', pp 285–300 in Caputo, Richard (ed.) *Basic Income guarantee and politics: International experiences and perspectives on the viability of income guarantee,* New York: Palgrave Macmillan, p 295

for the cash transfers by reducing subsidies on such basic goods and services as bread, water, electricity, natural gas, petrol and diesel, and not by using new revenue from oil extraction. The scheme is therefore revenue neutral. Seventy per cent of the former subsidies went to 30 per cent of the population, and resulted in wasteful consumption of energy and foodstuffs, lack of investment, pollution, and smuggling to countries that did not benefit from such subsidies. The plan was to phase out subsidies over five years and slowly increase the cash transfers, but in fact the subsidies have been phased out quickly and the quite sizeable universal benefit established more quickly than originally envisaged.[173]

When the replacement of subsidies by cash transfers was first discussed, the plan was to provide additional cash to poorer members of society via a means test, and seventeen million households completed means-test questionnaires. It was the public unrest resulting from the results of that exercise that led to the abandonment of the means test. As soon as the suggestion was made that the money should be given to everyone (since the wealthy are taxed more than they would receive from the cash transfer), it just seemed obvious. Most of the households that had not applied for the payment then did so.

In one respect the Iranian cash subsidy (the official designation) is not a Citizen's Income. The head of the household receives all of the household's individual entitlements, so although the individual is the claimant unit in relation to the benefit calculation, the individual is not the claimant unit in relation to the benefit's payment. The transfer is not truly universal, either. Afghan refugees, many of whom have lived in Iran for decades, do not receive the cash subsidy, but do suffer price rises related to the withdrawal of commodity subsidies. Neither is it clear how sustainable the cash subsidy would be if oil revenues were to decline, because the language of rights has played no part in the establishment of the scheme, which both the government and the population regard as a pragmatic measure. An interesting question is the extent to which a universal payment will itself generate a concept of rights and a broader acceptance of democratic government. The scheme is enshrined in law, and it is possible that the resulting economic efficiencies, new investment, poverty reduction, and particularly income security, will recommend the scheme to both government and public as a longer term necessity.

While the cash subsidy does not constitute a subsistence income, it is a substantial start. (For a family of five, it comes to something like two thirds of subsistence.) If the research opportunity that this evolution

---

[173] Hamid Tabatabai (2012), presentation, 15 September, 14th BIEN Congress, Munich

offers is taken up then we shall have available to us information that we do not yet have on how a Citizen's Income affects employment, consumption, and household patterns.

This Iranian development is hugely important. We had thought that the widespread European debate on the benefits of a Citizen's Income[174] might one day result in a Citizen's Income in a European country, so that Europe would be the first continent to see a genuine national universal, unconditional and non-withdrawable income. But it was not to be. Alaska has now paid a Citizen's Income (an annual one) for thirty years; and now Iran has something very close to a Citizen's Income. A possible conclusion is that this is one more signal of the end of US-European hegemony. The empire is dying, and new empires are taking shape, doing what new empires do: doing things in new ways, and in ways that the old empires (therefore) refuse, thus hastening their decline.

Namibia[175]

On the 27 January 2009 I attended a seminar at the School of Oriental and African Studies. In the audience were academics, staff members of Nongovernmental organisations working in Africa, and people like me, all wanting to know how successful a Citizen's Income pilot project had been. The seminar was led by Professor Guy Standing, who for many years worked for the International Labour Organization and is now Professor of Economic Security at the University of Bath and Professor in Development Studies, School of Oriental and African Studies, London. He cofounded BIEN (the Basic Income European Network, now the Basic Income Earth Network), and has authored numerous books, several of which have a clear Citizen's Income agenda.[176]

---

174 Blaschke, Ronald (2012) *From the idea of a Basic Income to the political movement in Europe: Development and questions*, Berlin: Rosa Luxemburg Foundation, tr. Katharina Messinger

175 Torry, Malcolm (2009) 'Can unconditional cash transfers work? They can', report of a seminar, *Citizen's Income Newsletter*, issue 2, pp 1–3

176 Standing, Guy (1999) *Global labour flexibility: Seeking distributive justice*, Basingstoke: Macmillan; Standing, Guy (2002) *Beyond the new paternalism: Basic security as equality,* London: Verso; Standing, Guy, with Michael Samson (2003) *A Basic Income grant for South Africa,* Cape Town: University of Cape Town Press; Standing, Guy (ed.) (2004) *Economic security for a better world,* Geneva: International Labour Organization; Standing, Guy (2005) *Promoting income security as a right: Europe and North America,* London: Anthem Press; Standing, Guy (2009) *Work after globalization: Building occupational citizenship,* Cheltenham: Edward Elgar; Standing, Guy (2011) *The precariat: The new dangerous class,* London: Bloomsbury

Standing started his presentation with the heart of his message: Poverty is primarily a lack of money, so giving people money will lift them out of poverty. He then discussed the options facing attempts at poverty reduction in the developing world, starting with social insurance, the chief method employed across Europe for the past century: but because globalisation leads to whole societies suffering economic shocks, and because such risks are essentially uninsurable, social insurance is now unlikely to be a viable means of preserving the economic security so essential to people's autonomy and freedom. We therefore need new ways of providing people with enough money to prevent poverty, and sufficient financial security to give them choice over how they relate to production.[177] In Professor Standing's view potential schemes must

- not be paternalistic
- be based on rights and not charity
- benefit the most disadvantaged
- encourage ecological restraint
- promote dignified work.

In Africa it has now been recognised that cash transfers can help to alleviate poverty. There are three types:

- Universalistic and unconditional
- Targeted (usually on groups deemed to be the poorest, often by means-testing)
- Selective (for instance: in Latin America, cash transfers are received by poorer families who send their children to school)

Means-tested systems (and proxy means-testing based, for instance, on the quality of a family's housing, as in Chile) suffer from problems familiar to developed countries, such as unemployment traps, poverty traps, and savings traps. So in Africa new methods must be sought. At a BIEN Congress in Cape Town in 2006, much support was expressed for unconditional cash transfers, especially among trades unionists and community and church representatives. And now in Namibia a pilot project involving two villages has answered some common criticisms of unconditional transfers: that they would reduce labour supply,

---

[177]   Casassas, David and Bailón, Sandra González (2007) 'Corporate watch, consumer responsibility, and economic democracy: forms of political action in the orbit of a Citizen's Income', *Citizen's Income Newsletter*, issue 3, pp 8–12

would go to the rich as well as the poor, would be wasted on alcohol and other undesirable expenditure, would be unaffordable, and would lower incentives to save.

The pilot project ran from 2007 to 2009. It built on an existing debate about the possibility of a Citizen's Income in Namibia,[178] and also on the existing Namibian universal pension. It gave to every one of the one thousand inhabitants of two villages a Basic Income Grant (a Citizen's Income) of N$100 a month for every man, woman and child (one hundred Namibian dollars is about US$12, or £7). The costs were borne by donors, mostly in the form of voluntary contributions. The project was carefully watched by potential donors, including the World Bank, which is finally willing to consider conditional cash transfers as a mechanism for distributing development aid and might one day be persuaded to think about unconditional transfers.

The team organising the pilot conducted a benchmark survey and an evaluation survey. The results are significant:[179]

- Household poverty dropped significantly. In November 2007, 76 per cent of residents of the two villages fell below a food poverty line. Within a year, this was reduced to 37 per cent. Those households that were not joined by family members from outside the project villages (an understandable migration) saw poverty levels reduced from 76 per cent to just 16 per cent.
- The proportion of people engaged in economic activity rose from 44 per cent to 55 per cent, often through own-account work of various kinds: and especially through such initiatives as the tending of vegetable plots and the building of latrines, which directly led to an increase in the community's health.
- Far from leading to idleness and a decrease in economic activity, the economic security that a Citizen's Income offered to people gave them the confidence to take the economic risks necessary for new productive activity.
- Child malnutrition fell. Children's weight-for-age improved in just six months from 42 per cent of underweight children to 17 per cent, and to just 10 per cent by the end of the project.

---

[178] Haarman, Claudia and Haarmann, Dirk (2007) 'From survival to decent employment: Basic Income security in Namibia', *Basic Income Studies*, vol 2, no 1, pp 1–7

[179] Basic Income grant coalition (2009) *Making the difference: The BIG in Namibia: Basic Income Grant pilot project, assessment report*, Namibia NGO Forum, pp 13–17, www.bignam.org/Publications/BIG_Assessment_report_08b.pdf, 23/09/2011

- Before the pilot project, almost half of the villages' children did not attend school regularly. Pass rates were at 40 per cent, and drop-out rates were high. This was mainly because parents had to pay fees for their children to attend school. By the end of the project, 90 per cent of parents were paying school fees, and most children now attend school. Drop-out rates fell from 40 per cent to almost zero during the project.
- The clinic, like the school, is funded by attendees' payments. During the project, residents could pay the attendance fee, use of the clinic increased six-fold, and the income of the clinic increased fivefold.
- During the first year of the project, average household debt fell from N\$ 1,215 to N\$ 772. Savings increased, as did ownership of livestock.
- Crime rates fell by 42 per cent during the project. Theft of stock fell by a similar amount, giving people the confidence to invest in assets.
- The Citizen's Income gave to women a new economic independence, and paid-for sex was reduced accordingly.
- There was no evidence that the Citizen's Income led to an increase in alcoholism.
- Administrative costs were just 3 per cent to 4 per cent of the total outlay.[180]
- The villages of their own volition elected an advisory committee of 18 residents, and among its achievements are the opening of a post office, the establishment of savings accounts, and the closure of shebeens on the day of the monthly distribution of the grants.
- New shops have opened.
- The number of people experiencing daily food shortages fell from 30 per cent to 12 per cent of the population in just six months
- The number of people who rarely experience food shortages rose from 20 per cent to 60 per cent of the population.
- Economic activity rose fastest among women.
- Average income rose in every earnings quintile, and proportionately more for lower quintiles.
- Average income rose a staggering 200 per cent in the lowest quintile *excluding* the N\$100 (US\$12) Citizen's Income, because people could now purchase the means for making an income, and they did.
- Low wage employment was in many cases replaced by better paid self-employment.

So the pilot project passed all of the tests:

---

[180] The following results were given at the seminar.

- it was based on rights, not charity;
- it was not paternalistic;
- it benefited the poorest most;
- it promoted dignified work; and
- the kind of activity that it promoted cares for the environment.

In addition, the project has refuted the critics of unconditional cash transfers:

- far from encouraging dependency, the Citizen's Income increased enterprise;
- far from leading to waste of resources, it encouraged productive use of resources; and
- far from being unaffordable, the level of Citizen's Income employed in the pilot project would, if extended to the country as a whole, cost just 2.2 per cent to 3.8 per cent of GDP, and the increased economic activity generated by the Citizen's Income would by itself pay the entire cost.

Standing speculated that one reason why policy makers in Africa and elsewhere do not like the idea of a Citizen's Income is that the scheme is emancipatory: it allows people to make choices for themselves, and it does not allow policy makers to interfere in people's lives by imposing conditions on cash transfers.

Additional significant findings of the pilot project were that in a context of supply elasticity a Citizen's Income is not inflationary; that women's economic status had risen relative to men's; that the Citizen's Income is more effective than conditional transfers partly because it cannot be removed by a local bureaucrat if someone upsets them, as a conditional cash transfer can be; that because unconditional payments limit the power of bureaucrats, more of the money reaches the poor; that in the context of today's more flexible labour markets, trade unions are more willing to support a Citizen's Income; and that surveys in Africa have found that 80 per cent of people favour unconditionality.

The most vigorous, and to some extent hostile, questioning at the seminar came from people who worked for nongovernmental organisations committed to providing goods and services in Africa and elsewhere. Is it not better to build schools for people than to give them money? Well, no, not necessarily: because if they are given the money then they will build the kind of school that they need, not the kind that someone outside the situation thinks that they need. The main achievement of the pilot project was that it proved that people *do not* waste money, on the whole. They invest it wisely: in their children's nourishment, health, and education, in income-generating activity, and in the infrastructure that their community needs.

The seminar ran out of time.

Since the end of the pilot project Namibia's government has shown no positive interest in the results, and the Prime Minister has dismissed the Citizen's Income idea: 'We can't dish out money for free to people who do nothing.'[181] Initially the trade union movement followed the government's lead and withdrew from the alliance that had sponsored the pilot project. A vociferous public reaction provoked trade union re-engagement, and for the first time the movement finds itself in opposition to the government. How this novel political situation will affect debate on a Citizen's Income in Namibia remains to be seen.[182]

India

In January 2011, two more pilot projects started: one in West Delhi's Raghubir Nagar slum, and the other in eight rural villages in Madhya Pradesh. The Self Employed Women's Association (SEWA) began planning and raising money for the rural project in 2008. The Delhi government joined in, and has worked with SEWA to organise the urban project. In the urban project a hundred households are receiving 1,000 rupees per month (about £12 or US$19) and are deprived of permission to use a current scheme designed to help the poor: the subsidised ration shop. Another hundred households get a bank account and continued use of the ration shop; a third group of 150 families neither receive cash nor a bank account and continue to use the ration shop; and a fourth group is of 150 families which did not wish to receive the cash transfers. All cash transfers are made to the woman of the family.[183] In the rural project, adults receive 200 rupees a month (between 30 per cent and 40 per cent of subsistence income) and each child under the age of fourteen 100 rupees a month. The economic

---

181 Haarmann, Claudia, and Haarmann, Dirk (2012) 'Namibia: seeing the sun rise – the realities and hopes of the Basic Income Grant pilot project', pp 33–58 in Murray, Matthew C. and Pateman, Carole (eds) *Basic Income worldwide: Horizons of reform*, New York: Palgrave Macmillan, p 55

182 Haarmann, Claudia, and Haarmann, Dirk (2012) 'Namibia: seeing the sun rise – the realities and hopes of the Basic Income Grant pilot project', pp 33–58 in Murray, Matthew C. and Pateman, Carole (eds) *Basic Income worldwide: Horizons of reform*, New York: Palgrave Macmillan

183 http://binews.org/2011/09/india-basic-income-pilot-projects-are-underway

and social effects are being studied in relation to control groups.[184] A further project involving a tribal village is now underway.

Interim results were announced at the 2012 BIEN (Basic Income Earth Network) Congress in Munich. Families have mainly spent their unconditional cash transfers on food, healthcare, and education. School attendance has increased threefold, school performance twofold, and, in particular, more girls are now in secondary school. Especially where SEWA is active, communities have pooled their benefits to create roads, drains, and toilets, with benefits to community health. New businesses have been founded, and families have worked together to improve their housing. A significant benefit identified by the researchers and by SEWA is the empowerment of women. Because they receive cash transfers of their own they are no longer entirely dependent on their husbands for income. This applies as much to wealthier women as to poorer ones.

UNICEF,[185] the pilot project's main funder, has now given additional money to enable further pilot projects to be established; and political interest is growing. SEWA's interest in the project was not to get women into the formal economy, but rather to give them greater financial security in the informal economy. The government's interest is to find a way of replacing numerous corrupt and inefficient existing social welfare programmes with a new scheme in which money reaches those for whom it is intended. The pilot project suggests that unconditional cash transfers can achieve both SEWA's and the government's aims.[186]

Social transfers in Latin America and elsewhere

A number of countries, particularly in Latin America, run social transfer programmes for children and older people.[187] Some of these,

---

[184] Shrinivasan, Rukmini (2011) 'Social insurance is not for the Indian open economy of 21st century', *The Times of India, Crest Edition*, 9 July, www.timescrest.com/opinion/social-insurance-is-not-for-the-indian-open-economy-of-21st-century-5775, 23/09/2011

[185] The United Nations International Children's Emergency Fund. In 1953 the name was changed to the United Nations Children's Fund, but the acronym UNICEF was retained.

[186] Interim results announced at the 14th BIEN Congress, Munich, 15 September 2012. See also Standing, Guy (2012) *Cash transfers: A review of the issues in India*, New Delhi: UNICEF India

[187] Conferences of the United States Basic Income Guarantee network often contain papers on moves towards Citizen's Income in various parts of the world. An early collection of papers can be found in Widerquist, Karl, Lewis, Michael Anthony, and Pressman, Steven (2005) *The ethics and economics of the Basic Income Guarantee*, Aldershot: Ashgate. See www.usbig.net/congresses.php

such as the *Bolsa Família* in Brazil, are conditional (for poor families, and conditional on children attending school and health clinics),[188] but the stated intention is universality and unconditionality,[189] and in that cause coverage is being extended and conditionalities are being whittled away.[190] It was regional experiments that gave rise to the *Bolsa Família*. A new regional experiment is a Citizen's Income for every newborn resident.[191] It is not impossible that this too might one day become a national programme. Similarly, Argentina's Universal Child Benefit is not in fact universal, but the intention is continual extension to new recipients;[192] and in 2009 a scheme previously only for families with a worker in the formal labour market was extended to the unemployed and to informal workers.[193] Some schemes are becoming more conditional on attendance at school or for health checks,[194] but

---

[188] Barrientos, Armando and Pellissery, Sony (2011) 'The road to global citizenship?' pp 6–14 in Barrientos, Armando, Davy, Benjamin, Davy, Ulrike, Dean, Hartley, Jacobs, Harvey M., Leisering, Lutz and Pellissery, Sony, *A road to global social citizenship?* Financial Assistance, Land Policy, and Global Social Rights Working Paper no 10, www.tinyurl. com/3n9jh5h, pp 7–8; Coêlho, Denilson Bandeira (2012) 'Brazil: Basic Income – a new model of innovation diffusion', pp 59–80 in Murray, Matthew C. and Pateman, Carole (eds) *Basic Income worldwide: Horizons of reform*, New York: Palgrave Macmillan

[189] Suplicy, Eduardo Matarazzo (1995) 'Guaranteed minimum income in Brazil?' *Citizen's Income Bulletin*, no 19, February, pp 4–6; Suplicy, Eduardo (2012) 'The best income transfer program for modern economies', pp 41–53 in Caputo, Richard (ed.) *Basic Income guarantee and politics: International experiences and perspectives on the viability of income guarantee*, New York: Palgrave Macmillan

[190] Law 10.853/2004, an initiative by Partido dos Trabalhadores, and approved by all parties of the National Congress and sanctioned by President Luiz Inácio Lula da Silva, 8 January 2004. Cf. Britto, Tatiana and Soares, Fábio Veras (2011) *Bolsa Família and the Citizen's Basic Income: A misstep*, Working paper no 77, Brasilia: International Policy Centre for Inclusive Growth, www.ipc-undp.org/pub/IPCOnePager124.pdf; Standing, Guy (2012) 'Social insurance is not for the Indian open economy of the 21st century,' *Citizen's Income Newsletter*, issue 1, pp 5–7, p 6

[191] Senator Eduardo Suplicy (2012), presentation, 14 September, 14th BIEN Congress, Munich

[192] Roca, Emilio (no title) (2010) pp 17–20 in *Asignación Universal por Hijo*, Buenos Aires: Asociación Argentina de Politicas Sociales, p 18

[193] Gasparini, Leonardo and Cruces, Guillermo (2010) Las Asignaciones por Higo en Argentina, *Económica*, La Plata, vol 61, pp 105–46, http://economica.econo.unlp. edu.ar/documentos/20110519025114PM_Economica_572.pdf

[194] Lund, Francie (2011) 'A step in the wrong direction: linking the South Africa Child Support Grant to school attendance,' *Journal of Poverty and Social Justice*, vol 19, no 1, pp 5–14; Barrientos, Armando (2011) 'Conditions in antipoverty programmes,' *Journal of Poverty and Social Justice*, vol 19, no 1, pp 15–26; Standing, Guy (2011) 'Behavioural conditionality: why the nudges must be stopped – an opinion piece,' *Journal of Poverty and Social Justice*, vol 19, no 1, pp 27–37

some new benefits have been a bit of a surprise, such as Greece's new near-universal pension established in the midst of its financial crisis.[195] A study by the International Labour Organization has found that the Latin American transfer programmes for families with children result in numerous positive outcomes for recipients, including higher net incomes, reduced amounts of child labour,[196] increased school attendance, higher educational achievement, increasing productive activity, and better nutrition. There are not enough unconditional social transfer programmes designed for working age adults to enable the researchers to draw conclusions as to their effects, but Orton can still legitimately draw the conclusion that 'the results of social pensions and a number of other unconditional transfers support the expectation that a [Citizen's Income] could generate similarly positive social and micro-economic effects'.[197] Guy Standing's conclusion, following a survey of cash transfers with varying degrees of conditionality, is that

> now conditional cash transfers are legitimized. But the flaws of all forms of targeting, selectivity and conditionality, as well as their unnecessary costs, are making more people question the need for them. What we can say is that only universalistic transfers, ... where they have been tried, including in some of the world's poorest countries, ... have proved an effective means to combat poverty and income insecurity while promoting livelihoods and work.[198]

The World Bank has evaluated unconditional schemes in Africa and discovered how effective they can be:

> Much can already be learned from Sub-Saharan Africa's experience with cash transfer programs. Evaluations of unconditional programs have found significant impacts on household food consumption ...; nonfood consumption ... ; and children's nutrition and education ... . A recent

[195] Matsaganis, Manos and Leventi, Chrysa (2011) 'Pathways to a universal basic pension in Greece', *Basic Income Studies*, vol 6, no 1, p 1–20

[196] Orton, Ian (2009) 'The Citizen's Income and child labour: two ships passing at night', *Citizen's Income Newsletter*, issue 1, pp 6–9

[197] Orton, Ian (2011) 'The International Labour Organisation's analysis of social transfers worldwide augurs well for a Citizen's Income in the context of middle and low-income countries,' *Citizen's Income Newsletter*, issue 2, pp 4–8, p 6

[198] Standing, Guy (2008) 'How cash transfers promote the case for Basic Income', *Basic Income Studies*, vol 3, no 1, pp 1–30, p 26

experimental evaluation found that a program for adolescent girls conditioned on their school attendance improved enrollment, attendance, and test scores in Malawi. Unconditional transfers in the same program decreased early marriage and pregnancy among girls who had already dropped out of school.[199]

Conclusion

If it is true that

in all likelihood, the social security institutions emerging in the South will be quite different from the welfare states of developing countries. Facilitating the emergence of these new institutions is a global responsibility. ... . (Armando Barrientos and Sony Pellissery)[200]

then maybe we could learn from the trajectories established in Brazil and Argentina. Given the runaway success of the UK's National Health Service[201] and Child Benefit, the popularity and beneficial effects of the Alaska Permanent Fund Dividend, the rapidity with which Iran has established a universal cash benefit as an entirely pragmatic measure, and the stunning results seen by those evaluating the Namibian and Indian pilot projects, is it not time for a developed country to establish a pilot project? There would be a difference. The Namibian and Indian pilot projects have been funded by donations, the Alaskan dividend has been funded by the proceeds of a permanent fund into which oil extraction royalties have been paid, and the Iranian Citizen's Income has been funded by redirecting oil revenues previously spent on subsidies, whereas, in a country like the United Kingdom, any eventual Citizen's Income would probably need to be funded by reducing tax allowances and means-tested and contributory benefits, so any meaningful pilot project would have to be funded in that way. Organising such a pilot project in a developed country would not be easy, but that is no reason

[199] Garcia, Marito and Moore, Charity M.T. (2012) *The cash dividend: The rise of cash transfer programs in Sub-Saharan Africa*, Washington DC: World Bank, p 8

[200] Barrientos, Armando and Pellissery, Sony (2011) 'The road to global citizenship?' pp 6–14 in Barrientos, Armando, Davy, Benjamin, Davy, Ulrike, Dean, Hartley, Jacobs, Harvey M., Leisering, Lutz and Pellissery, Sony, *A road to global social citizenship?* Financial Assistance, Land Policy, and Global Social Rights Working Paper no 10, www.tinyurl.com/3n9jh5h, pp 13–14

[201] See the appendix to this chapter at www.citizensincome.org

for not trying. In the UK, an ideal boundaried community would be the Isle of Sheppey off the north Kent coast. As David Purdy suggests, following a detailed discussion of whether a Citizen's Income might be viable in different political contexts:

> Desirability, viability and achievability, though logically distinct, must ultimately be considered together. Until and unless [a Citizen's Income] is actually tried, its advocates can only speculate about how people would respond to its introduction, just as in the early nineteenth century, advocates of universal suffrage could only speculate about how government and society would be affected if all adults acquired the right to vote.[202]

It is no doubt significant that debate on the desirability and feasibility of a Citizen's Income is lively in a variety of countries,[203] but there comes a point when theory must give way to verification via experiment. The only way to find out whether a Citizen's Income will benefit individuals, families, society, the economy, and the labour market, is to try it; and the only way to find out whether there will be detrimental effects on the labour market will be to try it.[204] The Namibian and Indian experiments offer us tried and tested ways of conducting pilot projects,[205] so nobody will need to start from scratch. Particularly

---

[202] Purdy, David (2007) 'Is Basic Income viable?' *Basic Income Studies*, vol 2, no 2, pp 1–26

[203] Caputo, Richard (ed.) (2012) *Basic Income guarantee and politics: International experiences and perspectives on the viability of income guarantee,* New York: Palgrave Macmillan

[204] Groot, Loek (2004) *Basic Income, unemployment and compensatory justice*, Dordrecht: Kluwer Academic Publishers, esp. ch.4, 'Why launch a Basic Income experiment?' pp 93–114; Groot, Loek (2005) 'Towards a European Basic Income experiment', *Citizen's Income Newsletter*, issue 2, pp 2–7; Groot, Loek (2006) 'Reasons for launching a Basic Income experiment', *Basic Income Studies*, vol 1, no 2, pp 1–7; Widerquist, Karl (2006) 'The bottom line in a Basic Income experiment', *Basic Income Studies*, vol 1, no 2, pp 1–5; Peters, Hans and Marks, Axel (2006) 'Lottery games as a tool for empirical Basic Income research', *Basic Income Studies*, vol 1, no 2, pp 1–7; Noguera, José and De Wispelaere, Jürgen D. (2006) 'A plea for the use of laboratory experiments in Basic Income research', *Basic Income Studies*, vol 1, no 2, pp 1–8; Virjo, Ilkka (2006) 'A piece of the puzzle: a comment on the Basic Income experiment debate', *Basic Income Studies*, vol 1, no 2, pp 1–5

[205] Standing, Guy (2012) *Cash transfers: A review of the issues in India*, New Delhi: UNICEF India. Members of the Namibian and Indian research teams presented a paper on how to conduct pilot projects on 14 September at the 14th BIEN Congress, Munich.

important is to keep the design of the project clear and constant. If it is a Citizen's Income that is to be tested then it must be a genuine Citizen's Income that is experienced by participants in the pilot, and not something similar or changing; and the pilot will need to be long enough for behavioural trends to emerge. Two years would be a minimum.

If the results from the Namibian and Indian experiments are as significant as we think they are, then a Citizen's Income is an opportunity for social and economic change that the UK must not neglect. If we do neglect it then surely other countries will not, countries across the world will follow Iran's lead, and it will be those countries that will reap the economic and social benefits. Namibia's government might extend their pilot project to other villages and towns, and then establish a nationwide Citizen's Income; the Indian government could well see a Citizen's Income as a way out of numerous current problems; a newly developing country like East Timor might use resources revenues to pay for a Citizen's Income;[206] Latin America could turn more of its conditional transfers into unconditional ones; and Central and Eastern Europe could be next.[207]

Seventy years ago the UK was a world leader in social policy innovation. The inventions of that time have served us well. We now need to innovate in a new context. The rapid changes affecting our economy, our labour market, and our society, demand a new approach to the tax and benefits systems. If we get this wrong then we shall all suffer, rich as well as poor. If we get it right then we could achieve the economy, labour market and society that we shall need in this still quite new millennium.

A substantial UK Citizen's Income pilot project is not a lot to ask, given the extent of our current economic and social problems and the possibly substantial benefits of a Citizen's Income.

What are we afraid of?

---

[206] Casassas, David, Raventós, Daniel and Wark, Julie (2010) 'The right to existence in developing countries: Basic Income in East Timor', *Basic Income Studies*, vol 5, no 1, pp 1–14

[207] Huber, Evelyne (1996) 'Options for social policy in Latin America: neoliberal versus social democratic models', pp 141–191 in Esping-Andersen, Gøsta (ed.) *Welfare states in transition: National adaptations*, London: Sage; Standing, Guy (1996) 'Social protection in Central and Eastern Europe: a tale of slipping anchors and torn safety nets', pp 225–55 in Esping–Andersen, Gøsta (ed.) *Welfare states in transition: National adaptations*, London: Sage

CHAPTER 6

Criteria for a benefits system: coherence and administrative simplicity

Criteria for a benefits system

In Chapter 1 we recognized that there are two ways to argue towards benefits system reform: we can invent tax and benefits systems, and then compare our current systems with the systems that we have invented; or we can ask how we might solve the problems that the current systems have bequeathed to us. Here we begin an exploration based on the former method. We shall list criteria for a good benefits system and then test both a current system (in this case, the United Kingdom's benefits system) and a reform proposal (in this case a Citizen's Income) against those criteria. The Reader might wish to evaluate their own national system against the criteria that seem relevant to them, and then see how a Citizen's Income would fare in relation to the same criteria.

Here we are taking a lesson from William Beveridge. In preparation for writing his report in 1942, he sought a greater degree of coherence, greater administrative efficiency, a system that reflected the family structure of his time, and a system that reflected the labour market of his time. His report assumed that the government would be able to maintain full employment, by which he meant a full-time job for every male of working age:[208] an assumption that reflected his lifelong obsession that people should not be 'idle' or 'useless'.[209] Such an obsession, and such an assumption, might now be more of a social and economic liability than a social and economic advantage, which suggests that his set of criteria are no longer serviceable, that we need to list a new set more coherent with our own social and economic

---

[208] Beveridge, Sir William (1942) *Social insurance and allied services*, Cmd 6404, London: Stationery Office
[209] Torry, Malcolm (1992) 'The two Williams', *BIRG Bulletin*, no 14, February, pp 15–17

situation, and that any criteria that we might list will, in their turn, become obsolete.

Closer to the needs of our own time is the detailed list of criteria for a tax and benefits structure in the report of the 1978 Meade committee: An income maintenance scheme should 'aim at guaranteeing an adequate minimum for everyone, … the design of the benefits, and of taxes necessary to finance them, should be such as to minimise any adverse effects on the incentive to work and save', the whole system should be 'as simple, as easy to understand, and as cheap to administer as possible', and the benefits from the system should be as little open to abuse as possible.[210]

A similar list coherent with the needs of our time might look something like this:

1. Our tax and benefits structure should be coherent: that is, its different parts should fit together.
2. Our tax and benefits structure should be simple to administer: to reduce employment disincentives, to reduce administrative costs, and because democratic accountability requires comprehensibility.
3. Our tax and benefits structure should reflect today's family and household patterns, and should remain serviceable as household and family patterns continue to change.
4. Our tax and benefits structure should not disincentivise public goods such as enterprise, training, long-term relationships between the parents of children, and the ability to provide financially for oneself and one's dependents.
5. Our tax and benefits structure should incentivise the efficient allocation of resources, and so contribute to an efficient economy.
6. Our tax and benefits structure should treat people with dignity, and not stigmatise individuals involved in any part of the system.
7. Our tax and benefits structure should reflect the labour market of today, and should remain serviceable as the labour market changes in the future.

---

[210] Meade, J.E. (1978) *The structure and reform of direct taxation*, Report of a committee chaired by Professor J.E. Meade, London: George Allen & Unwin, for the Institute for Fiscal Studies, p 269

Comparing the current system with a Citizen's Income

How do the current UK system and a Citizen's Income compare when we measure them against our criteria for a good tax and benefits structure? In this chapter I shall evaluate the systems against the first two criteria in the list, and then in subsequent chapters move on to the others.

> Our tax and benefits structure should be coherent: that is, its parts should fit together

As things stand, our tax and benefits structure does *not* fit together. Indeed, the tax system on its own does not fit together. As the report of the recent Mirrlees Review puts it:

> The UK system is ... unnecessarily complex and distorting. Tax policy has for a long time been driven more by short-term expedience than by any long-term strategy. Policymakers seem continually to underestimate the extent to which individuals and companies will respond to the financial opportunities presented to them by the tax system. They seem unable to comprehend the importance of dealing with the system as a whole. And real and effective reform remains politically extremely difficult.[211]

When we add the benefits system, the resultant tax and benefits structure is a very long way from coherence. 'Universal Credit' will combine 'Tax Credits' with other means-tested benefits, but there will still be different sets of rules for 'Universal Credit', National Insurance benefits, Income Tax, National Insurance Contributions, and such universal benefits as Child Benefit. This would not matter if the different sets of rules did not cause problems when people are subject to several of them, but they do. The only regulations that do not cause problems when in combination with other regulations are those for Child Benefit. Similarly, the regulations for a Citizen's Income would not cause problems for the administration of any other parts of the system. This is one of many good reasons for saying that a Citizen's Income would make a good basis for a future benefits and tax structure.

---

[211] Adam, Stuart et al (eds) (2011) *Tax by design: The Mirrlees Review*, Oxford: Oxford University Press, p 7

(It might be suggested that taking Child Benefit into account when means-tested benefits are calculated causes a complication, but the complication arises from means-tested benefits taking other benefits into account, not from the Child Benefit itself.)

Now let us suppose that we establish a Citizen's Income. If revenue neutrality is essential (that is, if there is no additional money available), then we shall need to pay for the Citizen's Income by reducing tax allowances and means-tested and most contributory benefits. If there is extra money available (for instance, through a tax on financial transactions), then the Citizen's Income could be paid on top of the current system. In either case, the fact that a Citizen's Income was being paid would create no additional incoherence in the current system. If it were decided that means-tested benefits should be reduced by the amount of a Citizen's Income, then, as a Citizen's Income rose, and as individuals and households found their Citizen's Income either equal to or approaching the value of their means-tested benefits, they would come off means-tested benefits, their lives would be a great deal simpler, and they would be able to make choices about employment patterns without taking into account their decisions' effects on their benefits. They would also begin to experience the tax and benefits structure as coherent, rather than as a complex tangle. If an individual's or a household's Citizen's Incomes were to be paid on top of the existing system, then households would be likely to leave behind their means-tested benefits and to seek employment or self-employment in order to top up their Citizen's Income to their desired income level and so escape from the disincentives and intrusions of means tests: so even if initial calculations made paying a Citizen's Income on top of the current system look expensive, in reality it would turn out to be cheaper than the figures would suggest.

An increasing Citizen's Income would by itself reduce means-testing, meaning that means-tested benefits would again take on the safety net function that Beveridge intended for National Assistance. The larger the Citizen's Income, the higher the number of people able to escape from means-tested benefits (including 'Tax Credits'); and however small the Citizen's Income, there would be some people entitled to not very much means-tested income supplement who would abandon the means-tested system, with its complex administrative systems and its requirement to report changes of circumstances, and would fill any income gap with small amounts of employment or self-employment.

There is no need to see 'means-tested' and 'universal' as an either/or choice,[212] nor to see adding a Citizen's Income to the current system as an increase in incoherence. If we take the coherence of the system to mean the sum of individuals' and households' experiences of the coherence of the system, then a Citizen's Income of any size would create greater coherence because more people would be able to leave means-tested benefits behind. The higher the Citizen's Income, the greater the coherence. This is very different from the effect of means-tested benefits, where higher means-tested benefits, or means-tested benefits to which more people become entitled, tend to increase incoherence, because the more people there are on means-tested benefits, the more people there will be who experience the incoherence of the system, and therefore the less coherence there will be.

> **Our tax and benefits structure should be simple to administer:**[213] **to reduce employment disincentives, to reduce administrative costs, and because democratic accountability requires comprehensibility**

Again starting with the UK's current benefits system,

> the methods used to provide income and other support for those in need are extremely complex and interactions between the various benefits themselves and the direct tax system can cause serious anomalies. ... The complexity of the system makes it a nightmare for those administering or analyzing it and a complete mystery to most claimants. The result is enormous administrative costs and low take-up of benefit entitlements. (C.N. Morris).[214]

Members of Parliament have noticed. On the 27 January 2010 the House of Commons Work and Pensions Committee published a

---

[212] Bennett, Fran (1988) 'Alternatives to Basic Income: a personal view', *BIRG Bulletin*, no 7, Spring, pp 8–10

[213] Hermione Parker chooses 'simplicity' as the first of the core issues against which she evaluates alternative reform schemes: Parker, Hermione (1989) *Instead of the dole: An enquiry into integration of the tax and benefit systems*, London: Routledge, pp 285–6

[214] Morris, C.N. (1982) 'The structure of personal income taxation and Income Support', *Fiscal Studies*, vol 3, no 3, pp 210–18, p 210

report, *Decision making and appeals in the benefits system*.[215] The last two paragraphs read as follows (bold type in the original):

We do not underestimate the difficulty of the task facing decision makers across DWP's businesses. The complex rules that govern the social security system increase the scope for both customer and official error and the challenge of decision making accuracy. We have previously recommended that the Department establish a body to examine complexity in the benefits system and this has been supported by a number of organisations, including Citizens Advice.

We reiterate a previous recommendation of this Committee, that the Government should establish a Welfare Commission to examine the existing benefits system and model possible alternative structures with the aim of creating a fair but simpler system that claimants and their representatives are able to understand more easily and DWP staff are able to administer more accurately.

But of course it is not just the Department for Work and Pensions' section of the benefits system that is too complex: it is 'Tax Credits', administered by Her Majesty's Revenue and Customs (HMRC), that complicate the financial affairs of large numbers of working households. It would be nice to think that a means-tested system, which adjusts the amounts of benefit paid as people's circumstances change, could be simple to administer: but it cannot be. As research published by the Joseph Rowntree Foundation has shown,

> income testing can never be both simple and responsive in practice. There is always a trade-off between a simple system that does not reflect exactly the current circumstances of the recipient and a more complex system that adjusts to the detailed profile of a recipient's needs. The challenge is to decide when the trade-off is worthwhile.[216]

---

[215] House of Commons Work and Pensions Committee (2010) *Decision making and appeals in the benefits system*, HC313, p 44, www.publications.parliament.uk/pa/cm200910/cmselect/cmworpen/313/313.pdf

[216] Whiteford, Peter, Mendelson, Michael and Millar, Jane (2003) *Timing it right? Tax credits and how to respond to income changes*, York: Joseph Rowntree Foundation, p 27

The researchers suggest that a simpler system would be preferable.

It is bad enough that duplication and complexity imposes substantial administrative costs: it is much worse that the complexity blights the lives of so many families and individuals. With means-tested benefits, a small change in circumstances can throw a household's income maintenance system into disarray. Adding self-employment to employment, for instance, can cause both metaphorical and literal nightmares for both claimants and benefits staff alike: so either the new enterprise is not attempted, or it is attempted and not reported. A Citizen's Income would change the picture for everyone. As Philippe Van Parijs puts it, a Citizen's Income would provide 'administrative security that will enable people to take the risk of accepting a job or creating their own.'[217]

But the clear benefits to households and individuals are by no means the only reason for valuing the extreme simplicity of a Citizen's Income's administration. Equally important would be a substantial saving in administrative costs. As the National Audit Office puts it:

> While means testing can reduce public spending through targetting of support, the costs *per claim* of delivering means-tested benefits tend to be higher than for contributory or universal benefits even where benefits have similar target groups. The Department for Work and Pensions estimates that maintaining existing claims for Pension Credit cost £47 per claim in 2010-11, compared to £14 per claim for the non-means-tested State Pension. This is largely due to the greater complexity of assessing eligibility and the need to take account of changes in the financial circumstances of claimants.[218]

To administer a claim for Housing Benefit costs £163, for 'Tax Credits' £78, for Income Support £181, for means-tested Pension Credit £351 (£91 for contributory state pension), and for Jobseeker's Allowance £92. Those astronomical sums are just for the administration of a new claim. Means-tested benefits require complex and expensive administration throughout the claim, whereas universal benefits do

---

[217] Van Parijs, Philippe (1996) 'Basic Income and the two dilemmas of the welfare state', *The Political Quarterly*, vol 67, no 1, pp 63–66, p 65

[218] National Audit Office (2011) *Means testing*, Report by the Comptroller General, HC 1464, Session 2010–12, London: The Stationery Office, p 19

not.[219] And it is not just the government that suffers the expense of administering means-tested benefits. The National Audit office lists the costs borne by claimants:

> financial, such as the cost of calling a government benefits hotline from a mobile phone, which can be as much as 40p per minute; time, such as the costs of filling in forms; and psychological, including the 'stigma' and uncertainty of claiming benefits. Claimants may also find it difficult to understand their obligations and the options that they have in claiming benefits. Citizens Advice Bureaux dealt with 1.2 million cases related to means-tested benefits in 2009-10, 17 per cent of their total caseload. These impacts are rarely considered in departmental reports on means tested benefits.[220]

> Based on the latest information available, the Department estimates that in 2009 it overpaid between £1.75 billion and £2.14 billion to [']tax credits['] claimants due to error and fraud and underpaid between £0.25 billion and £0.55 billion to claimants due to error. The levels of error and fraud are material within the context of the £28.1 billion spent on [']tax credits['].As this expenditure has not been applied to the purposes intended by Parliament and does not conform with the requirements of the Tax Credits Act 2002, the Comptroller and Auditor General has qualified his opinion on the regularity of the [']tax credits['] expenditure.[221]

The report in which this statement occurs makes no reference to Child Benefit, even though it is administered by the same department: an example of a benefit not appearing on an agenda because there are no problems to discuss.[222]

---

[219] National Audit Office (2011) *Means testing*, Report by the Comptroller General, HC 1464, Session 2010–12, London: The Stationery Office, p 19

[220] National Audit Office (2011) *Means testing*, Report by the Comptroller General, HC 1464, Session 2010–12, p 22

[221] National Audit Office (2011) *HM Revenue and Customs 2010–11 Accounts*, Report by the Comptroller and Auditor General, London: National Audit Office, p R10

[222] See a website appendix on the National Health Service, at www.citizensincome. org, for an example of a healthcare funding policy not appearing on a social policy agenda because it experiences none of the problems experienced by healthcare systems in other countries.

So current means-tested benefits (including 'Tax Credits') are far from simple or cheap to administer, and 'Universal Credit' will be no easier and no cheaper. Information on individuals' earnings will be regularly relayed from the HMRC Pay as You Earn Income Tax computer to the Department for Work and Pensions computer so that households with at least one adult in employment will receive the correct amount of benefit: but this will only work seamlessly for the stably full-time employed and for people in stable relationships. For people with two part-time jobs, or with part-time employment and variable self-employment, or with occasional employment, or with changing relationships, benefits staff will still have quite a lot of work to do to ensure that entitlements are correctly calculated. Such flexible employment patterns are becoming more common, will become even more common, and will need to become more common in tomorrow's globalised and flexible labour market. I do not envy Department for Work and Pensions staff, or Her Majesty's Revenue and Customs staff, as they attempt to administer changes in claimants' circumstances in relation to a benefit involving both departments, the two departments' computer systems, and complex relationships between claimants, departmental staff, departmental computers, and employers.

It costs £11 per annum to administer a claim for Child Benefit. A Citizen's Income would be as easy and cheap to administer as Child Benefit, and it might be even cheaper, as there would be no main carer involved in the claim. For argument's sake, let us suppose a Citizen's Income of £30 per week for each adult citizen. The administrative cost would then be about 0.6 per cent of the total budget. The government might decide that it wanted proof of address when someone declared a change of address. If so, then this would be the sum total of ongoing administration that a Citizen's Income would require. A simpler benefit could not be possible.

The basic inefficiency in the current system is that a task is being done twice, millions of times a year. If I am earning an income and also receiving 'Tax Credits' then my earned income is being taxed, on the basis of calculations undertaken by my employer and by HMRC, and my 'Tax Credits' are being calculated by HMRC on the basis of information about my household's earnings. The first calculation is designed to take money away from me, and the second to pay me the right amount of benefit. (The same will continue to happen when 'Universal Credit' replaces 'Tax Credits'.) As Atkinson and Sutherland put it, 'a number of benefits are based on income tests, in effect operating a parallel system of taxation. If an extra £1 of earnings leads to the loss of 25p of a social security benefit, then this is no different, as far as cash receipts are concerned, from paying 25p extra Income Tax.'[223] Why do the same job twice? Why not simply pay a universal benefit that is never withdrawn, and then tax all earned income? Two sets of calculations would then be replaced by just one.

This would be genuine 'integration' – which is interesting, because it does not look like it. Schemes that *look* like integration are those that combine all of the operations in a single system to produce a single payment or deduction, such as a Negative Income Tax (which we shall discuss later in Chapter 15); but, as we saw with the Heath government's attempt at Tax Credits, complexity can be the result, particularly where an employer's administrative systems are being used to make payments or deductions, and where workers move rapidly between employers. A Citizen's Income, by making payments directly to every citizen, and by leaving the tax system as the only form of calculation relating to earnings, efficiently integrates the tax and benefits systems without integrating their administrations. Keeping the administration of the universal benefit and of the tax system separate is the efficient thing to do.[224]

An increasingly important factor relating to the administration of the benefits system is the ease with which a system can be computerised. The current means-tested benefits system has proved difficult to computerise. As computer companies and civil servants are discovering, the greater the complexity of a system, the greater the difficulty involved in computerising it, leading to the strong possibility that companies that win contracts to computerise tax and benefits systems will suggest policy changes that would make the system easier for them to automate, particularly if they are already in the middle of a fixed price contract. Once a contract has started, it is difficult for the government to resist such pressure, because no department wishes to see a computerisation project fail. The National Audit Office always has something damning and public to say when that happens. The extent to which the convenience of software companies is driving tax and benefits policy, and thus subverting democratic process, would be an interesting issue to study. A recent book about the ways in which the government has wasted money on computerisation and consultants

---

[223]   Atkinson, A.B. and Sutherland, Holly (1988a) *Integrating incomes taxation and social security: Analysis of a partial Basic Income*, Tax, Incentives and the Distribution of Income paper no 123, London: LSE, p 1; Atkinson, Tony and Sutherland, Holly (1988b) 'Analysis of a partial basic income', *BIRG Bulletin*, no 8, Autumn, pp 12–14

[224]   Parker, Hermione and Dilnot, Andrew (1988) 'Administration of integrated tax/benefit systems', *BIRG Bulletin*, no 8, Autumn, pp 6–10

contains plenty of material on the deeply flawed computerisation of 'Tax Credits', but significantly makes no mention of consultants or failed computer systems in relation to Child Benefit.[225] A Citizen's Income would be equally easy to computerise successfully.

Increasing numbers of benefits and 'Tax Credits' claimants receive their benefits into their bank accounts; though, for various reasons, such as women's reluctance to see Child Benefit disappear into a joint account effectively controlled by their husbands, appreciable amounts of Child Benefit are still collected from Post Offices (one effect of which is to keep more Post Offices open). People could easily be offered the same range of options for payment of a Citizen's Income as they are currently offered for the payment of Child Benefit. Because someone's Citizen's Income would never alter from one end of a financial year to the other, whether payment would be made weekly or monthly could be an entirely individual choice.

Just in case you might leave this section with the idea that the simplicity of a Citizens Income is its most important characteristic, and the characteristic most likely to recommend it to politicians and public alike (though not necessarily to civil servants, as we have already recognized), there are at least two counterarguments, and it is only fair to explain them.

As Tony Walter puts it: 'Simplicity may not be a vote catcher.'[226] People not receiving 'Tax Credits' or other means-tested benefits might not wish to know how much redistribution is being achieved, and, if they did know, they might not like it. With a Citizen's Income, taxpayers might not like the fact that they were paying for everyone's Citizen's Income, and that some other people were choosing not to seek employment and were thus making no effort to contribute to the pot out of which Citizen's Incomes were being paid.

We have to recognise that taxpayers might not be rational. They might not understand the argument that currently their taxes are paying people means-tested benefits that impose high marginal deduction rates and complex administrative problems that between them make it less likely that claimants will seek employment, whereas a Citizen's Income would lower marginal deduction rates and simplify administration and so would make it more likely that people currently not earning a living would seek to earn one. All one can say to this is that public education is a necessity.

225 Craig, David, with Richard Brooks (2006) *Plundering the public sector*, London: Constable, pp 7–11
226 Walter, Tony (1989) *Basic Income: Freedom from poverty, freedom to work*, London: Marion Boyars, p 59

A second argument for not emphasising too much a Citizen's Income's simplicity is that reform schemes rarely reach the statute book in their original form. A Citizen's Income would be bound to be implemented in a corrupted form, would therefore not be a Citizen's Income,[227] and would not be simple to administer. As De Wispelaere and Stirton point out, identifying those people entitled to a Citizen's Income would be a necessary administrative task, and a variety of payment methods might be needed in order to reach the maximum number of payees: so administration of a Citizen's Income might not be as simple as some might think, even if a genuine Citizen's Income were to be implemented. More importantly, 'proponents can claim important administrative savings for basic income, *provided they restrict those arguments to the most radical paradigmatic form*, while simultaneously having to face up to the reality that this radical version of basic income may face insurmountable political obstacles' (their italics).[228] Equally, a partial Citizen's Income, which is the only form that we are likely to see initially,[229] would leave in place many existing means-tested benefits. The higher the Citizen's Income, the more households would no longer receive means-tested benefits: but there would still be large numbers of people still being means-tested, and therefore large numbers giving rise to *increased* administrative costs because they would be receiving both the Citizen's Income and means-tested benefits. In order to save money, attempts would be made to impose conditions, or to withdraw the Citizen's Income from some sections of society as their earnings rose; or a household scheme rather than an individualised one might be attempted, which would impose all kinds of complex administrative consequences. Because a Citizen's Income would be likely to be implemented slowly, or for some groups and not for others, the existing complex benefits system would continue to exist. Any Citizen's Income that was not itself simple would add substantially to the complexity of the whole system and thus to administrative costs.

While there is legitimate debate about the likely administrative savings that would accrue from establishing a Citizen's Income,[230] however the

[227] Walter, Tony (1989) *Basic Income: Freedom from poverty, freedom to work*, London: Marion Boyars, pp 59–61

[228] De Wispelaere, Jürgen and Stirton, Lindsay (2011) 'The administrative efficiency of Basic Income', *Policy & Politics*, vol 39, no 1, pp 115–32, p 122

[229] Parker, Hermione (1988) 'Are Basic Incomes feasible?' *BIRG Bulletin*, no 7, Spring, pp 5–7

[230] Stirton, Lindsay and De Wispelaere, Jurgen (2009) 'Promoting Citizen's Income without bashing bureaucracy? (Yes, we can)', *Citizen's Income Newsletter*, issue 2, pp 5–6; Miller, Anne (2009) 'Citizen's income and administration', *Citizen's Income Newsletter*, issue 2, pp 6–8

debate went it would never constitute arguments against establishing a Citizen's Income. The debate is entirely one *for* its simplicity, and for emphasising its simplicity, in the hope that implementation will be of a true Citizen's Income and that the level of the Citizen's Income would grow over time and thus reap substantial administrative savings.

Errors, fraud, and criminalisation

A benefits system with increased administrative simplicity would, of course, reduce some of the consequences of the complexity that characterises the current system. In particular, it would reduce administrative error, reduce fraud, and reduce criminalisation.

Errors cost money:

> Material levels of fraud and error in the payment of benefits have led to the Department [of Work and Pension]'s accounts being qualified for 21 consecutive years. The qualification arises because mistakes are made, either by customers or officials, in processing benefits or as a result of customer fraud. Every year the Department estimates that it overpays around £3 billion to benefit claimants and underpays around £1 billion. Where the Department makes the mistake, overpayments are not normally recoverable and are consequently lost to the taxpayer, costing nearly £1 billion every year.[231]

While a book of this nature would not normally quote from *Private Eye*, there is one quote that I cannot resist:

> Gordon Brown's Tax Credit policy isn't just driving claimants mad: it's thrown his own staff into a state of gibbering confusion too.
>
> After reporting changes in her childcare arrangements, one *Eye* reader had the temerity to question a demand for repayment of a Tax Credit overpayment. Not only did HM Revenue and Customs customer support unit respond that 'it is not possible to explain how the figure of [£x] per week was calculated', but she was also told the demand

---

[231] National Audit Office (2010) *The National Audit Office's work on the Department for Work and Pensions*, London: National Audit Office, p 8

would stand as 'we do not think it was reasonable for you to expect that your payments were correct.'

Quite right, too. Anyone who knows anything about tax credits would never believe they were being paid the right amount.[232]

The serious point being made, of course, is that the greater the complexity of a tax and benefits structure, the greater the likelihood that mistakes will be made.

Overpayment of benefits can result in anxiety for the claimants who have been overpaid, additional administrative costs as the government attempts recovery of the debt, and an additional cost to the Exchequer when it fails to achieve that. If the anxiety generated by a letter telling a family that they have been overpaid and that they have to pay back money that they no longer have were to be quantifiable, then the cost of errors would be astronomical. Without quantifying anxiety, errors related to the means-tested Pension Credit cost £140 million per annum, which is 1.7 per cent of the total budget, whereas official error related to the non–means-tested state pension costs £40 million, which is below 0.1 per cent of that budget. We would expect errors related to the payment of a Citizen's Income to be even lower than that.[233]

Fraud costs money, too. It costs money to detect, it costs money to prosecute offenders, and it costs money when fraudulent payments cannot be recovered. Fraud related to Jobseeker's Allowance costs £180 million per annum, which is 4.1 per cent of the total budget; fraud related to means-tested Pension Credit costs £190 million per annum, which is 2.3 per cent of the budget. Fraud related to the Basic State Pension is so low that it is listed as £0 million.[234]

Should we worry about fraud? In total, it costs the exchequer about £1 billion per annum, which is only half the cost of error. The problem with the existence of fraud is that it gives the press stories to write, and those stories generate an anti-claimant agenda that enables the government to cut benefits.[235] The only answer is to remove the

---

[232] *Private Eye*, September 2006

[233] DWP (2011) *Fraud and error in the benefit system: Preliminary 2010/11 estimates*, London: DWP, p 12

[234] DWP (2011) *Fraud and error in the benefit system: Preliminary 2010/11 estimates*, London: DWP, p 12

[235] Baillie, Richard (2011) 'An examination of the public discourse on benefit claimants in the media', *Journal of Poverty and Social Justice*, vol 19, no 1, pp 67–70

possibility of fraud, and at the same time to increase social cohesion in the income maintenance system.

A Citizen's Income would probably attract a level of fraud similar to that experienced by the state pension. If someone's Citizen's Income was simply a follow-on from their Child Benefit, then the only way in which fraud could occur would be for there to be two Child Benefit claims related to the child. This would have to have happened at birth, and would be rare. If, on the other hand, a new Citizen's Income claim had to be made at the age of 18, then a normal check of identity and address would be sufficient to prevent multiple claims. With a Citizen's Income the only fraud that could possibly arise would be related to multiple claims. When in payment, someone's Citizen's Income would be of an unchanging amount, whatever their circumstances. Earnings would never affect the amount of Citizen's Income paid, household structure would not affect it, and savings would not affect it. The vast majority of fraud related to means-tested benefits results from nondeclaration of earnings, of changed household structure, or of savings. None of this would be a problem with a Citizen's Income; and because a Citizen's Income would remove numerous individuals and households from means-tested benefits (because they would prefer to fill any income gap with earnings rather than with means-tested benefits), overall levels of fraud would drop.

Criminalisation is at least as much of a problem as fraud. Under the current system, if someone on Jobseeker's Allowance is offered a weekend of well paid work, then it is rational for them not to declare their earnings to the Department of Work and Pensions. The administrative hassle of doing so would render the brief employment not worth taking. The claimant would be able to persuade themselves that the Department's hard pressed staff would rather not be bothered with their brief labour market re-entry; and, if asked anonymously, the hard pressed staff would probably agree. The problem is with the system, not with the claimant.

During the 1980s, Bill Jordan and his colleagues studied the labour market decisions of low income families on a housing estate in Exeter. They found that each household had put together a rolling financial strategy made up of a variety of employments and self-employments, with casual cash earnings not declared to benefits authorities if they remained below a certain level. Both a pragmatic moral sense and a community consensus permitted such nondeclaration, so long as it did not go too far.[236] This was all very sensible, but it meant that activity that strictly speaking was criminal became a community norm. It does nobody any good for crime to be both rational and acceptable. It brings the law into disrepute, it lowers the psychological barrier to other criminal activity, and it encourages criminal nondeclaration of income to become a habit, depriving the Exchequer of tax revenue in the longer term.

A Citizen's Income would attract almost no fraud, and because it would enable numerous individuals and households to avoid means-testing, it would lower the overall rate of fraud, and would therefore reduce both claimant criminalisation and the current trend towards 'the blurring of boundaries between the worlds of welfare, criminal justice and civil society'.[237]

Conclusion

C.N. Morris, to whom the quote at the beginning of this section belongs, concludes his survey of the problems facing the current tax and benefits systems by recommending that in the short term Child Benefit levels should be increased, and in the longer term that integration of the tax and benefits systems is essential.[238] I think that we can now see why he makes these recommendations. We can also see why in 2007 the House of Commons Work and Pensions Committee made the following recommendations (I make no apology for quoting them at length):

> There is a direct correlation between the amount of means-testing and the complexity of the system. We recommend that the Government specifically evaluates the current caseload of means-testing in the system as part of its simplification efforts and, where possible, reduces it.
>
> The contributory principle adds an additional layer to the current system and research suggests it is no longer as relevant to the benefits system as it once was. We therefore recommend that the Government reviews whether or not

---

[236] Jordan, Bill, James, Simon, Kay, Helen and Redley, Marcus (1992) *Trapped in poverty? Labour-market decisions in low-income households*, London: Routledge, p 277

[237] Rodger, John J. (2012) ' "Regulating the poor": observations on the "structural coupling" of welfare, criminal justice and the voluntary sector in a "big Society"', *Social Policy and Administration*, vol 46, no 4, pp 413–31, p 429

[238] Morris, C.N. (1982) 'The structure of personal income taxation and Income Support', *Fiscal Studies*, vol 3, no 3, pp 210–18

the contributory principle remains a relevant part of the modern benefit structure.

There is no Government Minister, department or unit that is attempting to address the combined and overlapping complexities of the benefits and tax credits systems. This omission must be urgently addressed.

We recommend that the Government undertakes research to investigate whether there remain some groups of claimants for whom work does not offer the best route out of poverty, and more detailed analysis of the impact of high Marginal Deduction Rates in parts of the benefits system on overall work incentives.

It is not enough to rely on 'masking' complexity; there is a need to go further and address the rules of the different benefits and the structure of the system itself.

The Government should establish a Welfare Commission, similar in format and remit to the Pensions Commission, which can take a holistic view, model alternative systems, and come up with a considered blueprint for a way forward. A benefits system that DWP staff, claimants and welfare rights advisers have a hope of understanding is in everyone's best interests.[239]

Having claimed that a Citizen's Income would provide a good basis for a simpler 'structure of the system', I ought at least to ask whether a Citizen's Income might in fact cause additional complexity in the system. Paul Spicker suggests that there are different

types of complexity in the operation of social security benefits. The first is intrinsic complexity: some benefits are complex in their concept, structure or operation. The second is extrinsic: systems become complicated when several benefits or agencies have to be dealt with. Third, there are complex rules. Some are imposed for administrative reasons, but there may also be some 'conditionality', including moral

---

[239] House of Commons Work and Pensions Committee Report (2007) *Benefits Simplification*, HC 463, vol I, London: The Stationery Office, paragraphs 51, 55, 148, 176, 262, 381, www.publications.parliament.uk/pa/cm200607/cmselect/cmworpen/463/46302.htm. The Citizen's Income Trust's evidence to the committee can be found in volume II, p Ev 84: www.publications.parliament.uk/pa/cm200607/cmselect/cmworpen/463/463ii.pdf

conditions and rules about rationing. Fourth, there are complex management systems, including the proliferation of agencies and the problems of information management. Finally, there is complexity that arises through the situation of claimants. Benefits that try to adjust to people's changing circumstances require elaborate rules and procedures, and they are always slightly out of step. If we want to simplify benefits, we need to focus on conditionality, administrative rules and management procedures.[240]

Means-tested benefits are complex in all five dimensions. A Citizen's Income is simple in all five: it is intrinsically simple, there would be a single delivery mechanism, there would be no complex rules because no conditionality, management would be simple because very little information would need to be managed, and no adjustment to personal circumstances would be required. A Citizen's Income clearly passes the simplicity test.

---

[240] Spicker, Paul (2005) 'Five types of complexity', *Benefits*, vol 13, no 1, pp 5–9

CHAPTER 7

Criteria for a benefits system: the family, then, now, and in the future

In this chapter we shall explore our third criterion for an ideal benefits system:

> Our tax and benefits structure should reflect today's family and household patterns, and should remain serviceable as household and family patterns continue to change.

We shall begin with a discussion of the ways in which households and the family have changed during the past half century and then ask what kind of benefits system today's family requires and how that compares with the benefits system constructed in an era with rather different social structures.

The changing family[241]

Whereas a generation ago someone might have lived with their parents until they married and moved in with a partner, or moved in with a partner and then married, today the only generalisation that we can make is that the situation is diverse. A young adult might share a house or a flat with people they know, or with people they don't. If they have a girlfriend or boyfriend then they might live apart, they might live together, or they might rotate regularly through a variety of household patterns. A mother and her child might live with the child's father, might leave him and move in with the child's grandmother (on either side), and might then form a household with a friend and her child. Are we discussing families or households here? As I have written this chapter I have found myself employing the terms somewhat interchangeably. This is symptomatic of the fluid nature of today's social structures, and I shall not attempt precise definitions of either of the two terms.

---

241 Torry, Malcolm (1996) 'The labour market, the family, and social security reform: a dissertation for the Master of Science degree in social policy and planning at the London School of Economics', unpublished dissertation

We have known some of the basic trends for some time, but research undertaken for the Centre for the Modern Family, recently established by the Scottish Widows insurance company, has shown just how diverse families in the UK now are, and how diverse people's attitudes to the family are too. In 1961, 38 per cent of families consisted of a married couple with two or more children, but by 2011 'just 16 per cent of the UK population believe that they fit the "traditional model". In short, there has been a meltdown in the traditional nuclear family.'[242]

Average household size has decreased from 3.1 persons in 1961 to 2.4 persons in 2010. A smaller proportion of households in Great Britain had children living in them in 2010 than in 1961, and the average household with children had fewer children than before. The most common type of family in the UK in 2010 contained one child (46.3 per cent of all families in 2010). The number of people living alone increased from seven million to 7.5 million between 2001 and 2010; and more couples have delayed having children or have remained childless: another reason for smaller households. A woman in a reasonably well paid job, and particularly a woman in a career in which progress relies on staying involved, will now think twice about having children. Having children carries an opportunity cost: a loss of income and status if the mother looks after the children herself, or the costs of the tensions that she will face if she hires childcare. A woman might think the cost worth it, but she might not; and having decided not to have children, or not to have children yet, she might eventually decide to have them when she can no longer put it off, and might therefore have fewer children and face a greater risk of not being able to have children at all. In 1971 nearly four out of five births in England and Wales were to women aged less than 30, but by 2009 only just over half were to women in this age group.

A hundred years ago, extramarital births were comparatively rare, and the vast majority of marriages were ended by the death of one of the partners. Change has been substantial in both of these areas, and particularly recently. In 1971, 8.4 per cent of all live births were outside marriage; by 1991 it was 30.2 per cent; and now it is 46.2 per cent. Lone parent families increased from 14.8 per cent of the total in 2001

---

[242] Centre for the Modern Family (2011) *Family: Helping to understand the modern British family*, Edinburgh: Scottish Widows, Centre for the Modern Family, p 4; Hughes, Matthew (ed.) (2010) *Social Trends*, no 40, London: Palgrave Macmillian, for the Office for National Statistics, p 14, www.ons.gov.uk/ons/rel/social-trends-rd/social-trends/social-trends-40/index.html

to 16.2 per cent in 2010.[243] Patricia Morgan suggests that a major cause of this trend is the 'flexible labour market', which gives to men few prospects of secure employment, resulting in 'whole communities in which it is very difficult to establish and maintain families, with almost insuperable obstacles to family formation at the bottom of the socioeconomic ladder'.[244] It might well be true that

> the subject of family formation is clearly one of considerable complexity, where the role of economic factors should not be exaggerated. The mechanisms at work are more subtle than any simple relation between income support and marriage or separation (Tony Atkinson).[245]

However, it must also be true that a benefits system that makes it financially more worthwhile for some parents to separate rather than stay together is giving entirely the wrong message.

There might be reasons for providing extra benefits for lone-parent families, but the safest option socially, politically, and morally, is to seek policies that are neutral between different family types.[246] Obvious ways to achieve the required neutrality are to individualise benefit claims and to increase the employment and childcare options available. Research has shown that children whose parents are in employment have a better experience of childhood than children whose parents are not, *and* that parental childcare has considerable benefits. Enabling parents to balance both employment and sufficient time to care for their own children should therefore be a priority.[247]

One of the worst features of the current system in the UK is that it divides our society in two and imposes different sets of regulations on taxpayers and benefits recipients (though some people find themselves subject to both sets of regulations if they receive 'Tax Credits' and also pay Income Tax). Individuals pay Income Tax, but couples receive

---

[243] Beaumont, Jen (2011) *Households and families: Social trends 41*, London: ONS, pp 2, 16, www.ons.gov.uk, 04/10/11

[244] Morgan, Patricia (1995) *Farewell to the family? Public policy and family breakdown in Britain and the USA*, London: Institute of Economic Affairs, p 61

[245] Atkinson, A.B. (1985) *Income maintenance and social insurance: A survey*, Welfare State Programme, paper no 5, London: LSE, p 140

[246] Kirnan, Kathleen and Wicks, Malcolm (1990) *Family change and future policy*, York: Joseph Rowntree Memorial Trust / Family Policy Studies Centre, p 31

[247] Cusworth, Linda (2009) *The impact of parental employment: Young people, well-being and educational achievement*, Aldershot: Ashgate, pp 195–7

means-tested benefits, such as 'Tax Credits',[248] and the same will apply to 'Universal Credit'.[249] Why do more people not question this difference in treatment? If my wife's earned income was paid to me, or I needed to know her income in order to complete my tax return, or if a tax inspector were to come round to find out who I was living with, then I would be justifiably furious, and she might be too. But that is precisely how 'Tax Credits' operate. A joint claim has to be made, and whoever fills in the form has to know both partners' incomes. My wife chooses to tell me her income, and I tell her mine, but that is a choice that we make. If we were claiming 'Tax Credits' then we would not have a choice to make: one of us would have to know the other's income; and if someone is claiming Income Support or 'Tax Credits' as an individual, when they ought to be claiming as a couple, and someone who bears a grudge betrays them, then a fraud investigator might take a look at their relationship.

Calculating benefits on the basis of the household, rather than on an individual basis, reduces the employment incentive for the spouse of a full-time earner, reduces couples' incentive to live together, might reduce children's parents' incentive to live together,[250] and, alongside all of these difficulties, makes it necessary for benefits administrators to investigate the private lives of claimants in order to find out who is living with whom. Peter Esam and Richard Berthoud suggest that it would be possible to individualise current benefits, and that 'if the relationships between men and women ... continue to change at the pace of the last decade, the assumption of dependence built into the benefit system will have to be tackled eventually.'[251] It is a pity that 'Universal Credit' will be calculated on a household basis, and also a pity that Steven Webb's proposal for a universal benefit assumed calculation on the basis of the household.[252] There will be more opportunities

---

[248]   www.hmrc.gov.uk/taxcredits/start/claiming/get-started/joint-single-claim.htm, 11/09/2011

[249]   www.dwp.gov.uk/docs/universal-credit-full-document.pdf, 11/09/2011, p 33

[250]   There is some controversy over whether the regulations do in fact favour the separation of a child's parents. The benefits and child support regime regulations would suggest that there is no advantage to separation. What the figures cannot show is the advantage to a couple of the father moving out, the mother receiving Income Support, Jobseeker's Allowance, or 'Tax Credits', and the father continuing to earn (and maybe receiving his own Tax Credits) and supplementing the mother's income with undeclared payments.

[251]   Esam, Peter and Berthoud, Richard (1991) *Independent benefits for men and women*, London: Policy Studies Institute, p 71

[252]   Brittan, Samuel and Webb, Steven (1990) *Beyond the welfare state: An examination of Basic Incomes in a market economy*, Aberdeen: Aberdeen University Press, p 1

to get it right, and we must not miss them. When a government implements a Citizen's Income, the individual must be the claimant unit, not the household or the family.

To the objection that individualised benefits payments fail to promote marriage, I say this: It is household-based payments that might be driving couples apart, and driving apart the parents of children. If a couple were to be allowed to keep the economies of scale generated by living together, if my employment incentives had nothing to do with my spouse's earnings, and if I were to receive the income to which I was entitled rather than my spouse getting it, then I would be *more* likely to stay in the marriage or the relationship, not less. It is the *current* system that corrodes marriage and long-term relationships, not a Citizen's Income. At the moment, someone living alone and receiving means-tested benefits who moves in with someone earning a living is likely to lose the whole of their independent income (apart from Child Benefit if they have children). This is a big risk for people to take.[253] With a Citizen's Income, the nonearning woman or man would know that they would be able to leave the partnership with an independent income intact, thus making it more likely that they would stay; and the fact that a Citizen's Income would not be withdrawn as earnings rose would make it more likely that they would seek employment once in the new relationship.

As Paul Spicker puts it: 'We cannot ask claimants to live simpler, more orderly lives', so we need to rid the benefits system of its complexity by addressing its current 'conditionality, administrative rules and administrative procedures'.[254] Change in household and family structures can only accelerate. As we shall see later, a benefits system containing a Citizen's Income would go a long way towards meeting the needs of today's families and households, and also the needs of families and households of the future, whatever relational, labour market and economic structures they turn out to have; and a Citizen's Income would at the same time facilitate the kinds of stable families that children need, whatever other social changes were taking place.

---

[253] Lewis, Jane (2012) Seminar at the LSE, 15 February, on Bennett, Fran and Sutherland, Holly (2011) *The importance of independent income: Understanding the role of non-means-tested earnings replacement benefits*, ISER working paper no 2011–09, Colchester: Institute for Social and Economic Research, University of Essex

[254] Spicker, Paul (2011) *How social security works: An introduction to benefits in Britain,* Bristol: Policy Press, p 145

The changing role of women

While the changing role of women is of course bound up with the ways in which families and the labour market are changing, it is still important to discuss the ways in which the current tax and benefits systems affect women, and the ways in which a Citizen's Income might also affect them.

As a Citizen's Income Trust report has suggested in relation to the UK:

> Born in 1879 (when Queen Victoria had another 22 years to reign), Beveridge populated his visionary world with happily married, single-earner couples, widows (no widowers) and single people living either alone or with their parents … in devising his Plan, Beveridge also assumed that virtually all poverty was and would continue to be due to interruption or loss of earnings, or to the presence of children in the family. Reading the Beveridge Report one wonders how someone with so much experience in public life could have been so unaware of the low pay, irregular pay and no pay with which women's work has traditionally been rewarded; the poverty associated with lone parenthood, divorce and separation; the lifetime poverty of people born with disabilities; and the legendary poverty of students.[255]

Decreasing numbers of women live in the kinds of family that Beveridge envisaged; childcare and the care of older and disabled relatives is still mainly undertaken by women; and women are therefore more likely than men to take career breaks, pauses, or decelerations. For this and other reasons, the average full-time earned income of women is still well below that of men.[256] However, part-time hourly

---

[255] Parker, Hermione (ed.) (1993) *Citizen's Income and women*, London: Citizen's Income Trust, pp 14, 16. cf. Parker, Hermione (1989) *Instead of the dole: An enquiry into integration of the tax and benefit systems*, London: Routledge, pp 22–30: Beveridge assumed that 'society consists of happily married couples (no divorce), widows (no widowers) and heterosexual celibates living either alone or with their parents … that all married women are financially dependent on their husbands … that it is within the power of governments to maintain full employment … that full employment means regular, full-time work for men, from age 15 to 65, with minimal job changes and minimal need for training or re-training.'

[256] The UK has the fifth highest gender gap out of the twenty-six OECD countries; OECD Social Policy Division (2011) *Gender pay gaps for full-time workers and earnings differentials by educational attainment*, Paris: OECD, www.oecd.org/dataoecd/29/63/38752746.pdf

rates for women are higher than those for men. This suggests that women are more likely to be working part-time in the higher-paid occupations.[257] While the man in a marriage or partnership is not now the default claimant where claims have to be made on the basis of the couple rather than as individuals, the fact that claims are not made by individuals, and that distribution of money within the household is not always equitable,[258] means that women often do worse out of means-tested benefits than men do.[259] This effect persists into old age: a result of the increasing importance of private pension provision and of an earnings related state pension, as well as of the contributory nature of the Basic State Pension.[260] While more recent attempts to repair women's National Insurance Contributions records mean that younger women will now accrue records similar to those that men accrue, there are still older women with lower National Insurance pensions because they never paid full contributions and did not pay contributions for sufficient numbers of years. A particular problem is that people working part-time and earning below the primary threshold for National Insurance Contributions pay no contributions and end up with incomplete contribution records: a problem that affects more women than men.[261] Again, the result is that women do less well out of National Insurance pensions than men.[262] Equally important is the disadvantage that women experience in relation to occupational pensions. Because women tend to have fewer years in full-time employment, and their earned incomes tend on average to be below men's earned incomes, the pension rights they build up are not

---

[257] Office for National Statistics (2010) *2010 Annual Survey of Hours and Earnings*, London: ONS, www.ons.gov.uk/ons/rel/ashe/annual-survey-of-hours-and-earnings/2010-results/index.html

[258] Pahl, Jan (1983) 'The allocation of money and structuring of inequality within marriage', *Sociological Review*, vol 31, no 2, pp 237–62; Adelman, Laura, Middleton, Sue and Ashworth, Karl (1999) *Intra-household distribution of poverty and social exclusion: Evidence from the 1999 PSE Survey of Britain*, Working paper no 23, Loughborough: Centre for Research in Social Policy

[259] Addabbo, Tindara, Arrizabalaga, Marie-Pierre, Borderias, Cristina and Owens, Alastair (eds) (2010) *Gender inequalities, households and the production of well-being in modern Europe*, Aldershot: Ashgate

[260] Rein, Martin and Schmähl, Winfried (2004) *Rethinking the welfare state*, London: Edward Elgar; Ginn, Jay (2003) *Gender, pensions and the lifecourse*, Bristol: Policy Press; Twine, Fred (1996) 'What kinds of people do we wish to be?' *Citizen's Income Bulletin*, no 22, July, pp 16–17

[261] Workers in this position can pay voluntary contributions if they wish, but few do.

[262] Sainsbury, Diane (1996) *Gender, equality, and welfare states*, Cambridge: Cambridge University Press, pp 55–8

as substantial as those accrued by men. They therefore receive lower occupational pensions. As Jay Ginn puts it:

> Women employees' disadvantage in pension scheme membership is greater if they are married, have a child, work part-time, are employed in the private sector, have been in their job a short time and have low earnings ... women's pension scheme membership is reduced by the gendered division of domestic responsibilities, and the impact this has had on the type of employment women were able to undertake. Current gender inequality in occupational pension scheme membership suggests that, unless more generous state provision for retirement is made, the likelihood of poverty for elderly women will increase in the future.[263]

We are beginning to build up a picture of continuing inequality, and of a scenario in which women in the UK are more likely to be poor than men. In the United States the picture is similar because adequate benefits, both publicly and privately provided, are closely tied to people's employment records.[264] Readers elsewhere will be aware of the situations in their own countries. I suspect that it will be similar, whether that country is developed or developing.

But the world *is* changing, and many women now face more choices then they would have done in a previous century, or even decade. Catherine Hakim discusses three broad categories of lifestyle choice available to women: 1. a life centred on career opportunities, 2. a life centred on family obligations, and 3. a role in which women adapt or compromise at various stages in their lifecycle depending on the options available. She suggests that different social policy configurations will privilege or disadvantage different options.[265] Given that women are likely to want all three options to be available, an option–neutral policy bundle would clearly be preferable, and this suggests a benefits system based on a Citizen's Income. Like Child Benefit, a Citizen's Income would in no way constrain choice, and, in comparison to today's configuration, it would considerably enhance it.

---

[263] Ginn, Jay (1993) 'Pension penalties: the gendered division of occupational welfare,' *Work, Employment & Society*, vol 7, no 1, pp 47–70, p 47

[264] Alstott, Anne L. (2001), 'Good for women', pp 75–9 in Cohen, Joshua and Rogers, Joel, *What's wrong with a free lunch?* Boston: Beacon Press

[265] Hakim, Catherine (2003) *Models of the family in modern society: Ideals and realities,* Aldershot: Ashgate

A Citizen's Income would not on its own generate equal status and equal net incomes for women and men,[266] and because it would enable women more easily to follow their lifestyle preferences, and because those preferences are to some extent constructed by an unjust society that ascribes an unpaid caring role to women, it is possible to argue that a Citizen's Income could entrench gender inequality by implicitly valuing the caring role.[267] However, because a Citizen's Income would treat women and men equally, every individual woman would experience at least some equalisation of their situation in relation to the gender division of income, and therefore women's financial positions would improve in relation to men's;[268] and because a Citizen's Income of any size would reduce the marginal deduction rates that apply to additional earnings, it would be more worthwhile for a woman to seek employment or additional employment, and she would therefore be more likely to do so. A Citizen's Income would therefore value both the caring and the earning roles, and because it would be more possible for two members of a couple to decide that they would both work part-time rather than one of them full-time, both their caring responsibilities and their earned incomes could be more equally distributed if the couple chose to behave in that way. In the absence of such additional policies as the increased availability of childcare, and in the presence of continuing prejudice, we shall of course continue to see gender inequality:[269] but that is hardly the fault of a Citizen's Income.

Should the state treat women as different from men, or should it treat them in the same way as it treats men? This question defines 'Wollstonecraft's dilemma', which in more practical terms asks this: Should social policy recognise that typically male work and typically female work are in practice different, and find a way of rewarding them equally, or should it treat everyone the same, whatever activity they choose to undertake? An interesting characteristic of a Citizen's Income is that it avoids the dilemma:

---

[266] Baker, John (2008) 'All things considered, should feminists embrace Basic Income?', *Basic Income Studies*, vol 3, no 3, pp 1–8

[267] Gheaus, Anca (2008) 'Basic Income, gender justice and the costs of gender-symmetrical lifestyles', *Basic Income Studies*, vol 3, no 3, pp 1–8

[268] Elgarte, Julieta M. (2008) 'Basic Income and the gendered division of labour', *Basic Income Studies*, vol 3, no 3, pp 1–7

[269] O'Reilly, Jacqueline (2008) 'Can a Basic Income lead to a more gender equal society?', *Basic Income Studies*, vol 3, no 3, pp 1–7

Both the 'male breadwinner' and 'adult worker' models take masculine work patterns (continuous full-time employment) as their reference point. In the 'male breadwinner' arrangement women are viewed as *different from men* – carers as opposed to workers, while in the 'adult worker' welfare state women are encouraged to behave the *same as men* – workers. Fewer women than men fit exclusively into either category, and less so over time. Rather, large numbers combine the breadwinner and caregiver roles. A [Citizen's Income] extends the opportunity to make this work-care mix the norm for men as well as women. Should this opportunity be seized, Wollstonecraft's dilemma of how the state should incorporate women into its policies would be resolved. That is, no longer will it have to integrate women according to how their behaviour relates to that of men, since men will now be in a position to behave the *same as women*. Moreover, in achieving this fusion of gender roles into one worker-carer category, women's overall wellbeing ... need not be compromised.[270]

As the Citizen's Income Trust's report quoted earlier suggests:

Given the opportunity, more couples would opt for a more equal division of caring and wage-earning responsibilities. ... At present, because most women earn less than men, there is a clear disincentive for couples to reverse roles. A Citizen's Income would reduce ... that disincentive.[271]

In other ways, too, a Citizen's Income would provide women and men with a more level playing field by

enhancing women's financial independence, challenging the sexual division of labour (by recognising the value of care-work), challenging occupational segregation (by making part-time jobs pay) and debureaucratising the state.[272]

---

[270] Bambrick, Laura (2006) 'Wollstonecraft's dilemma: is a citizen's Income the answer', *Citizen's Income Newsletter*, issue 2, pp 3–10, p 9

[271] Parker, Hermione (ed.) (1993) *Citizen's Income and women*, London: Citizen's Income Trust, p 10

[272] Fitzpatrick, Tony (1999) *Freedom and security: An introduction to the Basic Income debate*, Basingstoke: Macmillan, p 174

Largely hidden from outsiders are the ways in which finances are managed within the household, in particular the ways in which men will often control the household resources, leaving women with the responsibility for budgeting and for caring for the children but with too few resources with which to do that. The author has quite enough experience of men who waste a family's resources on their addictions and obsessions to know that this is a problem. Increasing Child Benefit would increase women's control over resources, as would individualising means-tested benefits. A Citizen's Income would immediately help, of course, because each individual would be paid their own Citizen's Income.[273]

So a Citizen's Income would begin to address income inequality between women and men, and it would also contribute to putting right some other inequalities too.[274] Because a Citizen's Income would be paid to individuals and not to households, and because it would be unconditional, women not in the labour market because of their caring responsibilities would receive an income as of right, and thus a modicum of financial independence.[275] Women and men would be more able to share childcare and employment without the constraints imposed by today's benefits regulations; and women in the labour market, far from finding a Citizen's Income a handicap,[276] would find themselves with net incomes more equal with men's than they are now.[277]

---

[273] Pahl, Jan (1986) 'Social security, taxation and family financial arrangements', *BIRG Bulletin*, no 5, Spring, pp 2–4; Zelleke, Almaz (2008) 'Institutionalizing the universal caretaker through a Basic Income?' *Basic Income Studies*, vol 3, no 3, pp 1–9

[274] Mullarney, Maire (1991) 'The rights of children – a justification of Basic Income, hitherto unremarked', *BIRG Bulletin*, no 12, February, pp 30–2, p 32

[275] Parker, Hermione (ed.) (1993) *Citizen's Income and women*, London: Citizen's Income Trust, p 21

[276] Bergmann, Barbara (2008) 'Basic Income Grants or the welfare state: which better promotes gender equality?', *Basic Income Studies*, vol 3, no 3, pp 1–7

[277] If a Citizen's Income is paid for by reducing tax allowances, then part-time workers not currently paying tax would find themselves paying tax for the first time but would also be in receipt of a Citizen's Income. It is possible that a lower Citizen's Income and part-time earnings above a certain level could mean that some women could end up slightly worse off initially, though particularly in families in receipt of Tax Credits the net difference would be difficult to predict. Cf. Atkinson, A.B. (1989) *Basic Income schemes and the lessons from public economics*, Tax, Incentives and the Distribution of Income paper no 136, London: LSE, p 2

Conclusion

Hermione Parker's words are as relevant today as when she wrote them over twenty years ago:

> Many of the changes taking place, especially increased life expectancy, drudgery-avoiding automation and women's emancipation, could add to the sum of human happiness, but only if we quickly adapt to the new conditions they impose. If we do not, if we cling to institutions handed down from the past, then there are dangers of accelerating relative economic decline, continuing mass unemployment, further destabilisation of family life and social discord. ... Only governments can ensure that the tax and benefit systems match the economic and social conditions under which people actually live.[278]

The current system is a nightmare to administer when households are in transition from one configuration to another. If a couple receiving 'Tax Credits' separates, and the mother takes the young children and is no longer employed, then she needs to make a new Income Support claim, and her husband needs his 'Tax Credits' recalculated. Her boyfriend moves in. He is employed, and receiving 'Tax Credits'. Her benefit stops, and his 'Tax Credits' increase. He leaves. You get the picture ... . None of this will be any easier under 'Universal Credit'. Alternatively, the woman knows how complicated it will get if she tells the office that her boyfriend has moved in, so she fails to tell them. Her neighbour does it for her. There is a fraud investigation, at great cost. Who benefits from all of this?

We have seen the ways in which families are changing, and the difficult labour market decisions with which the current tax and benefits systems face many modern families. Particularly problematic is the situation of the female partner of a male on means-tested benefits, whether 'Tax Credits' or Jobseeker's Allowance (or, in the future, 'Universal Credit'). If she finds employment, then apart from a small disregard, most of her additional income is deducted from the means-tested benefits coming into the household. If there are work expenses to be paid, such as fares and childminding costs,[279] then

---

[278] Parker, Hermione (1989) *Instead of the dole: An enquiry into integration of the tax and benefit systems*, London: Routledge, pp 20, 21

[279] Owen, Sue and Mogridge, Martin (1986) 'The costs of working', *BIRG Bulletin*, no 6, Autumn, pp 21–24

employment could mean financial loss. This really is not sensible.[280] A Citizen's Income of any size would begin to tackle the problem, and would continue to make sense as households and families continue to change in the future.

---

[280] McGinnity, Frances (2004) *Welfare for the unemployed in Britain and Germany: Who benefits?*, Aldershot: Edward Elgar, p 185

CHAPTER 8

Criteria for a benefits system: incentives, efficiency, and dignity

In this chapter we shall explore the next three items in our list of criteria for an ideal benefits system:

Our tax and benefits structure should not disincentivise public goods such as enterprise, training, long-term relationships between parents of children, and providing financially for oneself and one's dependents.

Our tax and benefits structure should incentivise the efficient allocation of resources and so contribute to an efficient economy.

Our tax and benefits structure should treat people with dignity and not stigmatise individuals involved in any part of the system.

We shall again ask whether the current system or a Citizen's Income more nearly matches these criteria.

Incentives

The fourth criterion is this: Our tax and benefits structure should not disincentivise public goods such as long-term relationships among parents of children, enterprise, training, and providing financially for oneself and one's dependents.

Hermione Parker, in her *Taxes, benefits and family life: The seven deadly traps*, shows how our current tax and benefits systems between them bait seven traps: the unemployment, invalidity, poverty, lone parent, part-time, lack of skills, and savings traps.

The 'unemployment trap' refers 'to a situation in which people are encouraged to stay out of work for longer than is strictly necessary, or to move to the underground economy, because a return to work in the formal economy would either reduce their spending power or bring a net gain too small to make the effort financially worthwhile.'[281] The precise marginal deduction rates that will result from specified benefits or tax changes are often difficult for either an academic or a household to predict,[282] the extent to which high marginal deduction rates reduce employment incentives is debatable, and empirical experiment is difficult to achieve because the number of hours worked in full-time employment is relatively inflexible: but it would appear that full-time employment is relatively inelastic in relation to marginal deduction rates (that is, as the rate of withdrawal of additional earnings increases, employment participation does not go down very much), but there is more of an effect on part-time employment and on the employment of someone whose spouse loses their job.[283] Whether or not someone actively seeks employment after losing their job might depend more on whether they think they will experience uncertainty over the amount of future net income, and on whether they think they risk administrative difficulties over benefits and taxation, than on whether they have calculated how much financial benefit they will receive from returning to work.

The situation faced by both means-testing governments and people without employment could not be put better than at the beginning of a report published by the Joseph Rowntree Foundation:

> If you offer someone money on condition that they have a particular characteristic, you give them an incentive to acquire or keep that characteristic. That is the fundamental source of the trade-off between income redistribution and work incentives that confronts all governments with a dilemma.
>
> Concern for poverty or inequality motivates governments to want to redistribute income, but providing benefits on the basis of low income reduces the incentive for people on low incomes to work themselves out of that position (over and above additional disadvantages of means-tested benefits such as stigmatising recipients, requiring burdensome form-

---

[281] Parker, Hermione (1995) *Taxes, benefits and family life: The seven deadly traps,* London: Institute of Economic Affairs, p 27

[282] Parker, Hermione (1989) *Instead of the dole: An enquiry into integration of the tax and benefit systems,* London: Routledge, pp 318–30

[283] Atkinson, A.B. and Mogensen, Gunnar Viby (eds) (1993) *Welfare and work incentives,* Oxford: Oxford University Press, p 191

filling and achieving less than full coverage among the entitled population). ...

Thus the two main ways for a government to help people with low incomes – providing them with support directly and encouraging them to earn more themselves – are in head-on conflict with each other. How best to deal with this conflict has long been one of the central questions facing academic economists and economic policy makers.[284]

The report's authors recommend an increase in Child Benefit. This would not damage work incentives, because Child Benefit is not withdrawn as earned income rises; and a particular advantage of increasing Child Benefit is that 'benefits accrue disproportionately to the poor'.[285] The argument for a Citizen's Income could not have been put more cogently.

The 'invalidity trap' refers to a situation where, because of disability or long-term illness, someone's 'earnings potential net of tax is low in relation to out-of-work benefits'.[286] Chapter 16 includes a section on the higher costs experienced by people with disability. One of the problems related to long-term illness is the difficulty of employment market re-entry. Sometimes a flexible approach to the number of hours worked is required. This can be administratively difficult under the present benefits system. It would be a lot easier with a Citizen's Income, because the Citizen's Income would never change.

The 'poverty trap' refers to low gains from each extra £1 earned, which discourages attempts to increase earned income by seeking training or promotion, or by starting a business. For some households the poverty is not as deep now as it was when Parker was writing in 1995 (when some households suffered marginal deduction rates of 98 per cent, leaving them with only 2p out of each extra £1 earned): but more serious now is the 'poverty plateau': 'the disappearance of differences in spending power over a wide range of earnings ... Within

---

284 Adam, Stuart, Brewer, Mike and Shephard, Andrew (2006) *The poverty trade-off: Work incentives and income redistribution in Britain,* Bristol/York: Policy Press/Joseph Rowntree Foundation, p 1

285 Adam, Stuart, Brewer, Mike and Shephard, Andrew (2006) *The poverty trade-off: Work incentives and income redistribution in Britain,* Bristol/York: Policy Press/Joseph Rowntree Foundation, p 30

286 Parker, Hermione (1995) *Taxes, benefits and family life: The seven deadly traps,* London: Institute of Economic Affairs, p 35

that range people find themselves on a plateau where extra effort and extra skills go unrewarded. The size of the plateau depends on family composition and housing costs: the bigger the family, the older the children, the higher the rent, the broader the plateau.'[287] Whether the extension of the poverty plateau is more or less of a problem than the poverty trap itself will be a matter of opinion, but they both have the same disincentive effect: they make it less rewarding for people to pursue new skills, to start small businesses, or in other ways to improve their earnings in order to provide more effectively for themselves and their dependents: and therefore they make it less likely that people will work hard to do so.

An important source of evidence for the different outcomes generated by universal and means-tested benefits is New Zealand, where a Universal Family Benefit has been abolished in favour of an income-tested benefit. Research has shown that the new system has entrenched families in poverty in ways in which the universal benefit did not.[288] Equally interesting is research conducted in the United States. The earnings rule was abolished for workers above normal retirement age, and the probability of being gainfully employed after retirement age did in fact go up.[289] In Canada similar evidence was obtained when the marginal deduction rates of higher earners decreased, particularly for women in part-time employment. Part-time employment rose by 10 per cent among higher-earning women, and not at all among lower earning women.[290] While labour market participation *is* a complex matter, and is subject to numerous personal, household and labour market factors, the evidence suggests that the lower marginal deduction rates that a Citizen's Income would offer *would* promote greater labour market activity, and that the earnings ranges across which reductions in marginal deduction rates were highest would experience the greatest increased participation. This would particularly benefit part-time workers because of the high marginal deduction rates that

---

[287] Parker, Hermione (1995) *Taxes, benefits and family life: The seven deadly traps,* London: Institute of Economic Affairs, p 42

[288] O'Brien, Michael (2007) *Poverty, policy and the state,* Bristol: Policy Press, p 124

[289] Michaeu, Pierre-Carl and van Soest, Arthur (2008) 'How did the elimination of the US earnings test above the normal retirement age affect labour supply expectations?', *Fiscal Studies,* vol 29, no 2, pp 197–231

[290] Crossley, Thomas F. and Jeon, Sung-Hee (2007) 'Joint taxation and the labour supply of married women: evidence from the Canadian tax reform of 1988', *Fiscal Studies,* vol 28, no 3, pp 343–65

they suffer now and because a Citizen's Income – even quite a small one[291] – could significantly affect those deduction rates.

The 'lone-parent trap' – the additional costs associated with employment that make it less feasible for lone parents to seek employment – is not as serious now as it was when Parker was writing,[292] because the way in which childcare costs are now taken into account when benefits are calculated gives more recognition to the level of childcare costs incurred. However, 'lone-parent trap' can have two meanings, and in her *Taxes, benefits and family life* Parker deals with a second meaning as well: that the benefits system imposes penalties on marriage and other relationships. (See the previous chapter for more on this). 'Tax Credits' and Income Support regulations (and, in the future, 'Universal Credit' regulations) regard the household as the claimant, and therefore take into account both partners' earnings when means-tested benefits are being calculated. This creates an immediate incentive to separate, and a disincentive to form and maintain long-term stable relationships: which is a serious problem because long-term relationships are important for adults and are even more important for children. If the parents do decide to live together, then the regulations make it less likely that the unemployed partner of someone employed will seek employment,[293] making it difficult for many families to lift themselves out of poverty.

The 'part-time trap' refers to high deduction rates suffered by people employed part-time. If someone out of work takes part-time employment of a few hours a week and then increases their hours, say from 8 hours to 16 hours, then it makes almost no difference to their net income because Jobseeker's Allowance is withdrawn as earnings rise.[294] If they then take employment of say 18 hours per week, they find themselves on 'Tax Credits': but again they find themselves almost as badly off as when they were on Jobseeker's Allowance and working fewer hours. When 'Universal Credit' replaces both Jobseeker's Allowance and

[291] Parker, Hermione and Sutherland, Holly (1988) 'How to get rid of the poverty trap: Basic Income plus national minimum wage', *Citizen's Income Bulletin*, no 25, February, pp 11–14

[292] Parker, Hermione (1995) *Taxes, benefits and family life: The seven deadly traps,* London: Institute of Economic Affairs, p 43

[293] Evans, Martin and Harkness, Susan (2010) 'The impact of the tax and benefit system on second earners', *Journal of Poverty and Social Justice*, vol 18, no 1, pp 35–51

[294] See the website www.citizensincome.org for a research note on the high marginal deduction rates related to part-time employment.

'Tax Credits' this situation will improve, but not markedly. 'Universal Credit' will be withdrawn at 65 per cent, so, for every additional £1 in earnings, the worker will receive only 35p, and even less if they are paying Income Tax and National Insurance Contributions. This is no way to encourage someone not in employment to take a part-time job if that is all they can get or that is what their circumstances require.

The 'lack of skills trap'. If Britain is to compete in the global economy then it needs a highly skilled and highly educated adult population. We might disagree over some of the things that Tony Blair said and did, but he offered one commitment with which it is difficult to disagree: 'Our top priority was, is and always will be education, education, education. To overcome decades of neglect and make Britain a learning society, developing the talents and raising the ambitions of all our young people.'[295] But what we have now is a school system still posited on the assumption that academic ability is what is required, a higher education system that attracts students by offering degrees too easy to pass (– this is particularly true of postgraduate degrees in many of our universities), a student loans system that saddles young adults with a mountain of debt and therefore discourages young people from entering higher education,[296] and spasmodic and unconvincing attempts to reinvent apprenticeships. This is not the place to discuss how best to create an education and training system suitable for a modern global economy, but the morass of funding systems, and their accompanying prohibitions, really do not help. A simple unconditional income during any registered and inspected high quality training or education course would be a colossal incentive to people to educate and train themselves for the kind of economy that we shall need.

But just as important is encouraging people to retrain and to undertake continuing training. The problem is that there is little incentive to do so. Why spend time and money on training in order to retain employment or to move into new and growing industries when most of any increase in pay will be taken away? If an increase in earnings were to translate into an increase in net income then there would be rather more incentive to train or retrain. In the same way that Beveridge made Family Allowances a presupposition of his

---

[295]   Blair, Tony (2001) speech, 23 May, www.guardian.co.uk/politics/2001/may/23/labour.tonyblair

[296]   Berg, Gary A. (2010) *Low-income students and the perpetuation of inequality*, Aldershot: Ashgate

contributory benefits system,[297] we ought now to make a Citizen's Income a presupposition of both income maintenance and education and training policies.

The 'savings trap'. This is one trap that thankfully might soon be less of a problem. Many retired people today experience a complex pension system. Someone with a small occupational pension and a small private pension might be receiving four or more different pensions: a Basic State Pension, a state second pension (if they worked for an employer that was not contracted out), one or more occupational pensions, and a private pension. And if that is not enough to live on then they will receive a means-tested pension. It is this last item in the list that causes the problem. Any gap between pension income and a specified minimum (in 2012, £142.70 per week for a single person and £217.90 for a couple) will be filled by Pension Credit: so what is the point in forgoing current consumption in order to pay for a private or occupational pension if total retirement income is going to end up somewhere around the specified minimum? The sacrifice would not have been financially worthwhile. This problem has been somewhat reduced by Savings Credit (paid in addition to Pension Credit to anyone with savings). Savings Credit tapers the rate of withdrawal of Guarantee Credit, but still any risk of benefit withdrawal is a disincentive to pension savings for workers with low lifetime earning potential.[298]

An STP that exceeds the current minimum income, and is not withdrawn in respect of any other income, would end the savings trap for most of those who receive the new pension: that is, for those with thirty years of National Insurance Contributions or credits:[299] though means-tested Housing Benefit and Council Tax Benefit would continue to impose a savings trap for some pensioners.

Just as the savings trap would be substantially solved by an STP, so the other traps would be substantially or completely solved by a Citizen's Income: an unconditional, non-withdrawable income for every citizen. Because it would not be withdrawn as other income rose, any element of a trap currently related to the withdrawal of benefits

---

[297] Beveridge, Sir William (1942) *Social insurance and allied services*, Cmd 6404, London: Stationery Office, pp 154, 157, 163

[298] www.direct.gov.uk/en/Pensionsandretirementplanning/index.htm

[299] The Citizen's Income Trust's response to the Department for Work and Pensions' consultation on the future of the state pension, *Citizen's Income Newsletter* (2011) issue 3, pp 1–6. See Chapter 3 above for further details of the STP.

(including the withdrawal of 'Tax Credits') would disappear. Even a small Citizen's Income would reduce total marginal deduction rates somewhat, and so would ameliorate the traps, both by reducing their effects for everyone on means-tested benefits, and by abolishing them for those that it floated off means-tested benefits altogether. An increase in Child Benefit would ameliorate the poverty trap for all families with children,[300] and a Citizen's Income would do it for everyone.

We have decided that our tax and benefits structure should not disincentivise public goods. A rather different question is this: Should our benefits system positively promote certain public goods? To take an example: It is generally a good thing for children, older people, and disabled people, to be cared for by family members. It is therefore important that our benefits system should not discriminate against carers. Part-time rather than full-time employment is more likely to fit in with caring responsibilities. Our current system, based as it is on the assumption of full-time employment, disincentivises unpaid care work. A Citizen's Income, by making part-time employment more beneficial, would impose fewer disincentives.

But should our benefits system positively *value* otherwise unpaid care work? A Citizen's Income would make it easier for people to spend time on care work, but because the Citizen's Income would be paid to everyone, whether or not they were caring for family members, it would not ascribe a value to care work and would not be perceived to do so. It is for this reason that Ruth Lister is ambivalent towards a Citizen's Income. Only a benefit restricted to people undertaking care work within the family would positively ascribe a value to such work. However, Lister does recognise that a Citizen's Income would help to share employment more evenly across the working age population, and that it would break the income/work relationship, thus both economically and psychologically freeing carers, and particularly women carers, to pursue more varied work-life patterns.[301] She proposes a Participation Income as an intermediate step, and a Citizen's Income as a longer term option. Others take a somewhat different view. The word 'work' can encompass a wide range of activity, both paid and unpaid, both individual and corporate, and a Citizen's Income, by disconnecting

---

[300]   Brown, Joan (1988) *Child Benefit: Investing in the future*, London: Child Poverty Action Group, p 20

[301]   Lister, Ruth (1997) *Citizenship: Feminist perspectives*, Basingstoke: Macmillan, pp 189–90

---

work and income, would ascribe value to all kinds of work,[302] and would create a level playing field between paid employment, care work, and voluntary activity in and for the community.[303] A Citizen's Income would promote a more gender-inclusive citizenship 'without reinforcing the existing gendered distribution of labour or the primacy of the public sphere by equating care with work;'[304] it would 'increase the amount of work done both paid and unpaid, ... people would *willingly* be in the labour market, or *willingly* out of it; this surely cannot but help job satisfaction, productivity, and human welfare' (emphasis in the original);[305] it would give to people greater control over their use of time, and would therefore increase a country's level of equality;[306] and, because a Citizen's Income would be income received on the basis of one's citizenship, it would recognise every aspect of our engagement with society.

We have done enough to show that a Citizen's Income would not disincentivise public goods such as long-term relationships among parents of children, enterprise, training, and providing for oneself and one's dependents both financially and in terms of personal availability. This means that, in comparison with our present benefits system, a Citizen's Income would incentivise these public goods. We have also shown that a Citizen's Income would positively incentivise a number of public goods. It would therefore function as a 'production factor': as a driver of an 'investment state'.[307] After all, what is a benefits system for if not to promote the wellbeing of individuals and society by encouraging the creation of wealth of all kinds?

---

[302] McKay, Ailsa (2005) *The future of social security policy: Women, work and a citizen's Basic Income*, London: Routledge, ch.7, pp 182–224; Robertson, James (1988) 'If any would not work, neither should he eat', *BIRG Bulletin*, no 8, Autumn, pp 23–5

[303] Jordan, Bill (2008) *Welfare and well-being: Social value in public policy*, Bristol: Policy Press, p 250

[304] Zelleke, Almaz (2011) 'Feminist political theory and the argument for an unconditional basic income', *Policy & Politics*, vol 39, no 1, pp 27–42, p 38

[305] Walter, Tony (1989) *Basic Income: Freedom from poverty, freedom to work*, London: Marion Boyars, p 56

[306] Haagh, Louise (2011) 'Basic Income, social democracy and control over time', *Policy & Politics*, vol 39, no 1, pp 43–66

[307] Morel, Nathalie, Palier, Bruno and Palme, Joakim (eds) (2012) *Towards a social investment welfare state? Ideas, policies and challenges*, Bristol: Policy Press

Efficiency

Our fifth criterion is this: Our tax and benefits structure should incentivise the efficient allocation of resources and so contribute to an efficient economy.

The financial crisis that began in 2008 has revealed that there is something not quite right about the way that we run our economy: but it has not been easy to sift the plethora of commentary and discover a simple narrative about what happened and why. Reckless bank loans across the developed world left the banks with too much bad debt; debt had been sold as a commodity, and had been bundled with other financial 'commodities' into complex financial instruments, and because such instruments had values difficult to determine the banks left holding them could not sell them; and governments supported the banks financially so that they did not collapse, thus transforming financial industry debt into state debt, and leaving less revenue for public spending. This has meant jobs disappearing in both the private and the public sectors, making it difficult for even more households to repay their loans. This is part of the story, but it is not all that needs to be said. In Chapter 11 we shall ask whether a Citizen's Income would tackle the issues of poverty and inequality, but we must pre-empt that discussion to some extent by offering here Stewart Lansley's explanation for the financial crisis: that income inequality reduces productivity, and that growing inequality has therefore driven economic decline. As he points out, major economic crises have always been preceded by periods of growing inequality: and the reason for the crises has always been that when more of the financial rewards from productivity go to capital (and are paid in dividends, generally to the already wealthy), and less of the financial rewards go to wages, then inequality grows, wage-earners have less to spend than the economy is producing, demand drops, and recession is the result. 'Consumer societies suddenly find they lack the capacity to consume':[308] so the causal link is that an imbalance in the rewards to capital and labour leads both to lower demand and to growing inequality. The trend to suppress workers' wages, such as has occurred most noticeably in the US, must either reduce consumption, or increase household debt, or both. At the same time, larger amounts of money going to the already wealthy encourages them to buy scarce or

---

[308] Lansley, Stewart (2011) 'From inequality to instability: why sustainable capitalism depends on a more equal society', *Fabian Review*, Winter, pp 12–14, p 12; Lansley, Stewart (2011) *The cost of inequality: Three decades of the super-rich and the economy*, London: Gibson Square

unique assets, thus increasing asset prices. The money does not generally go to investment in productive capacity – because, after all, demand is falling. A further reason for the crisis is that with a lot of loose capital in the world, creative skills have been exercised in creating so-called financial products rather than on making things in the real economy. A consumer society can put off recession briefly by increasing personal debt, but eventually the debt mountain becomes unsustainable and repossessions begin. As Lansley puts it:

> It is now clear that a business system that fails to share the proceeds of growth will eventually self-destruct. Allowing the richest members of society to accumulate a larger and larger share of the cake has merely brought a dangerous mix of demand deflation, asset appreciation and a long squeeze on the productive economy which has ended in prolonged economic turmoil. The great experiment in unequal market capitalism has failed on its own terms.[309]

Lansley's prescription is that capitalism needs to share its output more evenly between shareholders and wage earners. As James K. Galbraith puts it more generally: '*Sufficient* equality in the distribution of income, within a country, is a proper goal of efficient economic policy, and is part of a strategy for shared prosperity and full employment; it is both effect and cause.'[310]

So our question is this: Is it possible to find a way of redistributing income so as to increase rather than decrease economic efficiency?[311]

Economic theory assumes that an economy without taxes or benefits is efficient: that is, prices are adjusting to enable resources to be exchanged in such a way that everyone's utility is maximized. There is just one way of taxing individuals that does not interfere with the working of the market: 'lump sum' taxes, which means the same amount of tax for everyone. A Citizen's Income would be a negative lump sum tax, and it would therefore have the same effect on the economy as a lump sum tax: that is, no effect at all. So a Citizen's Income must be the most efficient basis for a benefits system.

---

[309] Lansley, Stewart (2011) 'From inequality to instability: why sustainable capitalism depends on a more equal society', *Fabian Review*, Winter, pp 12–14, p 14

[310] Galbraith, James K. (2002) 'The importance of being sufficiently equal', pp 201–24 in Paul, Ellen Frankel, Miller, Fred D. Jr., and Paul, Jeffrey, *Should differences in income and wealth matter?* Cambridge: Cambridge University Press, p 224

[311] Spicker, Paul (2000) *The welfare state: A general theory*, London: Sage, p 169

But how large should a Citizen's Income be in order to maximise efficiency? Presumably quantity of supply needs to match quantity demanded.[312] This condition will be met if the level of the Citizen's Income is equal to a subsistence income. However, the revenue required to pay such a Citizen's Income needs to be collected in such a way as not to compromise economic efficiency, and it is difficult to see how lump sum taxes could achieve that. We shall therefore need to balance the efficiency offered by a Citizen's Income with the inefficiency created by Income Tax and other taxation. In spite of this problem, we should be encouraged by the fact that the Citizen's Income will contribute to efficiency in ways in which means–tested benefits do not, so even though taxation remains an efficiency problem, to move from a system of means–tested benefits to a system based on a Citizen's Income could not fail to improve economic efficiency. We can conclude that a Citizen's Income would provide a basis for reducing inequality at the same time as improving the efficiency of the economy:[313] a rare achievement.

But what if it is not necessarily the case that an economy without taxes or benefits is efficient?

> When we allow for real–world phenomena like incomplete information and the absence of markets, it is conceivable that the payment of basic incomes, and the levying of the associated tax, may improve the allocation of resources. (A.B. Atkinson)[314]

> Many versions of the 'equality-efficiency trade-off' ... do not survive closer scrutiny; ... abdication of the insurance function of the welfare state produces efficiency losses in our second-best world; ... progressive redistributions may not entail efficiency losses or higher costs because the alternative system of order maintenance, namely disciplinary enforcement, is also costly; ... distributive policies ... produce dynamic efficiency gains if, by reducing poverty and inequality, they positively influence the welfare and the cognitive abilities of children and hence human capital

---

[312] Spicker, Paul (2000) *The welfare state: A general theory*, London: Sage, p 169

[313] Zelleke, Almaz (2005) 'Distributive justice and the argument for an unconditional basic income', *The Journal of Socioeconomics*, no 1, vol 34, pp 3–15

[314] Atkinson, A.B. (1989) *Basic Income schemes and the lessons from public economics*, Tax, Incentives and the Distribution of Income paper no 136, London: LSE, p 13

> formation; … the under-provision of [care] services acts
> as an 'inactivating influence' on market participation and
> employment, particularly for women … (Lilia Costabile)[315]

Any tax and benefits structure might in practice improve social
wellbeing and the efficiency of the economy, but a Citizen's Income
would be more likely to achieve this than a means-tested one. This
is because, in terms of the factors listed by Costabile, a means-tested
system has to pay for coercion, it contributes to inequality, and it
disincentivises informal care work, whereas a Citizen's Income would
incentivise informal care work, would contribute to greater equality, and
would dispense with the need for coercion in the labour market and
with surveillance of family structures. This means that with a Citizen's
Income it might not just be individuals in particular circumstances who
would be better off: it might be that a more efficient economy would
see economic growth benefiting the whole of a society and creating
individual, social and corporate welfare. Farnsworth defines 'corporate
welfare' as those government activities that benefit businesses (such as
subsidies, tax allowances, and investment incentives). While there will
often be a trade-off between corporate and social welfare, some social
policies might be able to increase both social welfare and corporate
welfare.[316] A Citizen's Income would be one such policy.

  Even if a Citizen's Income scheme did not redistribute income on the
first day of its implementation, by lowering marginal deduction rates for
low earners it would enable them to increase their net incomes more
easily, and it would therefore increase the spending power of workers
in the lower earnings deciles. A Citizen's Income would therefore be
likely to share the output of the economy more evenly between the less
well off and the better off, and, because poorer people spend a higher
proportion of their incomes on goods and services in the national
economy, a Citizen's Income would increase the consumption of goods
and services, and it would at the same time create a more efficient
economy in which the real economy both produces what we need
and provides us with the means for obtaining it. Eleanor Rathbone
thought it an important argument for her proposed child allowances
that there would be 'an increased demand for cotton frocks and woollen

---

[315] Costabile, Lilia, 'Conclusion', in Costabile, Lilia (ed.) (2008) *Institutions for social well-being: Alternatives for Europe*, Basingstoke: Palgrave Macmillan, pp 222–34, pp 225–31
[316] Farnsworth, Kevin (2012) *Social versus corporate welfare: Competing needs and interests within the welfare state*, Basingstoke: Palgrave Macmillan, p 42

jerseys, for boots and coal ... Would that make no difference to the depressed industries?'[317]

Dignity

Our sixth criterion is this: Our tax and benefits structure should treat people with dignity, and not stigmatise individuals involved in any part of the system.

Stigma is a relationship between the person doing the stigmatising and the person being stigmatised, with the stigma being felt by the person stigmatised – though often the stigmatising is a collective and social action that is felt as stigma by the person or category of persons suffering the stigma. Goffman lists three types of stigma: 'physical deformities', 'blemishes of individual character', and 'the tribal stigma of race, nation, and religion'.[318] It is the second of these types that operates in the context of the benefits system. We stigmatise people who find themselves subject to means-testing, and we ascribe their being in that situation to their weakness of character.

Our stigmatising of others, and the experience of stigma, are complex psychological realities, but at their root is fear: fear of being in the situation of the person stigmatised, or fear of someone different from ourselves. So, if we are not on means-tested benefits ourselves, then we might stigmatise people who find themselves on means-tested benefits because we fear being in their situation. This means that we might stigmatise ourselves if we are on means-tested benefits and have no wish to be.

Research shows that

> the perception of the poor and unemployed [is] most negative in liberal [means-tested and selective benefits] regimes (maybe moderated by the fact that the recipients really are in need), more positive in conservative [i.e., contributory] regimes ... , and most positive in social democratic [more universal] regimes (maybe moderated by

---

[317] Rathbone, Eleanor 'Utopia calling! A plea for family allowances', from an address broadcast by Eleanor Rathbone MP, Family Endowment Society archives, quoted in Levitas, Ruth (2012) 'Utopia calling: eradicating child poverty in the United Kingdom and beyond', Minujin, Alberto and Nandy, Shailen (eds) *Global child poverty and well-being: Measurement, concepts, policy and action*, Bristol: Policy Press, pp 449–73, p 451
[318] Goffman, Erving (1990) *Stigma: Notes on the management of spoiled identity*, London: Penguin, pp 13–14

the fact that many of the potential poor have rather good living conditions). (Christian Larsen)[319]

But *why* do means-tested benefits regimes result in stigma? What is wrong with being on means-tested benefits? Why should we not wish to be on them, and why do we stigmatise people who are on them? Again, the cause is complex, but a factor must be the bureaucratic intrusion required by means-testing: an intrusion into our lives by people whom we do not know and probably have no wish to know. A typical claim for a means-tested benefit might begin with a face to face interview with someone younger than ourselves who asks us for detailed personal information about our household, our living arrangements, and the sources of our income. We have to provide them with evidence, which suggests that they do not believe us. Then a decision is made about how much benefit we will receive, and we do not know how that decision was made or who made it. 'Discretion' has been exercised in our direction,[320] setting up 'relationships of domination and subordination, within which supplication becomes a standard mode of conduct' (Richard Wagner).[321] All of this is demeaning, and it results in stigma: self-stigmatising if we are going through it, or the stigmatising of someone else if they are going through it. Particularly demeaning are the often perfunctory 'work-related' interviews[322] integral to so-called 'active labour market policies'. Underlying such interviews is the assumption that the person interviewed will only seek employment if they are coerced into it, whereas the truth is that the lack of employment opportunities has deprived them of employment and has demotivated them, and the complexities of the benefits system now make them hesitant about attempting any change in their labour market status. At the heart of 'active labour market' policies is a contradiction: 'external surveillance and sanctions, and encouragement to internal motivation and effort' – whereas 'genuine empowerment can only come from freely exercised choice, and ... this ... is the only realistic and socially just way of tackling labour market exclusion' (Carpenter, Freda and Speeden).[323]

[319] Larsen, Christian Albrekt (2006) *The institutional logic of welfare attitudes*, Aldershot: Ashgate, p 141

[320] Hill, Michael (1990) *Social security policy in Britain*, Aldershot: Edward Elgar, p 110

[321] Wagner, Richard E. (2007) *Fiscal sociology and the theory of public finance: An exploratory essay*, London: Edward Elgar, p 196

[322] Handler, Joel. F. (2005) 'Myth and ceremony in workfare: rights, contracts, and client satisfaction', *The Journal of Socioeconomics*, vol 34, no 1, pp 101–24, p 117

[323] Carpenter, Mick, Freda, Belinda and Speeden, Stuart (2007) (eds) *Beyond the workfare state*, Bristol: Policy Press, pp 5, 6

Given the aggravation and stigma attached to 'active labour market' policies, Hartley Dean wonders whether the government's plan to combine in-work and out-of-work means-tested benefits in the same 'Universal Credit' might have the unintended consequence of increasing the stigma attached to means-tested benefits. At the moment, the 'virtuous worker', who believes that work is a virtuous taking of responsibility, can receive a means-tested benefit, 'Working Tax Credit', and still separate their self-image from their image of the out of work recipient of means-tested benefits. This is possible because Working Tax Credit has a different name from Jobseeker's Allowance or Income Support, and it operates with a different set of regulations.

> Because the [']Universal['] Credit will remove the distinction between 'credits' for workers and 'benefits' for people out of work by unifying the administration of transfer payments for all recipients of working-age, it may be foreseen that, paradoxically, some low paid workers may feel less good about having their wages topped up by the state. Insofar as [']Universal['] Credit recipients may be virtuous workers, their virtuous status will in fact be less distinctively recognised.[324]

The way round this problem is to provide exactly the same 'benefit' for everyone. No stigma attaches to Child Benefit. The claim process is not intrusive, and everyone with a child receives Child Benefit. Similarly, receipt of a Citizen's Income would be entirely without stigma, and it would, as Tony Walter puts it, 'replace structural guilt with a universal structure of acceptance and forgiveness'.[325] If the non-earner, the low wage earner, and the highest paid executive in the country, were all to receive the same benefit, then receiving it could not possibly carry any stigma. The benefits in terms of social cohesion, social welfare,[326] individual welfare, and productivity, would be considerable,[327] not

[324] Dean, Hartley (2012) 'The ethical deficit of the UK's proposed Universal Credit: pimping the precariat?' *Political Quarterly*, vol 83, no 2, pp 353–9

[325] Walter, Tony (1989) *Basic Income: Freedom from poverty, freedom to work*, London: Marion Boyars, p 133

[326] Jordan, Bill (2010) 'Basic Income and social value', *Basic Income Studies*, vol 5, no 2, pp 1–19

[327] Lundvall, Bengt-Åke and Lorenz, Edward (2012) 'From the Lisbon Strategy to EUROPE 2020', pp 333–51 in Morel, Nathalie, Palier, Bruno and Palme, Joakim (eds) *Towards a social investment welfare state? Ideas, policies and challenges*, Bristol: Policy Press, p 347

to mention the significant increase in self-worth experienced by individuals and households able to come off means-tested benefits.[328] While a means-tested system imposes substantial loss of self-worth on everyone involved (including the civil servants who have to operate the system: something that this author discovered when engaged in administering means-tested benefits), a Citizen's Income would positively enhance self-worth: an important element in the 'minimal autonomy' that we require if we are to exercise basic liberties and experience social justice.

Because a Citizen's Income would impose no stigma or complexity, and because no benefit could be easier to understand, take-up would be almost 100 per cent[329, 330] and this universal benefit would therefore prove to be the most effective way to tackle poverty.[331]

[328] Birnbaum, Simon (2012), *Basic Income reconsidered: Social justice, liberalism, and the demands of equality*, New York: Palgrave Macmillan, pp 48–51

[329] Spicker, Paul (2011) *How social security works: An introduction to benefits in Britain*, Bristol: Policy Press, pp 14–15

[330] Darton, David, Hirsch, Donald and Strelitz, Jason (2003) *Tackling disadvantage: a 20-year enterprise: A working paper for the Joseph Rowntree Foundation's Centenary Conference, December 2004*, York: Joseph Rowntree Foundation, p 33

[331] Walker, Carol (2011) 'For universalism and against the means test', pp 133–52 in Walker, Alan, Sinfield, Adrian and Walker, Carol (eds) *Fighting poverty, inequality and injustice: A manifesto inspired by Peter Townsend*, Cambridge: Polity Press, pp 149–50

CHAPTER 9

Criteria for a benefits system: the labour market, then, now, and in the future

In this chapter we shall explore our final criterion for an ideal benefits system:

> Our tax and benefits structure should reflect the labour market of today, and should remain serviceable as the labour market changes in the future.

We shall begin with a discussion of the ways in which the employment market has changed during the past half century, and then ask what kind of benefits system today's employment market requires, and how that compares with the benefits system constructed in an era with a very different employment market.

The changing workplace[332]

I grew up in Dartford, on the edge of London, and for most of the time since then have lived close to the South Bank of the Thames: a microcosm of our changing economy and changing labour market during the past sixty years.

By the 1930s, the whole of the South Bank, the Central London area from Battersea to Erith, was dominated by manufacturing: heavy and electrical engineering, food processing, brewing, ship repairers, and printing; and the South Bank at Dartford and beyond by paper making, cement manufacture, and Littlebrook Power Station. What brought all of these industries to the area was a navigable river for the transport of heavy raw materials and finished products, and a growing population to provide labour. During the Second World War, in the engineering factories, as well as at the Royal Arsenal in Woolwich, much of the manufacturing capacity was given over to weapons manufacture, and

---

[332] Parts of this chapter draw on Torry, Malcolm (1996) 'The labour market, the family, and social security reform: a dissertation for the Master of Science degree in social policy and planning at the London School of Economics'.

during that period women frequently undertook work previously undertaken only by men.[333]

After the war, many of the firms had not updated their methods or machinery, and they became industrial dinosaurs; the large labour forces gave trade union leaders considerable power in relation to managers, enabling workforces to resist change; and managers were either authoritarian or unrealistically benevolent, and showed little interest in innovation or in the competition building up around the world.[334] Industries began to close. From 1961 to 1966 there was a decline of 20 per cent in the number of people employed in manufacturing in South London, while office and service industry jobs increased slightly.[335] During the late 1960s, warehouses and factories closed and remained empty, and a particularly traumatic event was the loss of 5,000 jobs at AEI in 1968. By the end of the 1970s, heavy engineering had almost completely disappeared from South London, and, with it, vast numbers of full-time, semi-skilled, male jobs. Office development mushroomed during the 1960s and 70s, and offices, homes, and empty land, now stand where major industrial premises once stood.

My grandfather worked for Vickers Armstrong, a major engineering company on the South Bank at Erith. He started as a machine shop apprentice, but during the Second World War the company expanded rapidly and he found himself in Manchester and in administration. He spent his entire working life in a single company. That is now a rare experience. No longer are there workforces of 5,000 on a single site, all in full-time employment. Increasing numbers of jobs are 'flexible'. They might be flexible geographically, in the sense that someone might work for the same company for a number of years but during that period work in a variety of countries; or they might be flexible organisationally: many college and university teachers are now sessional, teaching for a few hours a week, running their own businesses part-time, and sometimes working as consultants for other businesses. On the Greenwich Peninsula, where we live, employment still means a fair number of full-time employees, but also increasing numbers of job shares, short-term contracts, part-time employment, agency staff, and

---

[333] Avery, Michael D. (1963) 'Industry in South-East London (Bermondsey and Southwark)', thesis submitted for M.A. degree, University of London, p 148

[334] Sedwick, Robert C. (1974) *Interaction: Interpersonal relationships in organisations*, Englewood Cliffs, NJ: Prentice-Hall, p 127

[335] Keeble, David (1978) 'Industrial decline in the inner city and conurbation', *Transactions of the Institute of British Geographers*, New Series, vol 3, no 1, pp 101–14; Martin, J.E. and Seaman, J.M. (1974) 'The fate of the London factory: twenty years of change', *Town and Country Planning*, vol 43, pp 492–5

casual staff. Managing staff rotas, in the private, public, and voluntary sectors, is a vital contemporary skill; and another essential skill is the ability to manage contracts between organisations – because now employment will often mean the employment of other organisations rather than of individual employees.

For men, employment rates peaked in 1971 at 92 per cent and decreased to 76 per cent by 2011. During the same period, the employment rate for women rose from 53 to 66 per cent, and between 1996 and 2010 the gap in employment rates between women with and without children narrowed from 5.8 per cent to just 0.8 per cent. The increasing presence of women in the labour market might help to explain another significant trend: from full-time to part-time employment. Between 1995 and 2011, the average number of hours worked per week fell from 33.5 to 31.5, suggesting an increase in part-time employment. Between early 2008 and early 2011, that is, during the current recession, the number of people in full-time employment fell by 3.1 per cent, but the number in part-time employment increased by 5.6 per cent. Before the recession, 9.5 per cent of people in part-time work were looking for full-time employment and could not find it. In 2011 that figure stood at 15.2 per cent.[336]

So workforces are now smaller, institutional arrangements are diverse, no sector is immune from change, and the hardest hit have been the semi-skilled and those with skills related to particular industries.[337] What are the reasons for these changes? One of the reasons is technological change. The twentieth century saw colossal change: first of all the assembly line, with its alienating effects,[338] and then the explosion in communication and information technology that has enabled companies to ensure efficiency, calculability, predictability and control on a global scale, as in the McDonalds empire,[339] and has enabled the principle of the assembly line to be applied to such industries as call centres.[340] Now that complex processes can be

---

[336] Spence, Alison (2011) *Labour market: Social Trends 41*, London: ONS, pp 2, 9, 10, www.ons.gov.uk, 04/10/11

[337] Evans, Martin and Williams, Lewis (2009) *A generation of change, a lifetime of difference? Social policy in Britain since 1979*, Bristol: Policy Press, p 306

[338] Braverman, Harry (1974) *Labor and monopoly capital*, New York: Monthly Review Press; Blauner, Robert (1964) *Alienation and freedom: The factory worker and his industry*, Chicago: University of Chicago Press

[339] Ritzer, George (2000) *The McDonaldization of society*, Thousand Oaks, CA: Pine Forge Press, pp 13–14; Ritzer, George (2010) *McDonaldization: The reader*, 3rd edn, Thousand Oaks, CA: Pine Forge Press, p 77

[340] Taylor, Phil and Bain, Peter (1999) 'An assembly line in the head: work and employee relations in the call centre', *Industrial Relations Journal*, vol 30, no 2, pp 101–17

automated and computerised, relatively low skilled workers have been displaced. Low skilled workers are still employed if their wages are low enough to compete with the costs of automating work processes, so manufacturing has moved to countries where wage expectations and actual wages are low; and as we now live in a globalising economy, in which goods and services required in one place can easily be created in another, wage levels *will* harmonise around the planet, and wage levels for low skilled workers here will fall to the level of low skilled workers in Shanghai.[341] Highly skilled workers are still needed for complex design, cultural, policy and management tasks that cannot (yet) be automated. The outcome is job polarisation, particularly in countries like the UK that have put too little effort into maintaining manufacturing capability:[342] a bifurcation of the labour market into those with permanent, secure, fulfilling and well-paid employment, within which they can progress in 'careers', and those with less secure, less well paid, and generally less fulfilling, employment: that is, into 'insiders' and 'outsiders'.[343]

So yes, there has been change: but it might not have been as rapid or as deep as we might have thought. The labour market is in many ways quite resistant to change, and 'flexibility' might not be the best overall description. For instance: part-time employment, because it can be a way into full-time and stable employment, is not necessarily a signal of a more insecure labour market experience;[344] and while some labour market sectors have been contracting, others, such as education, healthcare, social care, media, retail, finance, and information and communications technology, have been expanding.[345] We might or might not be heading for more rapid change, and we might or might not be heading for a 'flexible' labour market. What we do seem to have is a more *diverse* labour market than the one that my grandfather knew.

As David Purdy suggests, for a stable labour market, and stable employment patterns, wage labour along with social insurance and

---

[341] Hawkins, Tim (2011) 'A perspective from Shanghai', *Citizen's Income Newsletter*, issue 3, pp 15–16

[342] Goos, Maarten and Manning, Alan (2007) 'Lousy and lovely jobs: the rising polarization of work in Britain', *Review of Economics and Statistics*, vol 89, no 1, pp 118–33

[343] Jordan, Bill (1998) *The new politics of welfare: Social justice in a global context*, London: Sage, p 65

[344] Doogan, Kevin (2009) *The transformation of work*, Cambridge: Polity Press, pp 1–21

[345] Doogan, Kevin (2009) *The transformation of work*, Cambridge: Polity Press, p 8; Coats, David (2012) 'Labour market myths and realities', pp 2–3 in Wallis, Ed (ed.) *New Forms of Work*, London: Fabian Society

---

means-tested safety nets might be appropriate: but now that the labour market is more diverse, and more people combine employment and caring, full-time jobs and full-time workers are no longer the only norm. Full employment in a rapidly changing and technological society is difficult to achieve, and might now be less appropriate. Purdy concludes that a Citizen's Income would reduce the average working week and would redistribute wage labour, thus giving to more people the experience of employment; and that it would also promote self-employment, and would generally give people more options for employing their creative gifts and earning an income.[346] No longer would losing one's job consign someone to a single option: finding another full-time employment. Part-time employment, self-employment, or a mixture of the two, would become more viable options, because the Citizen's Income's secure income floor would always be there. The same conclusion was reached thirty years ago by Keith Roberts, an engineer, who saw no reason why an economy should not be designed in the way in which an engineer designs a machine, starting with the goal to be achieved and then working out the means for achieving it:

> The most logical arrangement would be to provide [a] basic income to all citizens in a uniform way by means of a standard payment to be called the National Dividend, requiring no means test or other complex administration, and to allow the forces of the classical market to determine the equilibrium level of additional wages and other forms of income.[347]

Important consequences of this process would be that unemployment would be less feared, part-time employment would be more possible, and wages would more nearly reflect the economic value of people's work – thus creating the conditions for rational industrial planning, for the modernisation of both manufacturing and service industries, and for genuine wage bargaining based on the value of the worker's labour.[348] We could see more working lives characterised by 'variety

---

[346] Purdy, David (1988) *Social power and the labour market*, Basingstoke: Macmillan, pp 204–5, 234. See the website www.citizensincome.org for a research note on how a Citizen's Income would make part-time employment more viable.

[347] Roberts, Keith (1982) *Automation, unemployment and the distribution of income*, Maastricht: European Centre for Work and Society, p 13

[348] Walter, Tony (1989) *Basic Income: Freedom from poverty, freedom to work*, London: Marion Boyars, pp 101, 113

and stability, freedom and security ... true human flourishing consists in varied and integrated lives, overcoming the division of labour and the one-sided humans it produces, encouraging all to engage in many types of activity as far as possible, ...' (John Hughes).[349] In Chapter 12, on citizenship, we shall find Stuart White suggesting that the reciprocity necessary to citizenship requires people to participate in society as a condition of receiving an income,[350] and Philippe Van Parijs saying that what matters most is freedom, including the freedom to spend one's days surfing.[351] But who is contributing more to society: the man employed in a full-time post designing a machine to make cigarettes, or the unpaid volunteer taking older and disabled people to their hospital appointments?[352]

While permanent full-time and part-time employment might still be the normal labour market pattern, more flexible, not to say more chaotic, patterns are on the increase. 'Zero hour' contracts (with the worker being called in and paid only when they are required) are becoming common in the entertainment industry, and such terms as 'freedom', 'flexibility' and 'security' now characterise discussion on growing sectors of the labour market: but as Ursula Huws puts it:

> Flexibility may be perceived as autonomy, creativity, freedom of manoeuvre, responsiveness, convenience, adaptability or the ability to integrate activities from different spheres of life in new and mutually enhancing ways. On the other hand it may be perceived as precariousness, insecurity, contingency, marginalisation and instability. It may be experienced as chaotic and unpredictable, making it impossible for rational forward planning to take place and encouraging short-termism and opportunism.
>
> Similarly, security may be perceived positively, as a precondition for mental and physical well-being, social stability, mutual trust between the social partners and the creation of a social and economic infrastructure within which it is possible for rational long-term planning to take

---

[349] Hughes, John (2007) *The end of work: Theological critiques of capitalism*, Oxford: Blackwell, p 232

[350] White, Stuart (2003) *The civic minimum: On the rights and obligations of economic citizenship*, Oxford: Oxford University Press, p 168

[351] Van Parijs, Philippe (1995) *Real freedom for all: What (if anything) can justify capitalism?* Oxford: Clarendon Press, pp 2, 89, 96, 133

[352] Chandra, Pasma (2010) 'Working through the work disincentive', *Basic Income Studies*, vol 5, no 2, pp 1–20, p 7

---

place. It may also, however, be regarded as detrimental: as a form of rigidity which encourages dependence and bureaucratization, imposes unacceptably high costs on the dynamic sectors of society and is the enemy of creativity and initiative.[353]

Huws describes two interrelated kinds of labour market flexibility: 'internal' flexibility, meaning multiskilling and organisational innovation, and 'external' flexibility, meaning temporary and part-time employment, home-working, on-call working, and subcontracted and casual labour. On the basis of our discussion of the ways in which our current benefits system is ill-equipped to serve people flexibly employed, we can agree with Huws that 'the evidence points to a range of different traps and barriers that, taken together, either discriminate against flexible workers or create obstacles to entry into the labour market on a flexible basis'. She finds that the various forms of flexible employment are growing across the European Union:[354] and she suggests that a Citizen's Income might be appropriate to this situation.

Guy Standing comes to similar conclusions. He lists the many different levels of security available under pre-1980s 'industrial citizenship', and compares them with the insecurities experienced by the 'precariat': a new pattern of existence that has now infected most occupational groups, for all of which 'labour is instrumental (to live), opportunistic (taking what comes) and precarious (insecure)'.[355] The phenomenon is global,[356] and anxiety, alienation, and information overload, are some of the results.

Standing discusses the reasons for the precariat's growth: a global labour market, the weakening of social and trade union labour market protections, individual and temporary contracts replacing regulated permanent ones, and unemployment benefits being made more precarious so that they don't look more attractive than precarious employment. When he asks 'Who enters the precariat?' he finds that it can be any of us, from interns to post-retirement age employees who, subsidised by small pensions, deprive younger people of the

---

[353] Huws, Ursula (1997) *Flexibility and security: Towards a new European balance*, London: Citizen's Income Trust, p 13

[354] Huws, Ursula (1997) *Flexibility and security: Towards a new European balance*, London: Citizen's Income Trust, pp 21, 37, 39

[355] Standing, Guy (2011) *The precariat: The new dangerous class*, London: Bloomsbury, p 14

[356] On Canada's experience, see Swift, Jamie, Balmer, Brice and Dineen, Mira (2010) *Persistent poverty: Voices from the margins*, Toronto: Between the Lines, p 25

employment they need. Particularly welcome to mobile capital is ultra-precarious migrant labour. The 24/7 global market is changing our sense of time, and also our understanding of 'work', which is now not only 'labour', i.e., 'work having exchange value', but 'work for labour',[357] i.e., job-search and personal financial management. As Deborah Padfield puts it:

> A record number of people must 'take the plunge' again and again, never knowing colleagueship, never having hope of sustained progression, emotionally or professionally. Never being granted the respect we all deserve ... Most unemployed people I meet desperately want to work. They don't need sanctions and conditionality to force them into it. They need the security and opportunity which our economic model does not provide.[358]

How, in this situation, can we provide the sense of security necessary for constructive functioning in flexible labour markets and in a chaotic social environment?

Standing's well-argued response is 'universal provision', and particularly a Citizen's Income. As he shows in his *Work after globalization: Building occupational citizenship*,[359] the recommodification of labour – a shift from labour being rewarded by diverse social benefits to it being rewarded only financially – is an inevitable result of temporary contracts, because they offer fewer employment benefits than permanent contracts: a particular problem where healthcare is employment-based. The UK, with its healthcare free at the point of use, has been able to weather the change to precarious labour contracts better than many other countries, and Standing could have used this example to bolster his already persuasive argument for a Citizen's Income;[360] but without that his argument is sound enough: that in an era of labour market and income insecurity we need a firm base on which to stand if we

---

[357] Standing, Guy (2011) *The precariat: The new dangerous class*, London: Bloomsbury, pp 117, 120

[358] Padfield, Deborah (2011) 'The human cost of flexible labour', *Citizen's Income Newsletter*, no 1, pp 15–16, first published on the Open Democracy website, 24 October, www.opendemocracy.net/ourkingdom/deborah-padfield/human-cost-of-flexible-labour

[359] Standing, Guy (2009) *Work after globalization: Building occupational citizenship*, London: Edward Elgar

[360] Standing, Guy (2011) *The precariat: The new dangerous class*, London: Bloomsbury, pp 41, 171–3

are going to be able to take the risks that we shall need to take if we are to thrive as individuals and as a society.[361]

As Standing recognises, anxiety and freedom go together, and a more precarious lifestyle is not necessarily worse than one founded on a secure full-time job, and might offer possibilities which that did not. Whether labour is more or less commodified is rather beside the point if the bundle of income and services that we experience is sufficiently secure to make precarious living a positive experience.[362] A secure income to match secure healthcare would go a long way to making a more flexible employment market a creative reality for a lot more people.

How to characterise today's labour market is a problem. Is it still much as it was in my grandfather's time, but with a bit more part-time and flexible employment; or are we in the midst of seismic change? What are the factors controlling the ways in which we construct our images of the labour market? Is it in multinational companies' (and capitalism's) interest to construe the labour market as flexible and as a dangerous place to be?[363] What matters is that whether we are heading for a growing precariat and a generally less secure labour market, or for a still fairly stable but more diverse labour market, means-tested benefits are no longer the answer: because they are withdrawn rapidly if the unemployed person finds some casual employment and declares it, because they are so complex to administer and so complex for the claimant to manage, because they perpetuate the precarious worker's insecurity, and because they make it difficult for workers to be employed part-time or in a contract with variable hours.[364]

We might think that it is the level of unemployment benefit that has the most impact on people's employment market decisions: that the higher the unemployment benefit, the fewer the number of people who will look for employment, and therefore the higher the unemployment rate: but, as Tony Atkinson suggests, things are not that simple.

---

[361] Wong, Wilson (2012) 'The new deal for Britain?', *New Forms of Work*, London: Fabian Society

[362] Cf. Panitch, Vida (2011) 'Basic Income, decommodification and the welfare state', *Philosophy and Social Criticism*, vol 37, no 8, pp 935–45. Panitch argues that, far from decommodifying labour because it loosens the relationship between work and subsistence income, Philippe Van Parijs's Citizen's Income proposal further commodifies labour because it replaces service provision, such as healthcare, with a cash benefit. But if a Citizen's Income replaces means-tested cash benefits then it does decommodify labour because it loosens the link between work and out of work and in work benefits.

[363] Doogan, Kevin (2009) *The transformation of work*, Cambridge: Polity Press

[364] Dean, Hartley (2012) 'The ethical deficit of the UK's proposed Universal Credit: pimping the precariat?' *Political Quarterly*, vol 83, no 2, pp 353–9

> To judge whether the effect is likely to be important in
> a particular situation, one has to study the way in which
> the benefit is administered, the constraints to which the
> unemployed are subject, the prevailing social norms, and
> the nature of the labour market.[365]

It is not so much a rational comparison of the amounts of money
available from a variety of employment and benefits scenarios that
determines the decisions that workers make when considering entering
the employment market, or moving from one employment status to
another, but rather the fear that complex administrative systems[366] will
leave the household without any income at all and not knowing what
the family's net income will be if a particular employment decision
is made.[367]

In the UK and elsewhere, debate still occurs as to whether it is better
to provide everyone with employment or better to provide everyone
with an income:[368] but such debates are purely theoretical, and probably
irrelevant, because no national government will now be able to ensure
that every one of its citizens is in employment for the number of
hours that they need to work in order to provide themselves and their
families with a subsistence income. By globalising the economy, we
have 'manufactured risk' (Anthony Giddens),[369] and that risk is not
going to go away.

In 1994, Abbe Mowshowitz predicted that 'virtual organisation'
would come to characterise the global economy.[370] This would 'deliver

[365] Atkinson, A.B. (1985) *Income maintenance and social insurance: A survey*, Welfare State Programme, paper no 5, London: LSE, p 9; Atkinson, A. B. (1995) *Public economics in action: The Basic Income / flat tax proposal*, Oxford: Clarendon Press, pp 130–53

[366] McLaughlin, Eithne (1994) *Flexibility in work and benefits*, London: IPPR/ Commission on Social Justice, p 2: 'OECD comparisons of unemployment insurance and assistance systems concluded that it is the rules and administration of systems (e.g., seeking work tests) rather than the level of benefit paid which most affects the rate of unemployment.'

[367] Jordan, Bill, James, Simon, Kay, Helen and Redley, Marcus (1992) *Trapped in poverty? Labour-market decisions in low-income households*, London: Routledge; Smithies, Rachel (2007) 'Making a case for flat tax credits: income fluctuations among low-income families', *Journal of Poverty and Social Justice*, vol 15, no 1, pp 3–16

[368] *Basic Income guarantees and the right to work*, *Rutgers Journal of Law and Urban Policy*, vol 2, no 1, Fall 2005: a booklet containing the abstracts of papers given at the 10th BIEN congress held in 2004, with an accompanying CD containing the papers.

[369] Giddens, Anthony (1994) 'Brave new world: the new context of politics', pp 21–38 in Miliband, David (ed.) *Reinventing the left*, Cambridge: Polity Press, p 22

[370] Mowshowitz, Abbe (1994) 'Virtual organization: a vision of management in the information age', *The Information Society*, vol 10, no 4, pp 267–88

increases in efficiency and effectiveness on an unprecedented scale'.[371] Because virtual organisation would operate on a global scale, seeking production opportunities and resources globally (a process made possible by new information technology and by rapid transport), and embedding human knowledge in computer programmes and thus commodifying it, it would eviscerate the economy of such subjective goods as loyalty, and would presage massive social change.

The virtualisation of business has implications for every facet of human activity. Government, education, work, social relations, and cultural affairs are all likely to be transformed by this sweeping development.

One major effect will be

> the decoupling of wealth creation from job creation ... The adoption of interface standards, translation protocols, and information commodities in the production of goods and services will reduce dependence on human intellectual skills just as mechanization and the first stages of automation reduced industry's dependence on physical skills.

Mowshowitz's final paragraphs are worth quoting in full:

> Relatively few people will be employed by the global corporations of the future. Technical innovation in the production of goods and services may increase productivity or improve quality and thus stimulate higher revenues, but it is not likely – barring radical demographic changes – to generate enough jobs to keep pace with demand from new entrants in the labor market ... . On the contrary, the commoditization of information reduces labor requirements, and since no area of economic activity is immune to this labor-reducing effect, the net result, barring a decline in the workforce, must be steadily increasing unemployment.
>
> The long-term impact of virtual organization on employment and the nature of work, as well as other social consequences of this new type of organization, warrant more extensive discussion ... However, one general conclusion must be stated. Decreasing labor requirements in the global workplace will necessitate new ways of distributing wealth.

---

[371] Mowshowitz, Abbe (1994) 'Virtual organization: a vision of management in the information age', *The Information Society*, vol 10, no 4, p 267

Absent such social innovation, disorder will surely increase beyond our ability to control it.[372]

Those words were written nearly twenty years ago, when there were few signs of the changes that the economy and our society are now beginning to experience. If Mowshowitz is only half as right about the labour market and social effects as he was about virtual organisation, then it is high time that we started to plan for the new way of distributing income that he quite rightly regards as necessary.

The labour market, the family, and tax and benefits policy

We have given separate chapters to the family and the labour market, though perhaps we ought not to have done so. Changes in working patterns and changes in the family are of course connected. There is a further connection: If we were to understand the term 'relationship' more widely as referring to our engagement with our society's institutions as well as to other individuals, and if we were to understand entering a particular employment as entering a relationship, then, just as a Citizen's Income, by providing a level of autonomy, would make it easier to enter a new personal relationship, so a Citizen's Income would make it easier to enter a new employment relationship.[373] If you know that you will receive your Citizen's Income before, during, and after this new relationship, then the risk of entering the relationship will be reduced.

This final section of the chapter not only brings together our discussions of the changing employment market and the changing family: it also asks whether tax and benefits policy should adapt itself to changes in the economy and in society, or rather seek to change the economy and society. If we want to generate change then we shall need to work out what changes we want to impose on the labour market and on family structure, and then design tax and benefits systems accordingly. If we want to adapt to trends rather than to cause them, then every now and then we shall need to refashion our tax and benefits systems to match changes occurring in society; and if we want to follow social trends then it is not an option to leave the tax

---

[372] Mowshowitz, Abbe (1994) 'Virtual organization: a vision of management in the information age', *The Information Society*, vol 10, no 4, p 287

[373] Offe, Claus (2008) 'Basic Income and the labor contract', *Basic Income Studies*, vol 3, no 1, p 23

and benefits systems as they are, because the way they are might fit previous family and employment patterns, but it will no longer fit the way family and employment are now. The only occasion on which we can leave the structure as it is is if the way it is will impose changes on today's society and they are the changes that we want to see. This is rather unlikely, which means that, one way or another, the tax and benefits systems will need to change, and to change constantly.

Unfortunately, change is expensive and disruptive, and it also tends to be inefficient.[374] This raises an interesting question: If we do not wish to have to change the system too often, then what kind of system should we have? That is: What kind of system will serve the greatest possible variety of social and economic configurations? This is quite an easy question to answer.

Take household structure: tax and benefits systems modelled on a particular kind of household, or on a restricted bundle of possible households, will find it difficult to serve changing household patterns. So, for instance: our benefits system pays less to two people living together than it does in total to two individuals living separately. This is because people living together create economies of scale, and most governments want to profit from those economies rather than leave them with the couples that generate them. During and after the Second World War, family patterns were quite stable, there was moral and social pressure on married couples to stay together, and the fact that they would be paid more in total if they separated was hardly relevant.

---

[374] Because only government department insiders know the minimum resource requirements for efficient delivery of a public service, and because ministers do not know, and because insiders inevitably maximise resource requirements in order to maximise the size of their departments and to provide a cushion against future hard times, the only way for ministers to control budgets is to reduce the budget until the public service is seen to suffer. However, this only works if the service delivery structure stays the same. Change costs money, and ministers won't know how much, which gives departmental insiders yet another opportunity to maximise resources. What comes out at the other end will have unpredictable service levels and unpredictable resource requirements, and nobody will be able to tell whether resources are being efficiently deployed. We have seen this difficulty experienced by the National Health Service during recent reforms. The aim was to replace primary care trusts. Staff were made redundant, new structures emerged, and the staff were rehired. Some staff never came back, so NHS administration is suffering recruitment and training costs; and those staff members who have come back have of course retained their redundancy payments. This is hardly efficient. By constantly tinkering with the tax and benefits systems, successive governments have suffered frequent additional administrative costs, and often entirely unpredictable costs. Any major change ought to be towards a new system modelled on a known system, such as Child Benefit, so that costs can be confidently predicted, and thereafter change should be kept to a minimum.

Today, people (understandably) value their autonomy. A woman might no longer wish her husband or partner to know what she earns, or to have her benefits reduced because she is living with him. There is now less moral and social pressure for couples to stay together, so a benefits system originally designed for couples who were likely to stay together might now contribute to forcing them apart.

Similarly with the changing economy and the changing labour market. The power of multinational corporations, increasing mechanisation and computerisation, and the growth of international trade in raw materials, manufactured products, services, and labour, mean that we are facing a time of change, whether that be slow change through a series of stable patterns, or rapid change into a generally more precarious labour market. We can have no expectation that, as in the past, an individual's financial return on their labour will be sufficient to provide for the subsistence needs of themselves and their family. For much of the last century the male full-time wage just about covered subsistence needs for most families; and in our current economy wages and benefits between them provide enough for people to live on – though only at the cost of major disincentives and rigidities. This is not going to be an adequate framework for the future, particularly because during our working lives we all need to earn sufficient to fund pensions to support ourselves during increasingly protracted old age.[375] There is no reason to expect that earnings and subsistence income will match each other for the majority of individuals or households. A period of change in the labour market and in the economy requires a new approach to income maintenance in which the tax and benefits structure will actively distribute both employment and income,[376] and in which it will not need to change as the labour market changes. A Citizen's Income's ability to redistribute work at the same time as distributing buying power, and its suitability to a wide variety of labour market patterns, makes it an excellent candidate for the foundation of any future economy.

We can therefore conclude that if the family, the household, the economy and the employment market continue to move in the directions in which they are moving, then we shall need a different benefits system, and in particular one that would provide a secure

---

[375] Offe, Claus (2008) 'Basic Income and the labor contract', *Basic Income Studies*, vol 3, no 1, pp 1–30, p 4

[376] Esping-Andersen, Gøsta (1994) 'Equality and work in the post-industrial life-cycle', pp 167–185 in Miliband, David (ed.) *Reinventing the left*, Cambridge: Polity Press, pp 182–3

income floor that would satisfy our need for security.[377] Because it would not be taken away as earnings rose, a Citizen's Income would provide such a firm floor on which to build an income. Adding additional hours of employment, either short-term or long-term, would always be worth it; and people would find it more worthwhile to upgrade their skills, or to learn entirely new skills, because they would continue to receive their Citizen's Income while training, and they would keep more of every extra £1 that their new skills earned for them. In a changing employment market we are going to be more in need than ever of updated and new skills,[378] and it could only be helpful if the benefits system made skill acquisition more likely.

As with other innovations, it is the first movers who will reap the benefits of innovation. For the UK to replace the employment age social compact[379] with a postmodern one[380] before others get there first would enable our economy, our labour market, and our social structures, to adapt to new global conditions more quickly than would be possible for other countries. This would provide the UK with both economic and social advantages. And because the Citizen's Income will cohere with future changes in the family and the labour market, first mover benefits would continue to operate until other countries established their own Citizen's Incomes.

Conclusion

We have seen that a Citizen's Income would serve today's changing labour market and today's changing family, but that is far less relevant than whether it would serve the labour market and the family as both of them continue to change. Far more important than the detail of today's household structure and labour market is the fact of change. The one line that I can remember from Peter Gabriel's music for the central high wire show at the UK's Millennium Exhibition is 'The one

---

[377] Piven, Frances Fox (1994) 'Comment: economic imperatives and social reform', pp 186–91 in Miliband, David (ed.) *Reinventing the left*, Cambridge: Polity Press, p 189
[378] Mayhew, Kevin (1995) 'Basic Income and economic efficiency', *Citizen's Income Bulletin*, no 19, pp 13–15
[379] Ashdown, Paddy (1990) 'Breaking the poverty trap: a Basic Income', *BIRG Bulletin*, no 10, Autumn/Winter, pp 5–6; Ashdown, Paddy (1992) 'What the politicians say', *BIRG Bulletin*, no 14, February, pp 4–6; Silva, Francesco, Ponti, Marco, Balzarotti, Andres and Dore, Ronald (1995) 'Welfare and efficiency in a non-work society', *Citizen's Income Bulletin*, no 20, July, pp 4–6
[380] Robertson, James (1996) 'Towards a new social compact: Citizen's Income and radical tax reform', *The Political Quarterly*, vol 67, no 1, pp 54–8

thing that I'm sure about is the accelerating rate of change.' Whether that acceleration is rapid or slow is a matter for debate; but that change is accelerating is undeniable. A system designed for the ways in which our society, economy and labour market worked seventy years ago is unlikely to be useful today or tomorrow. Similarly, systems designed with today's household structures, labour market and economy in mind will be unlikely to be useful in ten years' time. It is time to stop discussing the detail of today's welfare state and to start discussing the income maintenance system that we shall need in a changing future. The only way to approach a world of change is to design systems with possible change in mind, and the only kind of system that will continue to be serviceable in a wide variety of possible future scenarios is a radically simple one. The more system variables there are that might or might not suit a future social and economic configuration, the less likely is the system to serve our future needs. We therefore need to remove variables. An individual-based, non–withdrawable and unconditional benefit is the only one to fit this condition. As Robert Goodin puts it: 'the best response to the destandardisation of life would be to abandon conditionality … Let's give up trying to second-guess how people are going to lead their lives and crafting [category-based] responses to the problems they might encounter. Instead, simply give them the money and let them get on with it.'[381]

There have been enough calls by committees of enquiry for the government to seriously consider a Citizen's Income. It is surely high time for the government to promote a well-informed and wideranging debate and the research necessary to make that debate intelligent.

Conclusions relating to the last four chapters

We have now compared both the UK's current system and a Citizen's Income with our list of seven criteria for an ideal benefits system. When James Meade compared the tax and benefits structure of his day with his list of characteristics of an ideal system, his verdict was that it failed the test.[382] Our verdict must be the same: that the tax and benefits structure of our own day fails the test of our list of criteria. We have also found

---

[381] Goodin, Robert E. (2001) 'Something for nothing?' pp 90–97 in Cohen, Joshua and Rogers, Joel, *What's wrong with a free lunch?* Boston: Beacon Press, p 93

[382] Meade, J.E. (1999) *The structure and reform of direct taxation*, Report of a committee chaired by Professor J.E. Meade, London: George Allen & Unwin, for the Institute for Fiscal Studies, p 279. cf Fitzpatrick, Tony (1999) *Freedom and security: An introduction to the Basic Income debate*, Basingstoke: Macmillan, pp 142–4

that universal benefits generally, and a Citizen's Income in particular, would fulfil all of our criteria. As Peter Townsend put it: universal benefits are 'an efficient, economical and socially integrative mechanism' to prevent poverty that 'have as ... by-products certain advantages, such as the reduction of social conflict, the greater integration of certain social minorities, and a strengthening of the earning incentives of low-income households, quite apart from any strengthening of social morals as a basis for a more productive economy'.[383] The argument of the last four chapters would support that verdict.

Robert and Edward Skidelsky have defined 'the good life' as consisting of seven 'basic goods': health, security, respect, personality ('the ability to frame and execute a plan of life reflective of one's tastes, temperament and conception of the good'), harmony with nature, friendship, and leisure. Good health in the UK is already served by a universal benefit: the National Health Service. The other elements of the good life would be served by a Citizen's Income, which would provide a secure income, would reduce stigma and thus generate greater respect, would give to individuals and to households greater freedom to create their own individual and community projects, would give to people more opportunities to develop friendships, and would enable people to choose their own preferred patterns of employment and leisure. As we show in Chapter 13, a Citizen's Income might also deliver greater harmony with nature. It is no surprise that at the heart of the Skidelskys' policy prescription is a Citizen's Income.[384]

---

[383] Townsend, Peter (1972) *The scope and limitations of means-tested social services in Britain*, Manchester: Manchester Statistical Society, p 29, quoted in Walker, Carol (2011) 'For universalism and against the means test', pp 133–52 in Walker, Alan, Sinfield, Adrian and Walker, Carol (eds) *Fighting poverty, inequality and injustice: A manifesto inspired by Peter Townsend*, Cambridge: Polity Press, p 149

[384] Skidelsky, Robert and Skidelsky, Edward (2012) *How much is enough? The love of money, and the case for the good life*, London: Allen Lane/Penguin, pp 154–66, 197–202

CHAPTER 10

Would people work?

The question which this chapter will tackle follows naturally from the discussion in the previous chapter, and it is this: Would a Citizen's Income make it more or less likely that someone unemployed would seek employment, or that someone in employment would seek to increase the hours they worked?

The vast majority of people wish to be in employment or self-employment. An important recent piece of evidence for this is that people with multiple needs still wish to be in employment even if society regards them as people who 'can't work'.[385] An important piece of evidence for the fact that people wish to be in paid employment, and that they wish to be properly rewarded financially for the work that they do, is that an unquantifiable but probably considerable amount of paid employment is never declared to tax and benefits authorities, because if it were declared then benefits would be reduced and the household would experience a period of budgetary uncertainty and little additional net income from their paid employment.[386] As we have seen in previous chapters, it is often the administrative complexity involved in changing one's labour market status, rather than any calculation of financial advantage or disadvantage, which discourages people from seeking employment, from seeking new employment patterns for themselves or for their households, or from declaring paid employment to government departments. Bill Jordan and his colleagues found that low earners would have an innate sense that a particular employment market decision was not worth taking because it would add nothing, or practically nothing, to the household budget: but also that careful calculation of financial outcomes of labour market decisions was not the norm. This was not because people did not understand the systems (for the most part they did), but rather because their earnings were too unreliable and unpredictable, and because the tax and benefits machinery was too slow and too fallible. Even if they had tried to work out the exact theoretical consequences of their decisions, these would

---

[385] Dean, Hartley (2012) 'Re-conceptualising welfare-to-work for people with multiple problems and needs', *Journal of Social Policy*, vol 32, no 3, pp 441–59, p 444

[386] Jordan, Bill, James, Simon, Kay, Helen and Redley, Marcus (1992) *Trapped in poverty? Labour-market decisions in low-income households*, London: Routledge, p 277

have been disrupted by subsequent unforeseen contingencies, or by the delays and mistakes characteristic of benefits administration – in several cases, couples had got quite severely into debt as a result of making otherwise sensible labour market decisions.[387]

Additional evidence for the fact that people wish to earn an income through employment is that workers in the UK believe that other people might need an incentive to seek employment, but that they do not. Because other people are perceived as needing an incentive to seek employment, and 'Working Tax Credit' is an incentive, 'Working Tax Credit' is experienced as stigmatising.[388] Also, 'Working Tax Credit' is a declaration to the worker that wages are not sufficient to meet subsistence needs, whereas wages higher up the earnings range do not need to be subsidised. This difference between the experience of low and subsidised wages and higher and unsubsidised wages is another of the causes of the stigma experienced by people who receive 'Working Tax Credits', or who would receive them if they found employment.

But this is only part of the story. Because at low wages the wage does not have to provide the whole of someone's subsistence income, the wage level and the value of the worker's labour to the employer will more nearly match each other than if the wage had to provide the whole of a household's subsistence needs. There is no evidence that increasing 'Working Tax Credit' depresses wages,[389] which suggests that the low wage is not far from the economic value of the worker's labour. A Citizen's Income would generate this effect across the entire earnings range, thus extending the free market character of the labour market.

While 'Tax Credits' might perform a useful function in matching some wage levels to work's economic value, they still ensure that low wages are perceived as insufficient, they can cause household budgetary chaos when circumstances change, and they are reduced by increases in the worker's or their partner's earnings. A Citizen's Income would solve these problems. It would not be experienced as a top-up for low wages because everybody would receive it; it would not be withdrawn as earnings rose, so it would enable the employment market to function more like a classical market across the entire earnings range, meaning that the economic value of work would be more accurately reflected in

---

[387] Jordan, Bill with James, Simon (1990) 'The poverty trap: poor people's accounts', *BIRG Bulletin*, no 11, July, pp 5–7, p 7

[388] Dean, Hartley and Mitchell, Gerry (2011) *Wage top-ups and work incentives: The implications of the UK's Working Tax Credit scheme: A preliminary report*, London: LSE

[389] Dickens, Richard and McKnight, Abigail (2008) *The impact of policy change on job retention and advancement*, CASE paper no 134, London: CASE, LSE

the wage rate across the entire earnings range; and the Citizen's Income, and the better functioning employment market, would mean that the less desirable jobs would have to offer higher wages in order to persuade people to do them, and the more desirable jobs would be able to offer lower wages because more people would want them. A particularly interesting development would be that internships would cease to be the preserve of children of wealthier parents and so could become a source of social mobility rather than of social rigidity. In general, the labour market would have a lot more space in it for individual choice and initiative in relation to the jobs that people chose to do and the ways in which households wished to organise their working lives, because not only would a better functioning market enable jobs' desirability and wages to match each other more closely, but it would also enable the hours of employment offered by industry, commerce and service industries to more nearly match the hours of employment that workers wanted. A Citizen's Income would 'provide a reliable income from some source other than earned income (thus making the rate of pay less important relative to other sources of income)' (James Meade), [390] thus enabling a more equal balance of power between employee and employer, and a labour market in which negotiation delivered benefits to all parties involved. An important result of this process would be increasing humanisation of workplaces in order to attract employees: a process that Götz Werner, a successful German entrepreneur, regards as one of the major benefits of a Citizen's Income.[391]

Economists normally assume a 'backward-bending' supply curve for labour. What this means is that, as wages rise, employment becomes more attractive, so the number of hours in employment rises; but as wages continue to rise, and needs are increasingly met, leisure again becomes more attractive, because someone might prefer to have more leisure in which to spend the money that they have already earned than to be employed for longer hours in order to earn money that they cannot spend. There is evidence to suggest that, as income continues to rise, utility, broadly understood in terms of wellbeing, is inversely

[390] Meade, J.E. (1995) *Full employment regained? An Agathotopian dream*, University of Cambridge Department of Applied Economics, Occasional Paper no 61, Cambridge: Cambridge University Press, p 57. On the development of James Meade's Social Dividend, in the context of others at work on similar ideas, see Van Trier, Walter (1995) *Every one a king*, Leuven: Departement Sociologie, Katholieke Universiteit Leuven, pp 343–407

[391] Werner, Götz W. and Goehler, Adrienne (2010) *1.000 Euro für jeden*, Berlin: Econ, Ullstein Buchverlage, pp 139–51

proportional to income.[392] Figure 10.1 shows the number of hours of employment on the horizontal axis, and the wage rate on the vertical axis. The curve first rises, then steepens to vertical, and then tips back on itself.

Figure 10.1: The backward-bending supply curve for labour

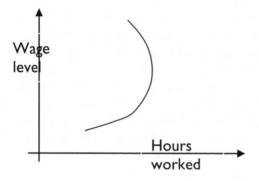

That is the theory: but research shows that among the poorest workers, and at the lowest wages, falling wages mean higher numbers of employment hours, and, conversely, higher wages mean lower numbers of hours of employment. This is simply because earnings are the only income, so falling wages means a higher number of hours worked in order to earn enough for the barest of subsistence needs. Because such workers are generally working extremely long hours, an increase in wages will mean that they choose to reduce working hours in order to relieve their mental and physical stress. This inverse relationship between wage level and number of hours of employment holds good at higher wage rates too, as in the theory: so either the whole curve tilts backwards, or the two ends tilt backwards and the middle part tilts forwards (as in Figure 10.2), representing a wage range when basic rising wages make employment attractive in relation to leisure, but workers are not already totally overworked and so have the capacity to work longer hours.[393]

The situation is of course different when there *is* a source of income other than wages. If that source is means-tested benefits, then, as we have seen, an increase in wages, or an increase in the number of hours

[392] Layard, R., Mayraz, G., and Nickell, S. (2008) 'The Marginal utility of income', *Journal of Public Economics,* nos 8–9, vol 92, pp 1846–57

[393] Sharif, Mohammed (2003) *Work behavior of the world's poor: Theory, evidence and policy,* Aldershot: Ashgate

Figure 10.2: Curve with two backward-bending sections

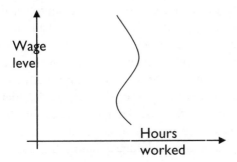

of employment, can make very little difference to net income. Under these circumstances, it is highly likely that an hour of leisure will be felt to be of more value than an hour of employment for miniscule financial gain – unless the job has an intrinsic value for the worker, which is less likely to be the case the lower down the earnings range we go.

There is evidence that higher tax rates make people less likely to involve themselves in the labour market, or in earnings-generating activity generally,[394] which means that high marginal deduction rates generated by the deduction of Income Tax and the withdrawal of benefits will have the same effect. A Citizen's Income would reduce these marginal deduction rates, making it more likely that adults without employment would enter the labour market, and that those already in it would seek to increase their earnings. When a group of researchers used the EUROMOD microsimulation programme (which employs family expenditure data to calculate redistributional and other effects of changes to tax and benefits systems), they found that in Denmark, Italy, Portugal, and the UK, a Citizen's Income or a Participation Income (like a Citizen's Income, but requiring participation in approved socially useful activity), along with progressive taxation, would offer outcomes better than means-tested and work-tested systems in terms of labour market participation and net income

---

[394] Davis, Steven J. and Henrekson, Magnus (2005) 'Tax effects on work activity, industry mix and shadow economy size: evidence from rich-country comparisons', http://ideas.repec.org/p/hhs/ratioi/0057.html. A version of this article also appears at pp 44–104 in Gomez-Salvador, Ramon, Lamo, Ana, Petrongolo, Barbara, Ward, Melanie and Wasmer, Etienne (eds) (2005) *Labour supply and incentives to work in Europe*, Cheltenham: Edward Elgar Publishing

equality, and that in Denmark and the UK a Citizen's Income or a Participation Income, again with progressive taxation, would offer better outcomes in relation to female labour market participation.[395] The labour market participation simulation relies simply on calculating the wage elasticity of labour supply (that is, the additional amount of labour market participation generated by a particular wage rate rise) from family expenditure data. This predicts the effect of the falling withdrawal rates offered by universal benefits. It does not tell us the additional effects of the income security offered by universal benefits, nor of the reduction in administrative chaos during changes in labour market status. These are all bound to have positive effects on labour market participation, suggesting that additional labour market activity will be even more likely with universal benefits than the model suggests.

But as a Citizen's Income rose, would there not be pressure in the opposite direction? If someone's subsistence needs are small, then would the provision of a Citizen's Income mean that they would be *less* likely to seek employment because no longer would earnings be the only route to a subsistence income? The answer to that question is this: *As things stand now*, earnings are not the only route to a subsistence income. Contributory and means-tested benefits are available, and these make it *less* likely that someone will enter the labour market because employment would often provide little additional net income and could burden the claimant and their dependents with domestic budgetary insecurity. So in the current circumstances labour market activity has to be coerced by such 'active labour market' policies as compulsory interviews with public officials, benefit cuts if employment offers are not taken up, and unpaid work to promote 'job readiness'.[396] (For a discussion of the related policy direction in the US, see the website appendix.[397]) A Citizen's Income would reduce the disincentives and would therefore make such 'active labour market' policies less necessary.

Motivation is a complex matter. Do some people *choose* not to seek employment? If so: why? Burchardt and Le Grand suggest that there are four 'layers' of factors involved in someone not seeking employment:
1. those factors over which an individual has no control (such as age);
2. those factors over which someone has no control at present (such

---

[395] Colombino, Ugo, Locatelli, Marilena, Narazani, Edlira and O'Donoghue, Cathal (2010) 'Alternative Basic Income mechanisms: an evaluation exercise with a microeconometric model', *Basic Income Studies*, vol 5, no 1, pp 1–31

[396] Handler, Joel and Babcock, Amanda (2006) 'The failure of workfare: another reason for a Basic Income guarantee', *Basic Income Studies*, vol 1, no 1, pp 1–22

[397] See the website appendix for this chapter at www.citizensincome.org

---

as educational achievement); 3. those factors that someone can change in the near future, but where high costs of various kinds might be experienced (such as place of residence); and 4. those factors that someone could change easily (such as starting voluntary work). On the basis of their research, Burchardt and Le Grand conclude that 'just 1 in 10 of non-employed men, and a similar proportion of non-employed women, can be unambiguously classified as voluntarily out of work'.[398] Others will of course be on the voluntary-involuntary spectrum: so for one tenth of non-employed workers the question of motivation is pivotal, and for a larger number it remains important.

One question that we might wish to address is this: Which is the most effective labour market motivator: the coercion related to means-tested out-of-work benefits, or the certainty of retaining a substantial proportion of every extra £1 earned? In a book to mark the centenary of Beatrice Webb's 1909 minority report on the importance of universal services, Peter Kenway suggests 'raising the level of the personal allowance to remove low earners from Income Tax altogether; raising the level of the income thresholds above which benefits and tax credits start to be tapered and/or council tax begins to become payable; reducing the rate at which tax credits and benefits are tapered away as earnings rise ... reintroducing a (lower) starting rate of Income Tax'; and Jonathan Bradshaw asks that Child Benefit should remain universal and shows how effective it is at reducing poverty. Steve Osborn adds that a serious problem looking for a solution is 'the uncertainties created by the current benefits system and its implications for moving poor people into employment.'[399] We can agree with all of these suggestions: but would it not be simpler to establish a Citizen's Income? It would achieve everything that these piecemeal suggestions would achieve, and a lot more besides; and it would take labour market coercion off the agenda. This is important, not least because, as coercion rises, the labour market will become less a free market in which price (in this case the wage) matches supply to demand, and will thus become even less efficient than it is now. Because a Citizen's Income would

---

[398] Burchardt, Tania and Le Grand, Julian (2002) *Constraint and opportunity: Identifying voluntary non-employment*, CASEpaper 55, London: CASE, LSE, p 24

[399] Kenway, Peter (2011) 'Stop taxing people into poverty', pp 49–57 in Knight, Barry (ed.) *A minority view: What Beatrice Webb would say now*, London: Alliance Publishing Trust, p 56; Bradshaw, Jonathan (2011) 'Hands off child benefit', pp 58–69 in Knight, Barry (ed.) (2011) *A minority view: What Beatrice Webb would say now*, London: Alliance Publishing Trust; Osborn, Steve (2011) 'People, places and poverty: getting away from the neighbourhood', pp 70–84 in Barry Knight (ed.) *A minority view: What Beatrice Webb would say now*, London: Alliance Publishing Trust, p 80

contribute to disconnecting subsistence needs from the wage level across the entire earnings range, and because it would take coercion out of the labour market,

> the quest for a fair wage (the very attempt to reward work fairly and take fully into account values based on the burdensomeness of work), far from leading to rejection of a universal benefit, becomes a justification for it.(Philippe Van Parijs)[400]

For supply and demand in the labour market to be more accurately coordinated through the price mechanism would be good for industry,[401] would be good for the efficiency of the economy, and would enable the worker to behave as a genuine participant in a market and able to refuse employment for which the wage did not sufficiently value the time, skills and activity on offer.[402] Even if this meant that some wages had to rise in order to attract sufficient people to take on the necessary work,[403] the greater efficiency would mean that firms and public sector organisations would make more rational decisions about mechanisation, postholders would have increased expectations of the training and development that an employer might provide (thus reducing the number of poor jobs and increasing the number of good jobs),[404] working age adults would be more likely to find the work that they wanted, industry and commerce would be more likely to find the workers that they needed, and every citizen would find themselves nearer to the 'democratic republican' ideal of autonomous individuals

---

[400] Van Parijs, Philippe (1990) 'Getting paid for doing nothing: plain justice or ignominy? The ethical foundations of a basic income', trans. Hermione Parker, *BIRG Bulletin*, no 11, July, pp 15–19, p 16

[401] Oubridge, Victor (1990) 'Basic Income and industrial development: an employer's viewpoint', *BIRG Bulletin*, no 11, July, pp 28–30

[402] Offe, Claus (2008) 'Basic Income and the labor contract', *Basic Income Studies*, vol 3, no 1, pp 1–30; Liebermann, Sascha (2012) 'Germany: far, though close – problems and prospects of BI in Germany', pp 83–106 in Caputo, Richard (ed.) *Basic Income Guarantee and politics: International experiences and perspectives on the viability of income guarantee,* New York: Palgrave Macmillan, pp 93–5

[403] Pech, Wesley (2010) 'Behavioral economics and the Basic Income guarantee', *Basic Income Studies*, vol 5, no 2, pp 1–17

[404] Mayhew, Kevin (1991) 'Basic Income as a lever for economic efficiency', *BIRG Bulletin*, no 12, February, pp 10–12

relating to each other and to institutions from a position of strength rather than from a position of weakness.[405]

It is not irrational to believe that if someone received a Citizen's Income then they might not wish to seek employment: but it is inconsistent to believe this at the same time as recognising that high benefit withdrawal rates disincentivise labour market participation. This common inconsistency is well represented by Karen Rowlingson's verdict on a Citizen's Income:

> There would be no direct disincentive to work and/or save, as individuals would keep the basic income even if they earned or saved large sums of money. However, it is argued that if basic income payments were set at a level to cover people's needs there might be no incentive for people to work at all.[406]

If means-tested benefits were replaced wholly or in part with a Citizen's Income, then some wages might rise in order to attract workers: but labour market incentives would also improve (without coercion having to be used), and supply and demand in the labour market would more nearly match each other across the entire earnings range. It rather looks as if a Citizen's Income would be unambiguously beneficial for both the labour market and for workers.

As we have seen, it is not just the actual marginal deduction rates that matter: rather more important might be not knowing the effect that a change in labour market behaviour might have on a household's income, and not knowing the bureaucratic difficulties that the household might face, if, for example, an employed person's spouse returned to employment. As Tony Atkinson has said, 'it's not just the actual but also the apparent disincentive that has to be avoided.'[407]

---

[405] Casassas, David (2007) 'Basic Income and the Republican ideal: rethinking material independence in contemporary societies', *Basic Income Studies*, vol 2, no 2, pp 1–7; Pettit, Philip (2007) 'A Republican right to Basic Income?', *Basic Income Studies*, vol 2, no 2, pp 1–8; Domènech, Antoni and Raventós, Daniel (2007) 'Property and Republican freedom: an institutional approach to Basic Income', *Basic Income Studies*, vol 2, no 2, pp 1–8; Pateman, Carole (2007) 'Why Republicanism?' *Basic Income Studies*, vol 2, no 2, pp 1–6; White, Stuart (2007) 'The Republican case for Basic Income: a plea for difficulty', *Basic Income Studies*, vol 2, no 2, pp 1–7

[406] Rowlingson, Karen (2009) '"From cradle to grave": social security and the lifecourse', pp 133–150 in Millar, Jane (ed.) *Understanding social security*, 2nd edn, Bristol: Policy Press, p 145

[407] Atkinson, A.B. (1985) *Income maintenance and social insurance: A survey*, Welfare State Programme, paper no 5, London: LSE, p 73

Household employment decisions can be extremely complex, involving such factors as the particular hours worked, educational or training possibilities or requirements, the care needs of children, aged parents requiring care, and more. A particularly complex factor is a psychological one that means that families in which the woman is the main breadwinner and the man is out of work are relatively rare:

> There remains a strong normative expectation against female breadwinners. Once the existence of such a taboo is hypothesised, many of the conundrums surrounding no-earner families fall into place. The number of non-working husbands has increased. Women are all but forbidden to work if their husbands have not got jobs, so the wives in these families cannot share in the general increase in employment experienced by women in other domestic situations. This means that the number of no-earner couples must increase. Such a process could entirely explain the apparent growth in within-family polarisation. (Richard Berthoud)[408]

In 2005, the Organisation for Economic Co-operation and Development found that 'a reduction of marginal effective tax rates [marginal deduction rates] by 20% ... implies a rise in the probability of moving from unemployment to employment by nearly 10% ....The strongest effects are found for the unemployed with a working partner, whose reemployment probability would increase by seven percentage points, from 51% to nearly 58%.'[409] This result corroborates Atkinson's and Sutherland's finding that 'the poverty trap tends to be discussed in terms of the effect of the husband earning an extra £1, but the marginal tax rate on the earnings of the wife may be quite different – and may well be more relevant, since the empirical evidence suggests that her decision may be more affected.'[410]

If a Citizen's Income made part-time employment more attractive for both men and women, might this make it more likely that both women and men in no-earner families would seek employment and feel more comfortable about the woman finding employment before the man managed to do so?

[408] Berthoud, Richard (2007) *Work-rich and work-poor*, Bristol: Policy Press, p 51

[409] OECD (2005) *Employment outlook, 2005*, Paris: OECD, p 127

[410] Atkinson, A.B. and Sutherland, Holly (1988a) *Integrating incomes taxation and social security: Analysis of a partial Basic Income*, Tax, Incentives and the Distribution of Income paper no 123, London: LSE, p 14

Conclusion

The current benefits system was modelled around a labour market in which a full-time employed worker provided for his family, and in which his wife might have a part-time job. The UK's 'Universal Credit' is modelled around the same kind of labour market; and the Jobcentre structure, which is at the heart of government labour market coercion policy, also assumes a labour market that is a given and into which individuals need to be propelled. Jobcentre Plus costs £3.56 billion per annum to administer. This looks rather high when compared to the Jobseeker's Allowance budget of £4.5 billion and the Income Support budget of £7.9 billion that Jobcentre Plus helps to administer.[411]

The desire to work (with work broadly defined) seems to be innate to our human nature: but it is still true that it needs to be in people's interests to exchange their labour for the wage on offer. First of all, money is an indicator of the value that society places on our work, and we wish to have our contribution properly recognised; and secondly, we work for pay in order to obtain for ourselves and our families the goods and services necessary to the lives that we wish to lead. Because we wish to work, and to exchange our labour for money, there is a market in labour. Unfortunately, the labour market we have does not work quite like a pure market. An employer might offer a wage of £10 per hour, but if all a worker would get out of working a few hours a week for that employer was 50p per hour then that worker might decide not to bother. That is the situation facing 700,000 employees. A full 13 per cent of employees face total deduction rates (not marginal deduction rates) of over 70 per cent: that is, for every hour they work at a wage of £10 per hour they will receive less than £3 per hour.[412] If they have to pay fares to get to work, then they might decide not to get on the train. A Citizen's Income would begin to put this right because a Citizen's Income of any size would reduce the total deduction rate for every worker, because the Citizen's Income would never be withdrawn as earned income rose.[413]

As J.K. Galbraith pointed out in 1999, the answer to poverty is that

---

[411] DWP (2011) *Jobcentre Plus annual report and accounts 2010–11*, London: The Stationery office, p 51

[412] Browne, J. and Phillips, D. (2010) *Tax and benefit reforms under Labour*, London: Institute for Fiscal Studies

[413] See the website www.citizensincome.org for an example of a Citizen's Income that could be implemented relatively easily and that would unambiguously improve labour market incentives for the three household types tested

everybody should be guaranteed a decent basic income. A rich country such as the US can well afford to keep everybody out of poverty. Some, it will be said, will seize upon the income and won't work. So it is now with more limited welfare, as it is called. Let us accept some resort to leisure by the poor as well as by the rich.[414]

While such debates in the fields of philosophy, ethics, and political economy might be important, they mean little if we have not previously answered the question: Would a Citizen's Income make people more or less likely to seek employment if they are unemployed, and more or less likely to seek additional employment or additional self-employment if already employed? Further research, and discussions like those offered in this chapter, are clearly going to be important to this process, but unfortunately that is not all that will be required. Prejudice remains a problem. However good the evidence that a Citizen's Income would increase rather than reduce work effort, we seem to find it difficult to believe that that could be true. We have already discussed the evidence for a Citizen's Income's positive effects on work effort generated by the pilot project in Namibia. A recent press release by the Namibian Basic Income Grant Coalition is instructive:

> Despite the positive results, the Namibian government has still not committed itself to the introduction of a BIG [Basic Income Grant: Citizen's Income] in Namibia. Instead, senior government leaders have raised concerns that the grant would make people lazy and dependent on hand-outs. Such perceptions are rooted in prejudices rather than being based on the evidence provided by Otjivero! We wish to point out that the BIG Coalition arranged for many Namibians, including Members of Parliament (MPs), to visit Otjivero and to witness the developments there first-hand. The honourable MPs were free to assess the impact of the BIG themselves and they were impressed with the results achieved in Otjivero. However, they preferred to express their views in private instead of speaking out publicly in support of a national BIG.[415]

---

[414] Galbraith, J.K. (1999) Speech, 29 June, and quoted in *Citizen's Income Newsletter*, issue 3, Autumn, p 7

[415] Basic Income Grant Coalition (2012) 'The Basic Income Grant (BIG) is government's responsibility', Press release, Namibia, 1 March, http://bignam.org/Publications/Press_release_March_2012_to_Government.pdf

CHAPTER 11

Would a Citizen's Income be an answer to poverty, inequality, and injustice?

First of all we shall disucss what we mean by 'poverty' and what we mean by 'inequality'; then we shall need to discuss the book *The spirit level*, by Wilkinson and Pickett, because it has had such an important effect on current debate about inequality; and finally we shall need to ask what a Citizen's Income would do about poverty and inequality.

Would a Citizen's Income be an answer to poverty?

First of all, what is poverty? We shall consider two fictional people:

Edna lives in a turn-of-the-century local authority house. She lives on Income Support as her husband, who is now dead, worked in the building industry and never paid National Insurance Contributions. She is now sixty, she belongs to pottery and singing classes at the local adult education centre, her children – all of them in low-paid employment and sometimes unemployed – come to see her once a week, and she tells her grandchildren about family hop-picking holidays spent living in wooden sheds and working from dawn to dusk in the fields. She will tell you how her mother helped to start the local co-op, and how she now has rheumatism but still enjoys visiting her old school at the end of the road: though it is now very different from the way it was when she left it at fourteen to work in a shop.

And there is Paul, thirty, who works in the design industry. He is single; his flat is worth 80 per cent of the mortgage and he can just about keep up with the payments; and he earns £30,000 a year, but he is not sure how long his job will last. He has a first-class degree and a master's degree, but his field is being taken over by younger people who can cope with computers better than he can. He is depressed, he never has any money, and he has started to drink too much.

Which of these two people is poor? Which of them is in poverty? The local authority tenant on Income Support who left school at fourteen? Or the owner-occupier who earns an above-average salary and has two degrees.

Might we be better off without the word 'poverty'?

1. There is no clarity as to its definition. Admittedly, this is true of all words. Since Ludwig Wittgenstein wrote his *Philosophical investigations*,[416] we have not been able to hide from the fact that no word has a univocal definition, that different uses of words bear 'family resemblances' to each other, if that, and that to choose a core definition is simply to add to the diversity of meanings. There are some words – and 'poverty' might be one of them – where the diversity of possible definitions is so broad as to be positively detrimental to clarity of thought and to constructive activity. The two scenarios that we have discussed reveal the possibility of situations in which we might use the word 'poverty' in ways opposite to the ways in which we might use it in relation to the general categories to which the anecdotes conform. This cannot be good for clarity, nor for analysis, nor for practical politics.

2. A second problem is that the general word 'poverty' is too often used in a specific fashion and thus leaves off the agenda some of those issues to which a more general definition might apply. For instance, Brian Abel-Smith and Peter Townsend, in *The poor and the poorest*,[417] use 'poverty' to mean 'income poverty', thus leaving off the agenda the question as to how important income is in relation to other social services, such as healthcare, social housing, and education (– and, in passing, it is surely of interest that general books on poverty are often more than 50 per cent about social security benefits and less than 50 per cent about every other kind of poverty put together). Jeremy Seebrook in his *Landscapes of poverty*,[418] and David Donnison in his *The politics of poverty*,[419] take specific definition and consequent exclusion of other definitions to its logical conclusion by relying on an anecdotal approach, and locating the definition of 'poverty' in the particular anecdotes that they happen to choose.

3. If we assume for the sake of argument that income poverty is at the heart of poverty, then we are still left with choices to make and difficulties to ponder. If we regard as 'income poor' any household with less than 60 per cent of median household income, then first of all this definition is somewhat arbitrary, and secondly it can lead to misleading conclusions. In the UK, the year 2010-11 saw pre-

---

[416] Wittgenstein, Ludwig (1967) *Philosophical investigations*, tr. G.E.M. Anscombe, Oxford: Basil Blackwell, part I, §§123–4, 654 , part II, p 226

[417] Abel-Smith, Brian and Townsend, Peter (1965) *The poor and the poorest: A new analysis of the Ministry of Labour's Family Expenditure Surveys of 1953–54 and 1960*, London: Bell

[418] Seebrook, Jeremy (1985) *Landscapes of poverty*, Oxford: Basil Blackwell

[419] Donnison, David (1982) *The politics of poverty*, Oxford: Martin Robertson

tax earnings fall on average by 7.1 per cent, and median household income fall by 3.1 per cent. The only conclusion to draw is that there is likely to have been more income poverty; but half a million individuals fewer than in the previous year found themselves in households with incomes below 60 per cent of median household income, leading to the conclusion that there was in fact less income poverty. There is clearly a flaw in the definition. Using the different income poverty measure of households with incomes below 60 per cent of the 1996-97 median, adjusted for inflation, gives a different result: that more individuals are in income poverty than during the previous year. This better reflects households' experience of falling incomes.[420]

4. A fourth problem is that 'poverty' can be defined in such a way that it can be stated that there is no poverty (as John Moore did when he was Secretary of State for Social Security). Any subsequent debate then turns on the definition of poverty, and on whether there is or is not any of this questionable commodity in the society in which we live. This means that political debate about the effects of specific policies fails to occur. To be without the word 'poverty' might turn our attention away from the sterile debate about whether poverty is absolute or relative, and about whether poverty exists, and towards the question as to whether every child should receive free preschool education, for instance.

5. A fifth problem is the all-embracing nature of most relative definitions of poverty. 'Poverty' defined in such a way as to include substandard housing, poor educational facilities, the poverty trap, Income Support rates, and long hospital waiting lists, not only fails to enhance the possibility of political action, but it positively disables it. It is never easy to see how to solve problems defined in large, amorphous ways. It is much easier to tackle the problem of whether there is an NHS dentist within a five mile radius of 95 per cent of the population.

6. A sixth problem is that any definition of poverty assumes an agreed understanding of what human beings need, whereas human need is always specific to an individual or to a particular situation. If need is regarded as 'inherent': that is, that we all share the same needs by virtue of our humanity (for instance, physical health and personal autonomy), then the ways in which such needs are expressed and met will always be culture-specific; and if need is understood as

---

[420] Cribb, Jonathan, Joyce, Robert, and Phillips, David (2012) *Living standards, poverty and inequality in the UK: 2012*, London: Institute for Fiscal Studies, pp 1–4

'interpreted': that is, as socially constructed, then the meeting of need will be equally socially constructed.[421] We might agree that sufficient food and water for survival are universal human needs, but that does not take us very far, and certainly fails to offer us a useful basis for any definition of poverty.

7. To my mind, the most serious problem with the word 'poverty' is that it encourages us to categorise people in ways in which they might not wish to be categorised. Edna does not regard herself as 'poor', and never has so regarded herself. Bill Jordan's work on how residents of an Exeter housing estate think about themselves[422] is perhaps the most useful evidence yet that we have no right to categorise any group as 'poor', or any particular bundle of circumstances as 'poverty', without first asking whether the people we have in mind wish to categorise themselves in that way. Those Exeter residents did as Runciman's research suggests that they would: they compare themselves with people socially and geographically close to themselves, rather than with people living different kinds of lives.[423]

We can combine these seven problems into a statement that poverty is 'socially constructed': that is, that we create the category and then we put people into it: either ourselves, or other people. A particularly difficult aspect of this realisation is that 'the spectre of poverty will not be eliminated as long as mechanisms for the relief or prevention of poverty remain in place, nor so long as such mechanisms make poverty an object of definition and regulation ... social policies calculated to relieve or prevent poverty in fact sustain poverty as a definable and manageable phenomenon and as a presence in the lives of everybody' (Dean and Melrose).[424] This suggests that individuals will understand themselves to be poor if their income arrives via a claim submitted to a government department and on which they await a decision with some anxiety. Nobody feels themselves to be poor because they receive Child Benefit.

There are thus substantial problems with the word 'poverty', and these lead to problems with the measurement of the extent of poverty.

---

[421] Dean, Hartley (2010) *Understanding human need*, Bristol: Policy Press, pp 24–6, 46–7

[422] Jordan, Bill, James, Simon, Kay, Helen and Redley, Marcus (1992) *Trapped in poverty? Labour-market decisions in low-income households*, London: Routledge

[423] Runciman, W.G. (1966) *Relative deprivation and social justice: A study of attitudes to social inequality in twentieth-century England*, London: Routledge and Kegan Paul, p 18

[424] Dean, Hartley and Melrose, Margaret (1999) *Poverty, riches and social citizenship*, Basingstoke: Macmillan, pp 27, 48

Even within particular fields such as 'income poverty' we have too little information about transfers within the family, or about the informal economy, to be able to make even an intelligent guess about the extent of income poverty.

Rather than trying to measure something that we cannot define, perhaps we should instead be measuring what we *can* define and *can* measure: the number of people living in conditions more crowded than permitted in local authority housing, the number of families living below half average income; the number of earners suffering marginal tax rates greater than 80 per cent, the number of families and individuals in negative equity whose mortgage payments leave them with less than 140 per cent of the Income Support scale-rates, the number of individuals with no qualifications at the end of their secondary schooling, or the growth in the inequality of incomes. These things we are able to discuss and to measure because we can define them with a reasonable degree of clarity. We can then develop policies and strategies to solve the problems thus defined and measured.

There are so many problems with the word 'poverty' and with the related concept of 'the poor' that we might well be better off without them, and without them we might find that we were more able to do something about the things that we *can* do something about.

While all of this might be true, the consequences of abandoning the word 'poverty' would probably be worse than the consequences of keeping it. Families and individuals often do face a bundle of difficulties: low or nonexistent earned income, low net income, poor quality housing, low educational achievement, poor health and so on. For such multiple deprivations the word 'poverty' might still be helpful. To abandon the word might be to suggest that multiple deprivations do not exist.

However, if we are going to keep the concept, we shall then need to discuss whether poverty is relative or absolute: If a school makes a charge for a school journey and one family cannot afford to pay, and so makes an excuse and their child stays at home, then that family is in relative poverty[425] – that is, relative to other families whose children

---

[425] Stouffer, Samuel A., Suchman, Edward A., DeVinney, Leland C., Star, Shirley A. and Williams, Robin M. Jr. (1949) *Studies in social psychology in World War II*, vol I, *The American soldier: Adjustment during army life*, Princeton, NJ: Princeton University Press. Stouffer surveyed half a million soldiers during World War II and found that feelings about hardship did not necessarily correlate with objective measures of hardship. Cf. Runciman, W.G. (1966) *Relative deprivation and social justice*, Berkeley: University of California Press; Fahey, Tony (2010) *Poverty and the two concepts of relative deprivation*, University College Dublin Working Paper, WP10/1, Dublin: University College Dublin

go to that school. 'Relative poverty' is 'exclusion from ordinary living patterns' because of a lack of resources:[426] hence today's preference for the term 'social exclusion'.[427] Absolute poverty is a recognition that for a family to fall below certain defined lines (such as a level of net income defined by Income Support scale rates) will mean that they and others regard them as poor. But as Ruth Lister suggests, notions of absolute and relative poverty are rather static ideas, and to understand poverty as social exclusion, and to understand social exclusion as a process rather than as a state, leads us to a more dynamic definition of poverty within which individuals and families are regarded as agents, that is, as actively seeking ways out of poverty. The interaction of social structures and people's own agency is probably the best way to understand how social exclusion works.[428]

If we look at our discussion about whether or not we should retain the word 'poverty', we might notice that we were discussing rather static notions of poverty or social exclusion. A first step beyond such static notions of poverty is to study both short term and long term poverty. Research by Jane Millar in 2006 showed that non-poor low-paid employees have less chance of staying out of poverty during the following year than non-poor employees in general (91 per cent as opposed to 96 per cent), and that

> tax credits and in-work benefits play an important role in keeping some low-paid people out of poverty, but are associated with a lower probability of avoiding poverty over time ... preliminary analysis of our data suggests the need to question the sustainability of relying too heavily on this type of fiscal strategy in preventing poverty over the longer term.[429]

Similarly, children living in poorer households do less well at school,[430] and therefore have fewer choices available to them as adults.

---

[426] Townsend, Peter (1979) *Poverty in the UK*, Harmondsworth: Penguin, p 131

[427] Hills, John, Le Grand, Julian and Piachaud, David (eds) (2002) *Understanding social exclusion*, Oxford: Oxford University Press

[428] Lister, Ruth (2004) *Poverty*, Cambridge: Polity Press, pp 94–7, 145–6, 178–83

[429] Research project by Professor Jane Millar, www.esrc.ac.uk/my-esrc/grants/RES-000-22-1071/read, reported in *The Edge*, issue 22, July 2006, London: Economic and Social Research Council, p 31

[430] West, Anne (2007) 'Poverty and educational achievement: why do children from low-income families tend to do less well at school?' *Journal of Poverty and Social Justice*, vol 15, no 3, pp 283–97, p 291

However, to take account of both short term and long term poverty still keeps us close to a static definition of poverty: that is, poverty understood as a state rather than as a process. If we were to extend Lister's understanding of the processes that lead into and out of social exclusion into a definition of poverty as 'an inability, either through the nature of social structures or personal resources or both, to climb out of a variety of deprivations', then we would have constructed a truly dynamic definition of poverty. Surely this is right. If we experience a variety of deprivations but are able to climb out of them – by our own agency, and/or by utilising social structures and processes – then we would be less likely to call ourselves poor than somebody unable to do that. We are only socially excluded if routes into social inclusion are closed to us.

Such a dynamic definition of poverty and social exclusion rather changes the debate about how poverty and social exclusion are to be defeated, because the required policy directions are now towards removing barriers to social inclusion rather than towards providing additional resources to people regarded as poor – though if the provision of resources contributes to the removal of barriers to social inclusion then such resources will still need to be provided. In this sense we should be discussing policy related to social inclusion rather than policy related to poverty or social exclusion, because policy is no longer about poverty or social exclusion in themselves but is rather about the increasing social inclusion that families and individuals will experience as they follow new trajectories that become available to them.

In the income maintenance field, one policy change surely required by a dynamic approach to social inclusion is the dismantling of means-tested benefits. As we have seen, these imprison people in their low net incomes (because benefits are withdrawn as earned incomes rise), they structure people's relationships and household arrangements, and they define people into social categories ('benefits recipients', 'free school meals recipients' and so on). All of these social processes constrain people's psychological motivation. The replacement of means-tested in-work and out-of-work benefits with a structure of universal benefits would provide low-earning and no-earning families with new routes out of social exclusion and into social inclusion. Poverty, whether understood as absolute, as relative, or as social exclusion, would be reduced.[431] As Peter Rosner has pointed out, the most important mechanisms for ensuring that poverty does not occur in the first place

---

[431] Dean, Hartley and Melrose, Margaret (1999) *Poverty, riches and social citizenship*, Basingstoke: Macmillan, p 172

are such universal systems as the National Health Service and universal free education. These are designed for the whole of the population and not just for the poor. This suggests that further universal systems would keep people out of poverty in the first place, and would therefore reduce both poverty and inequality.[432]

The static and process understandings of poverty, social exclusion, and social inclusion, relate closely to the distinction that Amartya Sen draws between 'process' freedom and 'capabilities' freedom. The latter occurs when the situation that we wish to be in is the situation that we find ourselves in. The former occurs when the process by which we reach that situation is a process of our own choosing. A Citizen's Income would provide people with a wide variety of new processes from which they could choose, and by which they could release themselves into new situations of freedom: that is, situations that they would choose.[433]

In 1987, the Citizen's Income Trust (then the Basic Income Research Group) replaced 'sufficient to meet basic living costs' with 'would help to prevent poverty' in its working definition of a Citizen's Income. This was because the earlier definition unnecessarily restricted the debate to a sizeable Citizen's Income, whereas a smaller one would offer many of the same benefits to the economy, the labour market, and society.[434] The change was made on the basis of a more static notion of poverty: a full Citizen's Income would abolish poverty, but a partial Citizen's Income, paid at a lower level, would not. If a more dynamic definition of poverty had been in view, then there would have been a richer understanding of the way in which a Citizen's Income tackles poverty. The same change in the definition would have been made, but it might have been worded rather differently: A Citizen's Income of any amount 'would contribute to the abolition of poverty'.

Would a Citizen's Income be an answer to inequality?

Income inequality has risen during the past thirty years, and the reason is that the least well off financially are doing worse than before, and

[432] Rosner, Peter G. (2003) *The economics of social policy*, Cheltenham: Edward Elgar, pp xiv–xv

[433] Sen, Amartya (2009) *The idea of justice*, London: Allen Lane, pp 225–52, 370–71. On capabilities, see also Burchardt, Tania and Vizard, Polly (2007) *Developing a capabilities list: Final recommendations of the Equalities Review Steering Group on Measurement*, CASE paper no 121, London: CASE, LSE

[434] Walter, Tony (1988) 'What are basic incomes?', *BIRG Bulletin*, no 8, Autumn, pp 3–5

the better off financially are doing better than before, the widening gap being mainly due to increased taxation at lower levels of earned income, increasing means-testing of benefits, and the bifurcation of the jobs market into high-skilled well-paid jobs and low-skilled low-paid jobs.[435] During the past fifteen years, there has been some growth in incomes among the poorer members of society, but this growth has been weaker than growth of incomes among wealthier people. Impending benefits cuts will cause the incomes of the poorest to fall from 2012 onwards.[436]

In 2009, Richard Wilkinson and Kate Pickett wrote *The spirit level*:[437] a book now rightly regarded as seminal.[438] Their message was simple: that in more unequal societies (by which they usually mean societies in which net incomes are more than usually unequal) other social ills, such as mental illness and imprisonment, are more common.

The authors are epidemiologists, and they bring to their task research tools normally applied to the study of how and why diseases spread in populations. The book is packed with useful and interesting data. It would have contained more if more had been available, but the authors found that data on wealth inequality and on educational attainment are less available for the whole range of countries that they were studying than is data on income inequality.[439] This is one reason for income inequality coming to stand for inequality in general.

Richard Layard has shown in his book *Happiness*[440] that, as GDP rises, happiness rises and then plateaus; and in their book, Wilkinson and Pickett show that the same applies to life expectancy, health, and other social indicators. But whereas *between* wealthier societies average income makes little difference to the levels of social indicators, *within* societies a very different picture emerges: 'Richer people tend, on average, to be healthier and happier than poorer people in the same society.'[441] This coheres with Runciman's finding that we compare

---

[435] Evans, Martin and Williams, Lewis (2009) *A generation of change, a lifetime of difference? Social Policy in Britain since 1979*, Bristol: Policy Press, p 313

[436] Jin, Wenchao, Joyce, Robert, Phillips, David and Sibieta, Luke (2011) *Poverty and inequality in the UK: 2011*, London: Institute for Fiscal Studies, p 2

[437] Wilkinson, Richard and Pickett, Kate (2009) *The spirit level: Why more equal societies almost always do better*, London: Allen Lane / Penguin Books

[438] Some of the material in this chapter appeared in a review article in the *Citizen's Income Newsletter* (2010) issue 1, pp 3–7

[439] Wilkinson, Richard and Pickett, Kate (2009) *The spirit level: Why more equal societies almost always do better*, London: Allen Lane / Penguin Books, p 27

[440] Layard, Richard (2006) *Happiness: Lessons from a new science*, Harmondsworth: Penguin

[441] Wilkinson, Richard and Pickett, Kate (2009) *The spirit level: Why more equal societies almost always do better*, London: Allen Lane / Penguin Books, p 13

ourselves with people 'in the same boat' as ourselves. A worker will compare their situation with that of other workers; I might compare my situation with those of other people in the same road rather than with the situation of people in the next one;[442] and we might compare our situations with those of people in the same country, rather than with the situation of people in a very different country. On the basis of a wide-ranging study of research literature on income and other inequalities, Karen Rowlingson has concluded that

> the most plausible explanation for income inequality's apparent effect on health and social problems is 'status anxiety'. This suggests that income inequality is harmful because it places people in a hierarchy that increases status competition and causes stress, which leads to poor health and other negative outcomes.[443]

Wilkinson and Pickett found that within any country levels of income inequality and levels of social and health problems correlate very closely with each other, and understandably assumed that income inequality causes a variety of other social inequalities.

There is one sense in which it hardly matters whether Wilkinson and Pickett are right or wrong about this causal link. A Citizen's Income would reduce income inequality (because households on lower net incomes would be more able to earn their way out of poverty) and this reduction would begin to tackle a more general inequality and would therefore reduce the social ills so well described in *The spirit level*.

However, there is one sense in which it does matter whether Wilkinson and Pickett are right about causality: If income inequality is the cause of other social ills, then reducing income inequality *by any available means* should begin to put things right. The available means would include an increase in means-testing. But if it is deeper social inequality that causes both income inequality and other social ills,[444] then attention needs to be paid to the deeper rifts in society and not just to the amounts of money that households receive. Means-testing divides society into the means-tested and the non-means-tested;

---

[442] Runciman, W.G. (1966) *Relative deprivation and social justice: A study of attitudes to social inequality in twentieth-century England*, London: Routledge and Kegan Paul, p 18

[443] Rowlingson, Karen (2011) *Does income inequality cause health and social Problems*, York: Joseph Rowntree Foundation, p 6

[444] See the website www.citizensincome.org for material that suggests that deeper social structures cause both income inequality and other kinds of inequality.

into those whose household structures are subject to examination by civil servants, and those whose household structures are entirely their own business; into those whose choices in the labour market are constrained by means-tested benefits regulations (including 'Tax Credits' regulations), and those whose choices in the labour market are relatively unconstrained; into those who have to report changes in personal circumstances to civil servants, and those who do not. These divisions in our society add up to a serious social rift: one that needs to be repaired if we are to experience ourselves as a single society – for only on the basis of knowing ourselves to belong together shall we begin to tackle the particular inequalities from which we suffer. Means-testing makes the rift worse. Universal benefits repair it. Therefore it matters whether it is deeper social inequality that is causing a variety of inequalities, or whether it is income inequality that is the culprit.

Wilkinson and Pickett call for a Citizen's Income.[445] They are right to do so. It would reduce net income inequality (though not by a lot), it would increase social mobility (by reducing employment disincentives), and it would push our welfare state in a more universalist direction. While in many ways a Citizen's Income would constitute a relatively small adjustment in our welfare state, its effect on labour market incentives would reduce net income inequality, and it would increase social cohesion. It is surely worth a try.

In every social policy area, changing the structure of provision will change outcomes. For instance: to remove private schools' charitable status would reduce the numbers going to them, which would bring more bright middle class children and their parents into the state system, which would improve state schooling, which would affect educational outcomes. To cease to allow voluntary aided schools to set their own admissions criteria would have a similar effect.

In the field in which we are most interested here, we therefore need policy change that will alter the *structure* of welfare provision, as this would change the ways in which the system redistributes income, which would change the national culture, which would increase social mobility, and which would therefore reduce both income and other inequalities. Changing only what might be a symptom – income inequality – could make matters worse if additional means-testing were

---

[445] Wilkinson, Richard and Pickett, Kate (2009) *The spirit level: Why more equal societies almost always do better*, London: Allen Lane / Penguin Books, p 264. This is in stark contrast to Jones, Owen (ed.) (2012) *Why inequality matters*, London: Centre for Labour and Social Studies, p 27, where reforms to the tax system are expected to reduce inequality, and the benefits system is ignored.

to be used to redistribute income: for that would increase marginal deduction rates (as more benefits would be withdrawn as earned income rose) and would thus dig people deeper into poverty. As Stuart White suggests, what is needed is a basic level of equality of resources administered in a way that does not treat some groups of people in condescending ways.[446] In this, as in all other policy areas, it is the structure that requires attention as well as the symptom. A Citizen's Income would do that.

In the end, what needs changing is the length of the 'social ladder'. The more equalities that we can introduce into our social infrastructure, and the more inequality-inducing structures we can turn into equality-inducing ones, the more the ladder will shorten, particularly for the next generation. While a Citizen's Income on its own would not complete that task, it would surely make a substantial contribution to it.

The spirit level is not just an exploratory work: it is a call to action. The authors have themselves set up a not-for-profit trust to disseminate their findings, deliver understanding of the connections that they have discovered, and promote action to reduce the inequality that they believe to be the root cause of social ills. The final part of the book is full of proposals for action: the kind of childcare that we are now seeing in the Sure Start programme; employee ownership of companies; reductions in CEO pay; and changing tax and benefits policies (– there ought to have been rather more on this because the authors themselves recognise that it is 'the most obvious way' to influence income differences).[447]

The importance of *The spirit level* is that no longer will anybody be able to say that income inequality does not matter: and, following the riots of summer 2011 in the UK, we can agree with Brian Barry that 'growing inequality means more envy, a growth of social exclusion, and a rise in antisocial subcultures'.[448] We need to take to heart the conclusion of Evans' and Williams' survey of social change during the past thirty years: 'We have lost and gained ... and we are mostly all hugely better off, but the losers and the gainers are further apart than ever. A new architecture for financial risk suggests new structures for sharing risk, and social policy must respond accordingly.'[449]

---

[446] White, Stuart (2007) *Equality*, Cambridge: Polity Press, pp 84, 93

[447] Wilkinson, Richard and Pickett, Kate (2009) *The spirit level: Why more equal societies almost always do better*, London: Allen Lane / Penguin Books, p 263

[448] Dore, Ronald (2001), 'Dignity and deprivation', pp 80–84 in Cohen, Joshua and Rogers, Joel, *What's wrong with a free lunch?*, Boston: Beacon Press, p 84

[449] Evans, Martin and Williams, Lewis (2009) *A generation of change, a lifetime of difference? Social policy in Britain since 1979*, Bristol: Policy Press, pp 315

Should we redistribute income?

Perhaps a prior question should be: *Can* we redistribute income? As Income Tax rates rise, tax revenue plateaus (because each hour of employment is now worth less, and additional free time might therefore be preferred), so there is a limit to the amount of redistribution that is possible. A limit is also imposed by the connection between inequality and social mobility. Social mobility can reduce inequality by enabling people earning less to earn more; but unfortunately, the greater the inequality in a country, the less social mobility there will be.[450] A further limit is political: Loss of income will be of interest to wealthier members of society, and wealthier members of society also tend to be more influential politically. There will therefore be political limits to the range of possible redistributions.[451] There would appear to be no self-righting tendencies within inequality, but only tendencies that exacerbate the situation: which means that redistribution of income, wealth, or opportunities, will need to be by purposeful policy change, and will rarely happen of its own accord. In this section we shall assume that we are working within a range of redistribution options which are feasible in relation to these constraints.

So far we have not answered the question as to whether or not we *should* redistribute income through tax and benefits systems. Do we do it because we share convictions about liberty, equality, fraternity, justice, or human rights? Because the poor have sufficient power to extract money from the rich? Because the social consequences of not redistributing income are too awful to contemplate? Because a religious or ethical tradition still informs our social policy? Or for all of these reasons? The differences that people experience in earning power are as much a matter of chance as of moral effort, and the same sum of money added to the net income of a poorer person is likely to increase their welfare more than that sum's loss will reduce the welfare of the wealthier person from whom it has been redistributed. We might or might not count this as a good reason for redistributing income.[452]

[450] Dorling, Danny (2012) *The no-nonsense guide to equality*, London: New Internationalist,. pp 47–8. The UK is suffering from falling social mobility: Dickens, Richard and McKnight, Abigail (2008) *Changes in earnings inequality and mobility in Great Britain 1978/9 – 2005/6*, CASE paper no 132, London: CASE, LSE

[451] Atkinson, A.B. (1995) *Public economics in action: The Basic Income / flat tax proposal*, Oxford: Clarendon Press, pp 5–11

[452] Arneson, Richard J. (2002) 'Why justice requires transfers to offset income and wealth inequalities', pp 172–200 in Paul, Ellen Frankel, Miller, Jr., Fred D., and Paul, Jeffrey, *Should differences in income and wealth matter?* Cambridge: Cambridge University Press

Any tax and benefits structure does redistribute income, and in a variety of ways. Redistribution from rich to poor or from poor to rich is 'vertical' redistribution; redistribution between differently constituted households receiving the same earned income is 'horizontal' redistribution (– it is important to evaluate reform proposals for their effects on such horizontal redistribution); and redistribution across the lifecycle is precisely that: we tend to be net recipients when we are young and when we are old, and net contributors during the years in between.[453] This chapter concentrates on vertical redistribution, which is not to say that other types are not important; and we start with a discussion of the notion of justice.

Would a Citizen's Income be an answer to injustice?[454]

John Rawls' *A theory of justice* has provided a framework for the debate in which both the overall level of happiness, and the idea that equality and liberty are self-evidently good things, are to some extent reconciled with each other.

Rawls suggests two 'principles of justice':

1. Each person is to have an equal right to the most extensive basic liberty compatible with a similar liberty for others.
2. Social and economic inequalities are to be arranged so that they are both (a) reasonably expected to be to everyone's advantage, and (b) attached to positions and offices open to all.[455]

The second principle implies that inequality is a necessary condition of society, and the first principle privileges liberty, suggesting that all that is possible is ameliorative activity rather than tackling the root causes of inequality. Norman Daniels suggests that Rawls' book became popular because it was 'a welcome return to an older tradition of substantive rather than semantic moral and political philosophy.'[456] That is only half the story. The book also became popular because it uses words like 'justice' and 'equality' while offering no real challenge

---

[453] Parker, Hermione (1989) *Instead of the dole: An enquiry into integration of the tax and benefit systems*, London: Routledge, pp 303–17

[454] A discussion of wider ethical considerations relating to a Citizen's Income will be found among the website appendices at www.citizensincome.org

[455] Rawls, John (1971) *A theory of justice,* Cambridge, Mass.: Belknap Press of Harvard University Press, p 60

[456] Daniels, Norman (1975) *Reading Rawls: Critical studies on Rawls'* A theory of justice, Oxford: Basil Blackwell, p 3

to the status quo. Its primary concern is with the freedom of the economic agent, and to this end it accepts the status quo in relation to the original distribution of wealth and income generated by the free market. Daniels notes that liberty is the only thing that is in fact to be equal, and that in general the project is individualist: 'the common good is measured in terms of a very restricted basic set of benefits to individuals: personal and political liberty, economic and social advantages, and self-respect.'[457] It is a monocultural approach, not recognising that different cultures and lifestyles will understand words like 'equality', 'liberty' and 'justice' differently. Rawls's theory is a 'liberal' theory of justice in the sense that it stems from 'a vision of society as made up of independent, autonomous units who co-operate only when the terms of co-operation are such as make it further the ends of each of the parties'.[458]

Almaz Zelleke takes a rather different approach. We are largely formed by our circumstances, and particularly by our upbringings, and in that sense we are not free: 'individuals in subsequent generations begin their lives advantaged or disadvantaged for morally arbitrary reasons of birth, not for being industrious'.[459] This is why Zelleke argues that 'in a system that generates winners and losers as part of its normal functioning, are the winners morally entitled to impose conditions like work requirements on its losers in return for income support?'[460] – and argues that a Citizen's Income is therefore a necessary policy and institution.

There is clearly no such thing as value-free freedom: rather, there are many different kinds of freedom, some of which are community freedoms that require loss of freedom on the part of individuals, some of which are individual and require a community to lose some freedom, some of which can be increased absolutely, and some of which can only be transferred from one free being to another. The market redistributes some of these freedoms, but it is far from being a perfect mechanism. As James Meade suggests: if people were

> i) equally endowed with income-earning assets, ii) if they were free to move themselves and their property without

---

[457] Daniels, Norman (1975) *Reading Rawls: Critical studies on Rawls'* A theory of justice, Oxford: Basil Blackwell, p xi

[458] Barry, Brian (1973) *The liberal theory of justice: A critical examination of the principal doctrines in* A theory of justice *by John Rawls*, Oxford: Clarendon Press, p 166

[459] Zelleke, Almaz (2005) 'Distributive justice and the argument for an unconditional basic income', *The Journal of Socioeconomics*, vol 34, no 1, pp 3–15, p 10

[460] Zelleke, Almaz (2005) 'Distributive justice and the argument for an unconditional basic income', *The Journal of Socioeconomics*, vol 34, no 1, pp 3–15, p 4

cost from any low-reward to any high-reward occupation, and iii) if everyone had the same needs and tastes, then free competition would simultaneously achieve all of the [following] five distributional objectives ... 1. the equalization of opportunity, 2. the equalization of actual income and wealth, 3. the maximization of the minimum level of consumption, 4. the equalization of enjoyment, 5. the maximization of total enjoyment.[461]

But the initial three presuppositions do not hold. Families transfer endowments of various kinds between generations, thus perpetuating a situation in which the market fails to redistribute opportunities. This is why the government redistributes some of them, and some of them we voluntarily redistribute:

[Market or government] redistribution does not preempt or replace ... voluntary exchanges. Rather it adjusts the structure of freedoms and unfreedoms from which people enter into voluntary exchanges. Thus the relevant comparison is not between voluntary exchanges and coercive transfers, but between the distribution of freedoms and unfreedoms with and without redistribution. (Peter Jones)[462]

The redistribution of income is always a redistribution of freedoms, and not necessarily in the same direction. If the redistribution is paternalistic then someone's freedom has been reduced: a consequence of numerous government-imposed redistributions. So to increase a freedom might be to reduce the level of justice in society, and to decrease a freedom might create a more just society. This means that to redistribute income might be to increase justice or to reduce it.

Do we *want* to reduce inequality?

For a further way of understanding the necessity to redistribute income, we can turn to Paul Spicker's general theory of welfare states. At a bare minimum, 'each person needs to be protected against eventualities'.

---

[461] Meade, J.E. (1976) *The just economy*, London: George Allen & Unwin, pp 142, 141

[462] Jones, Peter (1982) 'Freedom and the redistribution of resources', *Journal of Social Policy*, vol 11, no 2, pp 217–38, p 229

Greater coverage of the population reduces the number of people not protected against eventualities, so progressive universalisation occurs. 'As long as the marginal risk is not negligible, the argument for extending coverage continues to apply ... This means that although social protection may not be truly comprehensive, it will grow to be as comprehensive as possible in particular circumstances.'[463] There will always of course be pressures in the opposite direction, but as an argument for progressive universalisation of coverage it is difficult to fault this one.

We have discussed arguments for reducing inequality, and we have recognised a significant level of inequality in the UK: but will we ever *want* to do anything about it? The signs are that we will not. The abolition of inequality has never been an aim of our social security system. Means-tested benefits are intended to relieve poverty, and the effect of their earnings rules has *prevented* them from creating greater equality. Social insurance equalises income over the lifecycle to some extent (for instance, by providing state pensions), and between times of employment and times of unemployment and sickness: but it was never intended to minimise inequality between one person and another.

The reason that income maintenance mechanisms have not created greater equality is that the majority of people do not want them to. Many of us are content with market inequalities, and provided people are not starving, and we ourselves are protected from ill fortune, many of us are generally quite content to allow substantial inequality to persist. We only object when its levels are obscene and appear to be the result of redistribution from ourselves to the wealthy (– hence the recent fuss over bonuses for bankers). As Vic George and Paul Wilding summarise the political realities: 'In the last analysis, egalitarian policies will only succeed if they are desired and supported by the general public. Without such public support egalitarian governments have to resort to excessive authoritarianism that can destroy the very notion of true equality that it hopes to achieve.'[464] R.H. Tawney recognised that public opinion was unlikely to support equality of income, even though 'those who dread a dead-level of income or wealth, which is not at the moment a very pressing danger in England, do not dread, it seems, a dead-level of law and order, and of security for life and property.'[465] Tawney believed that it was worth working towards greater

---

[463] Spicker, Paul (2000) *The welfare state: A general theory*, London: Sage, pp 96–7

[464] George, Vic and Wilding, Paul (1984) *The impact of social policy*, London: Routledge and Kegan Paul, p 117

[465] Tawney, R.H. (1964) *Equality*, 5th edn, London: George Allen & Unwin (first published 1931) p 86

equality of opportunity in the hope that greater equality would be the result,[466] perhaps recognising that there will always be more people who do not want greater equality than people who do; and that many of the people with power will be among those who want to see just enough equality to head off social unrest, but no more than that. All of this means that those who wish to pursue equality are doomed to pursue it by policies for which they have to argue on other grounds.

So how come redistribution has sometimes occurred? Immediately after the Second World War 'reconstruction' was the mood, and it was possible to create a structure that redistributed income. Such circumstances as war are mercifully rare in Europe now.

So where might we find foundations for a policy of redistribution? After all, we *do* shift a lot of money from taxation to social security benefits. On what basis? Is it because there is something deeper underlying it all, such as a religious tradition that has still not had all of its teeth drawn by the secularisation process? Or an ethical sense stemming from such a tradition? Or is our desire to prevent the most embarrassing poverty, and to contain social risk, a sufficient explanation for the transfers that take place?

An important question is how long any of these partial foundations for redistribution are likely to maintain popular appeal in a globalising world suffering from increasing numbers of financial crises. Inequality is rising, and, if the shaky foundations under a minimal consensus about redistribution give way, then we can look forward to accelerating inequality, greater absolute and relative poverty, untapped human potential, and multiple deprivations affecting more families, more children, and therefore more future adults. We need a new – or at least a rediscovered – foundation for income redistribution, and perhaps in this secular age the autonomous ethic suggested by Marshall will have to provide for this:

> Welfare decisions ... are essentially altruistic, and they must draw on standards of value embodied in an autonomous ethical system that, though an intrinsic part of the contemporary civilization, is not the product either of the summation of individual preferences (as in a market) or of a hypothetical majority vote. It is impossible to say how these ethical standards arise in a society or are recognised by its members. Total consensus with regard to them is

---

[466] Tawney, R.H. (1964) *Equality*, 5th edn, London: George Allen & Unwin (first published 1931) p 42

unthinkable outside a devout religious community, but without a foundation of near-consensus, no general social welfare policy would be possible.[467]

We now live in a plural society, so it is not easy to see how such a foundation is to be rebuilt once the old one has started to crumble and the house is still built on top of it. David Collard's attempt to establish a theory of economics on the basis of altruism is a brave one,[468] and one based on a natural human inclination to cooperate and to be generous: but these tendencies are nothing like strong enough to combat individuals' and nations' inclinations to compete in a world in which the winners are wealthy and the losers are increasingly left behind. Within communities, people will continue to cooperate, but I see little hope that the wealthy and the poor will cooperate across our society when the income differences between them are great and growing.

We shall only be able to maintain policies that redistribute income if those policies can be shown to improve the efficiency of a market economy, to relieve poverty, and to redistribute resources across the lifecycle. If they improve equality, liberty and justice (however defined) then that will be a bonus: but this will not be the reason for the acceptability of such policies. As Philippe Van Parijs puts it, a Citizen's Income would 'both boost the national product and distribute resources in a more egalitarian way,'[469] and it is that combination that is perhaps the idea's greatest virtue.

If we want more egalitarian policies then we shall need to choose the ones that will make markets more efficient, and we shall need to argue for them on the basis of market-related aims. We shall need to choose policies that take seriously everyone's wish to be treated as an individual – which is why individual taxation is more popular than joint taxation; and we shall need to advocate policies that treat all of us the same, as the criminal law and the National Health Service do, and then argue for policies on the basis that we expect equal treatment in many areas of our lives and ought to expect it in others.[470]

---

[467] Marshall, T.H. (1981) *The right to welfare and other essays*, London: Heinemann, p 109

[468] Collard, David (1978) *Altruism and economy: A study in non-selfish economics*, Oxford: Martin Robertson

[469] Van Parijs, Philippe (1992) 'The second marriage of justice and efficiency', pp 215–240 in Van Parijs, Philippe (ed.) *Arguing for Basic Income: Ethical foundations for a radical reform*, London: Verso, p 227

[470] Horton, Tim and Gregory, James (2009) *The solidarity society: Why we can afford to end poverty, and how to do it with public support*, London: Fabian Society

As we have seen, it is not possible to argue for means-tested benefits on these bases, but it is possible to argue for Child Benefit, a Citizen's Income, or any other universal benefit on grounds such as these. A Citizen's Income would make the labour market more efficient, it would encourage engagement with the labour market, it would encourage own-account economic activity, it would reduce family break-up, it would encourage training and education, it would improve our freedoms, it would increase social mobility, it would be demonstrably just, it would treat us all the same, it would be based on the individual – and, depending on the precise parameters of the scheme, it would redistribute from rich to poor and thus create additional demand in the national economy. Parker and Sutherland have shown that child tax allowances would redistribute towards the rich, that to raise Child Benefit would redistribute towards the poor, and that to introduce a Citizen's Income would also redistribute towards the poor;[471] and they conclude that a small Citizen's Income would redistribute from rich to poor in such a way that poorer families would gain significant amounts and wealthier families would lose insignificant amounts. This would

> move net incomes in the directions necessary to reduce dependence on means-tested and work-tested benefits by low-income families (including young single people), thereby setting them freer (though not yet free) to take whatever work or training was available, without fear of prosecution and without affecting the tax or benefit situation of spouses or partners.[472]

Simply in terms of immediate economic efficiency, microsimulation research in the United States has shown that a Citizen's Income 'is not necessarily a less efficient way of accomplishing redistributive goals and that it could well be more efficient.'[473] As Andrew Harrop has shown on the basis of research conducted in a range of countries, the more targeted the social security system (in terms of means-testing), the less

---

[471] Parker, Hermione and Sutherland, Holly (undated) 'Child tax allowances?', London: STICERD / LSE; Parker, Hermione and Sutherland, Holly (1991) 'Child benefit, child tax allowances and basic incomes: A comparative study', *BIRG Bulletin*, no 13, August, pp 6–13

[472] Parker, Hermione and Sutherland, Holly (1994) 'Basic Income 1994: redistributive effects of transitional BIs', *Citizen's Income Bulletin*, no 18, July, pp 3–8, p 8

[473] Bryan, James B. (2005) 'Targeted programs v. the basic income guarantee: an examination of the efficiency costs of different forms of redistribution', *The Journal of Socioeconomics*, vol 34, no 1, pp 39–47, p 39

money is redistributed to the poor. This is probably because the level of means-tested schemes provided for the poorest is of little interest to most of the population. Because it is in the interest of the majority to pay less in Income Tax, the level at which benefits are paid drops, and the scheme becomes even more residual in nature and therefore becomes of even less interest to the majority. A universal scheme, on the other hand, provides money for everyone, everyone is interested in its value,[474] and it is more likely to retain its value.

Maybe we should put the question the other way around: Is there any reason for *not* redistributing income? If the response is given: 'because greater income inequality damages economic growth', then we can refute that charge, on the basis of empirical findings that 'income equality does not harm economic growth',[475] on the basis that the evidence base for concluding that income inequality drives economic growth is weak,[476] and on the logical basis that people with lower net incomes spend higher proportions of their incomes on consumption of local goods and services than do people with higher net incomes.

'Universal Credit' will redistribute more from rich to poor than the current means-tested system does.[477] It should therefore be no problem that a Citizen's Income would do the same.

Redistributing the ability to raise one's net income

The decision as to whether we should or should not redistribute income has to be a political one: but just as we have already asked whether 'poverty' should be discussed in static or in dynamic terms, so now we surely need to ask whether it might be more important to redistribute the opportunity to increase one's income than it is to redistribute income.

As we have discovered, numerous households find it difficult to increase their net incomes, not because they are lazy or because they do not wish to do so, but because the UK's benefits system (including 'Tax Credits') makes it very difficult to do so. Marginal deduction rates of over 90 per cent are not unusual, and marginal deduction rates of

---

[474] Harrop, Andrew (2012) *The coalition and universalism*, London: Fabian Society, p 9

[475] Pressman, Steven (2005) 'Income guarantee and the equity-efficiency tradeoff', *The Journal of Socioeconomics*, vol 34, no 1, pp 83–100, p 97

[476] Rowlingson, Karen (2011) *Does income inequality cause health and social problems?*, York: Joseph Rowntree Foundation, pp 35–6

[477] Brewer, Mike, Browne, James and Jin, Wenchao (2011) *Universal Credit: A preliminary analysis*, Institute for Fiscal Studies Briefing Note no 116, London: Institute for Fiscal Studies, pp 67–68, www.ifs.org.uk/bns/bn116.pdf

85 per cent are common. When 'Universal Credit' is implemented, marginal deduction rates should fall to 76 per cent, but this still means that for every additional £1 earned, the individual receives only 24p. For someone earning £25,000 per annum, Income Tax is paid at 20 per cent and National Insurance Contribution at 12 per cent, so, if they are not on 'Working Tax Credit', and don't have children, their marginal deduction rate is 32 per cent and for every additional £1 earned they keep 68p. Among the highest earners, Income Tax is paid at 45 per cent and National Insurance Contributions at 1 per cent, so for every additional £1 earned, the individual keeps 54p. For someone earning £40,000 per annum, Income Tax is paid at 40 per cent and National Insurance Contributions at 12 per cent, so for every additional £1 earned, they keep 48p. Strangely, if you are earning £100,000 per annum, because Income Tax is at 40 per cent and National Insurance Contribution at 1 per cent, you can keep 59p for every additional £1 you earn.[478] Median gross earnings in 2010 were £25,000.[479] Some people above median earnings will be receiving 'Child Tax Credit', Housing Benefit, and Council Tax Benefit, so their marginal deduction rates will be higher, but everyone else above median earnings – including everyone in the highest one tenth of earners – will be keeping at least 48p of every additional £1 earned. Yet there are people in the lowest one tenth of earners keeping a good deal less than half of this, and this situation will not change when 'Universal Credit' is implemented.

This is surely unacceptable. We might wish to discuss whether or not someone should be earning a great deal more than someone else, and we might wish to discuss whether the tax system should redistribute income by imposing higher tax rates on higher earners: but for the government to be taking away from many of the lowest earners more than three quarters of additional earnings, but only half of the additional earnings of the highest earners, has got to be wrong.

On the 7 September 2011, twenty economists wrote to the *Financial Times* to say that the 50 per cent tax rate should be abolished because it inhibited growth.[480] There was no suggestion that the marginal deduction rates suffered by low earners might be damaging growth,

---

[478] www.hmrc.gov.uk

[479] Chamberlin, Graeme (ed.) *Economic and labour market review*, vol 5, no 3, London: ONS, p 14

[480] 'Coalition must ditch 50p tax rate for growth', letter, *Financial Times*, 7 September 2011: www.ft.com/cms/s/0/d92b0bc4-d7e9-11e0-a5d9-00144feabdc0.html#axzz1cje51OoH

but surely they do. As we have seen, there is little incentive for people on low or no earnings to improve their skills, or to seek additional or more lucrative employment.

It is equally unacceptable that the lowest earners, and those on no earnings, experience far higher costs than higher earners when they interact with the tax and benefits structure. The smallest change in circumstances (it might be an increase in the weekly amount charged by a childminder) can cost hours in administrative hassle, particularly if 'Tax Credits' or Housing Benefit staff make a mistake (– I am not here blaming the staff for making mistakes: it is the system that they are working with that is the problem. Civil servants do an amazing job getting right as many claims as they do).

It really is time for some redistribution, and particularly of the ability to increase one's net income. The administrative burden imposed on low earners and on people not able to earn an income needs to be reduced, and the amounts extracted by the government from people on low or no earnings needs to come down, so that high earners, low earners, and those earning nothing, can experience equal administrative burdens and equal deduction rates. If that were to happen, then unequal earned incomes would be less of a problem, and unequal net incomes would be less of a problem, because it would be easier for people with no or low earnings to increase their net incomes. We might then begin to worry less about income inequality, because far more people would have the ability to earn their way out of poverty, and would thus have the ability to reduce inequality by themselves without anyone else needing to do it for them.

Multiple redistributions

So we need to reduce poverty, understood in dynamic rather than in static terms, and we need to equalise marginal deduction rates and reduce claimant administrative costs, so as to enable people to create their own ways out of poverty. A Citizen's Income, of whatever size, would reduce marginal deduction rates for anyone on means-tested benefits or 'Tax Credits', and for those able to escape from means-testing it would reduce their administrative burdens.

Depending on the precise Citizen's Income scheme, we might of course see some immediate redistribution of income:[481] preferably

---

[481] See the website www.citizensincome.org for an example of a revenue neutral Citizen's Income scheme that redistributes in such a way that the ten per cent of the population with the highest earnings lose 4 per cent of their net income and the ten per cent of the population with the lowest earnings gain 25 per cent.

with the lowest earners gaining net income, and the highest earners losing not too large amounts (say below 5 per cent for the highest ten per cent of earners).

It thus appears that we can achieve *multiple* redistributions: of net income, of the ability to increase one's earned income, and of administrative burden, and all without imposing too much pain on high earning households. This *has* to be good for low-earning households, it has to be good for society, and it has to be good for the economy.

Implementation of new redistributive policies

One question still to be answered is whether implementation of new redistributive policies is a practical possibility. Because ongoing household expenditure, whether on a basic weekly shopping basket or on fee-paying schools, is constructed around existing household income, any policy change designed to redistribute income will only be implemented with universal approval if no individual household will suffer an immediate reduction in disposable income. Where a policy change is generally desirable, but would cause a definable group to lose net income, transitional arrangements are possible: but then any greater simplification that the new policy is designed to deliver is likely to be lost.[482] Alternatively, a scheme can always be designed to ensure that no household loses money, but then there will be a net cost to the scheme as a whole, and in straitened financial times that might mean non-implementation.

There are two possibilities:

1. The new scheme could be implemented gradually, thus ensuring that no household could suffer an appreciable loss in net income. For instance, a Citizen's Income could be implemented at a very low level, and tax allowances, means-tested benefits and most National Insurance benefits reduced accordingly. The Citizen's Income could then be raised in each subsequent year, and tax allowances and benefits reduced each year.[483] Changes to household net income would therefore be gradual, and the Citizen's Income's social,

---

[482] Atkinson, A.B. (1984) *Review of the UK social security system: Evidence to the National Consumer Council*, Tax, Incentives and the Distribution of Income paper no 66, London: LSE, p 32

[483] Dickens, James and Vince, Philip (1997) *How Citizen's Income could become a practical reality: A Citizen's Income Position Paper*, London: Citizen's Income Trust. This detailed paper shows how in 1997 a small transitional Citizen's Income could have evolved into a larger Citizen's Income over ten years.

economic and labour market benefits would be experienced as an evolutionary process.

2. A Citizen's Income could be implemented one age cohort at a time, possibly even for individual year cohorts. While there would be a cost to ensuring that no household would suffer an immediate net income loss, the cost would be manageable within each individual year. The problem with this approach would be complexity, because households are composed of individuals of different ages, so implementing the change would be complex, and calculating the effects on different households would be complex.

But perhaps there is a third possibility. While for many changes in tax and benefits legislation or regulations there is not much that a household can do to ameliorate any consequent drop in net income, this might not be the case in relation to the implementation of a Citizen's Income. Because a Citizen's Income of any size would have an immediate effect on overall benefit withdrawal rates, increasing one's engagement with the labour market would have more of an immediate effect on household net income. This means that even if a household were to experience a loss of net income the day after the implementation of a Citizen's Income because of the ways in which the current tax and benefits systems relate to the household's particular circumstances, they would be able to take action to repair the loss, and would know that action taken would be more likely to have the desired effect than it would have done before the implementation of a Citizen's Income. A particularly significant effect of a Citizen's Income relates to the labour market decisions available to the unemployed spouse of an employee.[484] At the moment, it is difficult to predict whether the spouse's labour market participation will increase the household's net income, particularly if there were costs related to seeking and accepting employment. A Citizen's Income could only improve the spouse's incentive to participate in the labour market, or, if already participating, to seek greater participation.

This is a unique characteristic of universal benefits: An increase in the proportion of universal benefits in a household's total income package will always offer an increased ability to add to net income through additional earnings. It is this characteristic that means that implementing a Citizen's Income is always a practical proposition even if some households might suffer a small immediate loss in disposable income.

---

[484] Atkinson, A.B. (1984) *Review of the UK Social security system: Evidence to the National Consumer Council*, Tax, Incentives and the Distribution of Income paper no 66, London: LSE, p 33

CHAPTER 12

Who should receive a Citizen's Income?[485]

A 'Citizen's Income' is an unconditional, non-withdrawable income for every citizen: but who is a 'citizen'? – and what does it mean to be a 'citizen'? This matters, because, as Tony Fitzpatrick has pointed out, 'the ideological debate concerning [Citizen's Income] is, at its heart, a debate about citizenship'.[486]

A 'citizen' is 'a member of a state,'[487] but 'citizenship' can also have a broader meaning in terms of our membership of a variety of communities.[488] Some countries' residents are formally citizens but have few rights, and it must be asked whether they really are citizens at all. In most of the UK we are formally subjects of the monarch rather than members of a state, but a variety of rights and duties have evolved that constitute a degree of citizenship.[489] In addition, we now experience elements of both global citizenship and regional citizenship, as in the European Union.

The history of the citizenship debate in the UK

The terms of the modern debate on citizenship were set by T.H. Marshall when he formulated his three stages of civil, political and social rights: legal rights relating to contracts, followed by rights to participate in a representative democracy, in turn followed by rights to the benefits of a welfare state:

> By the social element I mean the whole range from the right to a modicum of economic welfare and security to the right to share to the full in the social heritage and to

---

[485] Much of the content of this chapter is drawn from the report of a working party, 'Citizenship and a Citizen's Income', *Citizen's Income Newsletter* (2003) issue 3, pp 3–10.
[486] Fitzpatrick, Tony (1999) *Freedom and security: An introduction to the Basic Income debate*, Basingstoke: Macmillan, p 15
[487] *Chambers twentieth century dictionary*
[488] Dwyer, Peter (2004) *Understanding social citizenship*, Bristol: Policy Press, p 17
[489] Oliver, Dawn and Heater, Derek (1994) *The foundations of citizenship*, New York: Harvester Wheatsheaf, p 5

live the life of a civilized being according to the standards prevailing in the society.[490]

Thus the National Health Service is

a general enrichment of the concrete substance of civilized life, a general reduction of risk and insecurity, an equalization between the more and the less fortunate at all levels – between the healthy and the sick, the employed and the unemployed, the old and the active.[491]

A rather different picture emerges in Martin Golding's discussion of the history of rights. He points out that the oldest known discussions of rights in Roman legal texts are about concrete property rights, suggesting that welfare rights, broadly defined, came first. He also finds them to be primary theoretically:

If there are any rights at all, there are welfare rights ... I see no reason whatsoever for respecting liberty as such, or for conceding option rights as such [i.e., the right to dispose of one's property as one wishes, which relies on a right to own property], as something separate from an individual's personal good ... The primary notion that underlies any theory of rights is that of welfare.[492]

Whatever the historical or theoretical process, the establishment and maintenance of rights is always a conflict-driven process, and it is by no means an irreversible one. Similarly complex is the citizenship that has emerged from the process: it is a many-layered reality involving the many different communities to which we all belong: local, sectional, economic, national, European, and global.[493] Citizenship is therefore a reality experienced differently by every individual.[494] While it is undoubtedly true that each person's citizenship is a web of rights and duties in relation to the different communities to which they belong,

---

[490] Marshall, T.H. (1950) *Citizenship and social class and other essays,* Cambridge: Cambridge University Press, pp 10–11

[491] Marshall, T.H. (1950) *Citizenship and social class and other Essays,* Cambridge: Cambridge University Press, p 56

[492] Golding, Martin p (1972) 'The primacy of welfare rights', *Social Philosophy and Policy,* vol 1, no 2, pp 19–136, pp 135–6

[493] Held, David (1984) *Political theory and the modern state,* Cambridge: Polity Press, p 203

[494] Lewis, Gail (2004) *Citizenship: Personal lives and social policy,* Bristol: Policy Press

the civil, political and social rights relating to a nation state still remain the bedrock of other citizenship rights and duties. It is therefore nation state citizenship on which we shall concentrate: a citizenship that 'refers to a status enjoyed by all full members of a ...... nation state,' a status that combines elements of universality, equality, and participation.[495]

The reversibility of citizenship's evolution has been amply demonstrated recently by both ideological and structural challenges to the welfare state. The New Right's fear of dependency, and an economy in which increased investment frequently means a drop in employment, have between them made rights to welfare and employment problematic. Maurice Roche sees the combined effects of contemporary changes as a rolling back of social citizenship[496] (Marshall's third category) and the new economic situation that we are in as a challenge to completely reinvent social citizenship.[497]

So the history of citizenship in the UK during the past two centuries has been one of increasing civil, political and social rights, and subsequently of the decline of some of those rights, and particularly of the social rights that constituted the welfare state and the full employment policies of the post-war political consensus.

Citizenship economic rights

T.H. Marshall's summary ignores any concept of economic rights: that is, rights to economic resources by virtue of one's citizenship. This is an important omission, for, without a certain amount of income, it is impossible to exercise rights and duties. If van Gunsteren is correct in saying that 'effective citizenship does not only require a political say and a legally protected status, but also a certain level of

---

[495] Purdy, David (1990) 'Citizenship, Basic Income and democracy', in *BIRG Bulletin*, no 10, Autumn/Winter, p 9

[496] Roche, Maurice (1992) *Rethinking citizenship: Welfare ideology and change in modern society*, Cambridge: Polity Press, pp 4, 16, 167. See also Jordan, Bill, Redley, Marcus and James, Simon (1994) *Putting the family first: Identity. decisions, citizenship*, London: UCL Press, p 205: a conclusion (based on interviews) that 'there is ample evidence that respondents were aware of the changes from a social democratic polity, in which social rights to universalistic services formed one of the main elements of common membership, to a different kind of order, where families were required to provide more for their own from their private resources.'

[497] See Coote, Anna (1996) 'Social rights and responsibilities', *Soundings*, issue 2, Spring, pp 203–12, for a contemporary discussion of the necessity of social rights if we are to exercise civil and political rights.

socioeconomic security,'[498] and if Melden is right to suggest that if certain material conditions are not met then other rights are 'empty moral possessions',[499] then the welfare state's guarantee of a minimum income is the foundation of civil, political and social rights, even though the history and current reasons for our complex system of benefits is not explicitly about either the prevention of poverty or the foundation of citizenship rights.[500] However, Fred Twine suggests that because citizenship is about the relationship between individuals and institutions, the stigma attached to means-testing means that 'a means-tested benefit cannot provide a social right of citizenship because it threatens the integrity of the self.'[501] Means-tested benefits (including 'Tax Credits') divide people off from those citizens who earn an income, or who otherwise receive an income without claiming benefits that involve the state intruding into their relationships or their daily activities. This means that if economic rights are indeed a prerequisite of civil, political and social citizenship rights, then a positive right to resources must be established that does not rely on a process that excludes people from a sense of citizenship.

The Commission on Citizenship, which reported in 1990, recommended

> that a floor of adequate social entitlements should be maintained, monitored and improved when possible by central government, with the aim of enabling every citizen to live the life of a civilised human being according to the standards prevailing in society.[502]

Two major criteria for the provision of such social rights are administrative simplicity and a lack of stigma.[503] In the income

---

[498] van Gunsteren, H. (1978) 'Notes on a theory of citizenship', pp 9–35 in Birnbaum, P, Lively, J. and Parry, G. (eds) (1978) *Democracy, consensus and social contract*, Beverly Hills: Sage

[499] Melden, A.I. (1981) 'Are there welfare rights?' pp 259–78 in Brown, Peter G., Johnson, Conrad and Vernier, Paul (eds) *Income support: Conceptual and policy issues*, New Jersey: Rowman and Littlefield, p 276

[500] Barry, Brian (1990) 'The welfare state versus the relief of poverty', *Ethics*, vol 100, no 3, pp 503–29

[501] Twine, Fred (1994) *Citizenship and social rights: The interdependence of self and society*, Beverly Hills: Sage, p 97

[502] The Speaker's Commission on Citizenship (1990) *Encouraging citizenship*, London: Stationery Office, p xix

[503] The Speaker's Commission on Citizenship (1990) *Encouraging citizenship*, London: Stationery Office, p 21

maintenance field, current legislation leaves much to be desired in these respects, for means-tested benefits are far from simple in their administration, and they are also highly intrusive, thus delivering plenty of opportunity for social stigma.

Citizenship duties

A welfare right in the absence of anyone having an obligation to provide for someone's needs is meaningless, so the 'human right to welfare [implies] a duty to support government welfare measures' (Raymond Plant),[504] and the welfare state is therefore a system of duties (to honour contracts, to vote in elections, and to contribute taxation according to one's means) as well as a system of rights.[505] Duties formalized in the seventeenth century Poor Law, and still enshrined in National Insurance and means-tested benefits legislation, are the obligation to seek employment, and the obligation to take employment if it is offered. In the period of reconstruction and full employment following the Second World War this obligation made sense, but now that technological and employment market change is as rapid as it is, much employment is short-term, new investment often results in a *loss* of employment, and the health of the employment market does not directly correlate with a country's economic performance.[506] The duty to work is now problematic, for how can there be a duty to work when for many people there is no opportunity, and when often what is available is part-time employment and what is required to lift a family off means-tested benefits is well paid full-time employment?[507] High marginal deduction rates extract from the worker a high proportion of any additional income earned, compromising the obligation to work for an income.

In this new situation, should we alter the definition of 'work' to mean 'beneficial activity', so that it covers paid and unpaid work, and

---

[504] Plant, Raymond (1988) 'Needs, agency, and welfare rights', pp 55–74 in Moon, T. Donald, (ed.) *Rights and welfare: The theory of the welfare state*, Boulder, Connecticut: Westview Press, p 73

[505] See Culpit, Ian (1992) *Welfare and citizenship: Beyond the crisis of the welfare state,* Beverly Hills: Sage, on the New Right's attack on both the rights and the duties of the welfare state.

[506] Sherman, Barrie and Jenkins, Phil (1995) *Licensed to work*, London: Cassell, p 57; Standing, Guy (2009) *Work after globalization: Building occupational citizenship,* Cheltenham: Edward Elgar

[507] Chandra, Pasma (2010) 'Working through the work disincentive', *Basic Income Studies*, vol 5, no 2, pp 1–20, pp 7–9

particularly caring work in the family and in the community? It is always easier to change one's attitudes when financially and socially secure, and many of those most in need of being able to re-evaluate their own unpaid work are those who take their obligations to their families seriously and yet have the least secure incomes. For them, financial security is both more of a necessity and more difficult to achieve.[508] Citizenship entails obligations, but those obligations must be amenable to being met. If an obligation to be gainfully employed is no longer amenable to being met for a growing proportion of the population, then the obligation needs to be reframed as a broader obligation to contribute to society by paid work, by unpaid work in the community, or by unpaid work caring for others.

Stuart White suggests that

> where institutions governing economic life are otherwise sufficiently just, e.g., in terms of the availability of opportunities for productive participation and the rewards attached to these opportunities, then those who claim the generous share of the social product available to them under these institutions have an obligation to make a decent productive contribution, suitably proportional and fitting for ability and circumstances, to the community in return. I term this the fair-dues conception of reciprocity.[509]

White's arguments for requiring such reciprocity are that self-esteem is a good thing, and that self-esteem depends on reciprocity in social arrangements. Non-reciprocation burdens other people, which is a bad thing, because to expect not to reciprocate is a statement of superiority, to expect others not to reciprocate is a statement of servility, and (– a more instrumental argument) a welfare state is more likely to remain politically acceptable if it is founded on reciprocity. Citizenship obligations can be met through paid labour, care work, and voluntary community activity, all of which is 'civic labour'; and it is through such civic labour that the resources are found to create the 'civic minimum'

---

[508] Sherman, Barrie and Jenkins, Phil (1995) *Licensed to work*, London: Cassell, London, pp 156–7

[509] White, Stuart (2003) *The civic minimum: On the rights and obligations of economic citizenship*, Oxford: Oxford University Press, pp 59

of income and healthcare that is the right of every citizen, and is even more of a necessity in the face of growing 'market vulnerability'.[510]

'In a context of otherwise sufficiently fair economic arrangements, everyone should do their bit': but the corollary of this is that if economic arrangements are *not* otherwise fair, then not only is it difficult for a society to sustain citizens' rights, but it is equally difficult to sustain citizenship duties. In the context of an adequate civic minimum, *and* in a context in which obligations apply equally to all – including the asset rich – a work test 'can be defended as a necessary device for protecting citizens against the unfair resource claims of those who are unwilling to meet the contributive obligations they have to the community':[511] but it is questionable whether in the UK we do experience an adequate civic minimum, it is questionable whether society holds the idle rich to any obligations at all, and it is in general questionable whether a context in which we can demand reciprocity exists when there is unequal access to employment opportunities, when it is difficult to determine what a fair distribution of employment opportunities might look like, and when we have no access to someone else's relative willingness to expend effort.[512]

As White suggests, 'some resources are properly seen as belonging to a common citizens' inheritance fund, and it is implausible that the individual's entitlement to a share of this fund is entirely dependent on a willingness to work.'[513] A share of the income that someone in

---

[510] White, Stuart (2003) *The civic minimum: On the rights and obligations of economic citizenship*, Oxford: Oxford University Press, pp 99, 131, 132. Daniel Shapiro develops a similar argument: If choice and responsibility are important elements in any ideology, and particularly in an egalitarian one, then a coercive redistribution of income compromises the choice available to someone from whom redistribution is made: Shapiro, Daniel (2002) 'Egalitarianism and welfare-state redistribution', pp 1–35 in Paul, Ellen Franklin, Miller, Jr., Fred D. and Paul, Jeffrey, *Should differences in income and wealth matter?* Cambridge: Cambridge University Press, p 35. This argument only holds water if opportunities to earn income are equally shared, which they are not.

[511] White, Stuart (2003) *The civic minimum: On the rights and obligations of economic citizenship*, Oxford: Oxford University Press, pp 18, 152

[512] De Wispelaere, Jürgen (undated) *Universal basic income: Reciprocity and the right to non-exclusion*, London: Citizen's Income Trust. Cf Phelps, Edmund S. (2001) 'Subsidize Wages', pp 51–59 in Cohen, Joshua and Rogers, Joel, *What's wrong with a free lunch?* Boston: Beacon Press. Phelps suggests that it might be just to share out a social surplus, but only to those who contribute to creating it through employment. This position fails to recognise the many ways in which unpaid activity contributes to the social surplus. Phelps' alternative to a Citizen's Income is wage subsidy, which would unfortunately make the labour and other markets even less efficient than they are now.

[513] White, Stuart (2006) 'Reconsidering the exploitation objection to basic income', *Basic Income Studies*, vol 1, no 2, pp 1–24, p 13

employment earns comes from resources that belong to all of us, so it is not exploitative to tax earnings in order to fund a Citizen's Income;[514] a Citizen's Income calculated on this basis would at least establish one of the necessary bases for just reciprocity because it would provide a secure income floor: an income as of right, establishing a reciprocal obligation;[515] and, because a Citizen's Income would make it easier for someone to refuse demeaning or poorly paid employment, and would therefore improve the employment opportunities on offer, it would provide 'opportunity for self-realisation in work': one of the conditions for just reciprocity.[516] White therefore argues for a Citizen's Income of a larger amount than that warranted by the 'common citizens' inheritance fund' on the grounds that

> 1. Even if basic income is bad for reciprocity, this is outweighed by its positive effects on other concerns of fairness, such as the prevention of market vulnerability.
> 2. Even if basic income is bad for reciprocity in one way, it is also likely to have positive effects in terms of this same value.[517]

We might therefore be able to reframe a familiar discussion: Is it the welfare state's role to seek to change people's behaviour by applying conditions to the receipt of welfare benefits? Politicians, social scientists, philosophers and others have offered a wide spectrum of answers to this question:[518] but their answers are generally ideologically driven and based on the assumption that the link between behaviour change and the receipt of benefits is constituted by regulations requiring that conditions should be met before benefits can be received. A redistributive system based on a Citizen's Income would pose the

---

[514] Birnbaum, Simon (2012), *Basic Income reconsidered: Social justice, liberalism, and the demands of equality*, New York: Palgrave Macmillan, pp 89–116. On pp 117–41 Birnbaum treats jobs as gifts and therefore the income derived from them as legitimately taxable because it is gained from gifts that belong to all of us.

[515] White, Stuart (2003) *The civic minimum: On the rights and obligations of economic citizenship*, Oxford: Oxford University Press, pp 155–62

[516] White, Stuart (2003) *The civic minimum: On the rights and obligations of economic citizenship*, Oxford: Oxford University Press, pp 166–8. Cf. Birnbaum, Simon (2008) *Rawlsian liberalism and the politics of Basic Income*, Stockholm Studies in Politics 122, Stockholm: Stockholm University

[517] White, Stuart (2006) 'Reconsidering the exploitation objection to basic income', *Basic Income Studies*, vol 1, no 2, pp 1–24, p 14

[518] Deacon, Alan (2002) *Perspectives on welfare: Ideas, ideologies and policy debates*, Maidenhead: Open University Press / McGraw-Hill, pp 118–34

question differently: Given a universal benefit, will people's behaviour change, and, if so, how? Here the answers will stem from empirical study rather than from ideological commitments, though how a philosopher would view the situation would still of course depend on their viewpoint. Philippe Van Parijs recommends a Citizen's Income on the basis of the 'real freedom' that it would offer, including the freedom to spend one's days surfing:[519] 'real freedom' because a Citizen's Income would offer not only the theoretical right to choose one's way of life, but also the financial security to turn the right into reality.[520] White would prefer to see a bit more reciprocity in the situation – though he is still happy to recommend a Citizen's Income, because while free riding is against the idea of just reciprocity, a small number of people not fulfilling their obligations would be a small price to pay for a secure income floor that would establish one of the main criteria for a *just* reciprocity.[521]

Today's layered citizenship

So who is a citizen? That is, who are the people to whom we grant rights and from whom we expect the fulfilment of duties? There are some things that do *not* constitute the boundary between citizens and non-citizens of the UK: for instance, not all British passport holders have a right to reside here; and in relation to those provisions that do determine the boundary (the Nationality Act, the Asylum Bill), the boundary is far from fixed. For instance: Child Benefit is paid to parents who are physically present in the UK together with their child, who are 'ordinarily resident' in the UK, who have a 'right to reside' in the UK, and who are responsible for the child living with them. Being present and being ordinarily resident in the UK are determined by relatively short lists of criteria: but having a right to reside can depend on which country you are from and whether or not you are employed.[522]

---

[519]   Van Parijs, Philippe (1995) *Real freedom for all: What (if anything) can justify capitalism?* Oxford: Clarendon Press, pp 2, 89, 96, 133. For critiques of Van Parijs' 'real libertarianism', see Reeve, Andrew and Williams, Andrew (eds) (2002) *Real libertarianism assessed: Political theory after Van Parijs*, London: Palgrave Macmillan, and Barry, Brian (1996) 'Surfers' saviour?' *Citizen's Income Bulletin*, no 22, pp 2–4

[520]   Solow, Robert M. (2001) Foreword, pp ix–xvi in Cohen, Joshua and Rogers, Joel, *What's wrong with a free lunch?* Boston: Beacon Press, p xi; Van Parijs, Philippe (2001), 'A Basic Income for all', pp 3–26 in Cohen, Joshua and Rogers, Joel, *What's wrong with a free lunch?* Boston: Beacon Press, p 3

[521]   White, Stuart (2003) *The civic minimum: On the rights and obligations of economic citizenship*, Oxford: Oxford University Press, p 168

[522]   www.hmrc.gov.uk

In the UK, there would therefore appear to be *degrees* of citizenship. Some people possess civil rights, but some do not (– for instance, residents awaiting adjudication on asylum requests cannot enter into a contract of employment); some people have political rights, but some do not (– some foreign nationals have permission to live and work here but cannot vote); and some people have more social rights than others (– a foreign student might be entitled to Child Benefit but not to means-tested benefits, and to free education for their children but not to NHS healthcare for themselves).

A category of people with varying degrees of citizenship in different countries is of course that of migrants. As Hartley Dean suggests, national boundaries are contingent things, nation states and their citizenships are the products of migration, and yet today's migrants are frequently denied the citizenship rights that other residents now enjoy.[523] Dean suggests a fourfold categorisation of regime models, each with a different basis and a different consequent treatment of welfare provision for migrants:

1. A regime model based on a moral-authoritarian justification that is hostile to migrants and is reminiscent of the Poor Laws: this favours minimum welfare provision.
2. A regime model based on a social-conservative justification that is capable of compassion for migrants, but does not recognise their right to belong: this favours protective (albeit measured) welfare provision.
3. A regime model based on a form of social liberalism, which (perhaps reluctantly) concedes the rights of migrants but expects them to play a part in society if they are to enjoy such rights: this favours conditional welfare provision.
4. A regime model based on a social-democratic justification that is capable of welcoming migrants and including them as citizens: this favours universal welfare provision.[524]

---

[523] Dean, Hartley (2011) 'The ethics of migrant welfare', *Ethics and Social Welfare*, vol 5, no 1, pp 18–35, pp 20–2

[524] For a survey of different countries' benefits systems' treatment of migrants, see Carmel, Emma, Cerami, Alfio and Papadopoulos, Theodoros (eds) (2012) *Migration and welfare in the new Europe: Social protection and the challenges of integration*, Bristol: Policy Press

These are, of course, ideal types; and a further ideal model is that of a 'global citizenship': the only model within which 'migration without borders' makes sense. Such a global citizenship presents challenges in relation to the four regime types listed:

1 The threat it poses to the moral-authoritarian construction is that 'aliens' would compete with natives for scarce resources.
2 The threat it poses to the social-conservative construction is that too many 'guests' would place strains on social solidarity and the social order.
3 The threat it poses to the liberal construction is that unproductive 'settlers' might drag down economic competitiveness.
4 The threat it poses to the social–democratic construction is that the diversity of new 'members" needs might challenge the principles of universality on which social provision is founded.[525]

Each of the four ideal types represents the nation state layer of someone's citizenship: but, as the example of global citizenship shows, additional layers can challenge the national layer. So a French citizen moving to the UK possesses citizenship rights and duties as much determined by their European citizenship as by their French or British citizenship statuses; and someone moving to the UK from a former British colony now in the Commonwealth will possess citizenship rights and duties relating to their national citizenship, their Commonwealth citizenship, and their British citizenship.

There is thus no univocal answer to the question 'Who is a citizen?' Each of us possesses a layered citizenship,[526] made up of different rights and duties relating to different layers. An immigrant will possess citizenship rights and duties relating to the particular model operated by the country to which they have moved, to their citizenship in the country from which they have moved, and to regional and global layers of citizenship.[527]

---

[525] Dean, Hartley (2011) 'The ethics of migrant welfare', *Ethics and Social Welfare*, vol 5, no 1, pp 18–35, 25–6, 32, 33

[526] On multiple citizenship see Handy, Charles (1994) *The empty raincoat. Making sense of the future*, London: Hutchinson, pp 101ff; and Oliver, Dawn and Heater, Derek (1994) *The foundations of citizenship*, New York: Harvester Wheatsheaf, p 7

[527] Lister, Ruth (1997) *Citizenship: Feminist perspectives*, Basingstoke: Macmillan, p 65

The Universal Declaration of Human Rights implies global rights and duties, and thus for all of us it establishes something akin to a global citizenship, and certainly to a global layer of a complex citizenship. We might possess other citizenship layers related to a regional citizenship (as in the European Union), to a global federation (such as the Commonwealth), or to multilateral or bilateral agreements (for instance, those relating to the payment of British state pensions to British citizens who have moved to other countries). Article 25 of the Universal Declaration of Human Rights grants to an individual a right to a 'standard of living adequate for the health and wellbeing of himself and his family'.[528] Does such a global right imply that some global institution has an obligation to ensure that such a 'standard of living' is provided? Can the United Nations duck that responsibility?

Such a layered citizenship poses interesting questions in relation to the administration of any new universal benefit, such as a Citizen's Income. For instance: Should a Citizen's Income be established on a national basis, or for a wider federation of countries? If a Citizen's Income is established in one country, then to whom should it be paid? To what extent would the existing regime model determine to whom the Citizen's Income should be paid, and to what extent would the existence of an in-principle universal payment shift the regime model towards a more universalist one? Or would a Citizen's Income act as a migration magnet more effectively than the current means-tested and contributory system, and thus lead to more strictly controlled migration and a residence requirement for the receipt of the Citizen's Income?[529]

The list of questions relating to a one-country Citizen's Income might pose challenges to the policy's implementation and to the existing regime model, but such challenges ought not to prevent implementation: rather, they should encourage it. The reason for this is that the challenges arise from the way in which the world is changing. A globalising market in goods and services implies a global market in labour, and so for economic efficiency we should both expect and encourage the migration of labour. Such migration would be encouraged both by the payment of a Citizen's Income within a destination country, and would be very much facilitated by a Citizen's Income paid on a regional or global basis. A European Citizen's Income

---

[528] Copp, David (1992) 'The right to an adequate standard of living: justice, autonomy, and the basic needs', pp 231–61 in Paul, Ellen Frankel, Miller, Fred D. and Paul, Jeffrey (eds) *Economic Rights*, Cambridge: Cambridge University Press, p 231

[529] Howard, Michael W. (2006) 'Basic Income and migration policy: a moral dilemma?' *Basic Income Studies*, vol 1, no 1, pp 1–22

would offer on a European basis all of the labour market, economic and social benefits that a Citizen's Income would offer in any nation state, and, in particular, because workers would carry it with them to whichever European country they travelled, it would promote the free movement of labour as well as a more flexible labour market across Europe. A global Citizen's Income might be difficult to imagine, but if we could implement even a very small one, then the development consequences would be profound. Tyler Cowen argues that if the welfare state's aim is to assist the poor, then there is no reason for restricting our attention to the territory within our own national boundaries.[530]

However much some might wish to arrest the process, we shall increasingly experience a layered citizenship, with local, national, regional, and global elements. The trend is towards the regional and global (and to some extent the local) elements, and to that extent away from the national. As Hartley Dean suggests:

> Citizenship is not something bestowed upon us by the various tiers of government, but something that is socially negotiated in a multiplicity of ways and at a multiplicity of sites.[531]

One day our social policy will need to catch up with the way in which citizenship is becoming multilayered. It must therefore be an open question as to whether we should seek the implementation of a Citizen's Income on a regional basis or on a one-country basis, and, in the UK, whether we should seek a Citizen's Income for the UK, a separate Citizen's Income for each country in the United Kingdom, or a Citizen's Income for the European Union; and it must be a long term open question as to whether to seek a global Citizen's Income:

> If global social citizenship is predicated on the idea of recognising the value of each individual, then social cash transfers could be an avenue of materialising that

---

[530]   Cowen, Tyler (2002) 'Does the welfare state help the poor?' pp 36–54 in Paul, Ellen Frankel, Miller, Fred D. Jr., and Paul, Jeffrey, *Should differences in income and wealth matter?* Cambridge: Cambridge University Press, p 53

[531]   Dean, Hartley (2011) 'What role for social solidarity?' p 16 in Barrientos, Armando, Davy, Benjamin, Davy, Ulrike, Dean, Hartley, Jacobs, Harvey M., Leisering, Lutz and Pellissery, Sony, *A road to global social citizenship?*, Financial Assistance, Land Policy, and Global Social Rights Working Paper no 10, www.tinyurl.com/3n9jh5h

recognition, by global standard setting and institution building in the field of social security. (Hartley Dean)[532]

A global Citizen's Income would be the result of an understanding of our global citizenship, and of that citizenship defined as a global social solidarity in search of global wellbeing; and it would contribute to the formation of our global citizenship. However small a global Citizen's Income might be, it would bind us together into a common solidarity in a way in which no other social policy could, and that would have to be good for the abolition of poverty and the establishment of peace and justice.

Who would get a UK Citizen's Income?

Clearly a UK Citizen's Income should be paid to UK citizens: but we have already seen that it is no easy matter to determine who is a citizen and who is not. Because a Citizen's Income would to some extent define a citizenry, the decision as to who should receive it would be a particularly important one.

One possibility would be to pay a Citizen's Income to anyone on the electoral register (and to under-18s if they would be on the electoral register if they were not under 18). If the current register were used then this would clearly pose problems: Someone with no address cannot be on the register, so to give a Citizen's Income only to people on the register would leave those without an address still on means-tested benefits rather than in receipt of a Citizen's Income. Of more importance numerically is the current state of the register. Electoral registers are only about 90 per cent accurate when they are at their most accurate after the annual October canvass: but some local registers are only 85 per cent accurate, particularly in the larger urban areas outside London. 'Under-registration is notably higher than average among 17–24 year olds (56% not registered), private sector tenants (49%) and black and minority ethnic (BME) British residents (31%).'[533]

---

532   Dean, Hartley (2011) 'What role for social solidarity?' p 16 in Barrientos, Armando, Davy, Benjamin, Davy, Ulrike, Dean, Hartley, Jacobs, Harvey M., Leisering, Lutz and Pellissery, Sony, *A road to global social citizenship?* Financial Assistance, Land Policy, and Global Social Rights Working Paper no 10, www.tinyurl.com/3n9jh5h

533   The Electoral Commission (2010) *The completeness and accuracy of electoral registers in Great Britain*, London: The Electoral Commission, pp 2–3; cf. Vince, Philip (2004) 'Second thoughts on the report *Citizenship and Citizen's Income*', *Citizen's Income Newsletter*, issue 1, pp 2–3

It is of course possible that to use the electoral register as the criterion for payment of a Citizen's Income would encourage people to register and would thus improve democratic participation,[534] and for this reason the suggestion should be given careful consideration; but the related problem of who should and who should not be on the electoral register would still need to be addressed. Some way would have to be found of including people with no fixed abode; decisions would need to be taken as to whether British citizens permanently abroad should a) be on the electoral register, and b) receive a Citizen's Income; and decisions would need to be taken as to which foreign nationals resident here would be entitled to a Citizen's Income. European Union citizens living here are allowed onto the electoral register and are entitled to a variety of existing benefits, and would presumably receive a Citizen's Income.[535]

A good reason for considering a link between the electoral register and a Citizen's Income is that legislation for a Citizen's Income would need voter support, and to link receipt of a Citizen's Income to the electoral register might achieve this, as it would clearly link the right to a Citizen's Income to the fulfilment of duties (and especially to the duty to vote) as well as to the rights of citizenship (and especially to the right to vote).[536] As we have seen, by encouraging both paid and unpaid work, and offering enlarged possibilities for care work, a Citizen's Income would encourage an active citizenship; and to link its payment to the electoral register would make this point plain.

But again: such a link would not of itself determine who should receive a Citizen's Income. One possibility is to model the criterion for receipt on that for receipt of Child Benefit. Just as a Citizen's Income is a comprehensible and simple payment, so the definition of who receives it should be comprehensible and simple, which rather suggests that regulations should be even simpler than those for Child Benefit. This might give entitlement to some people who perhaps ought not to receive a Citizen's Income (such as foreign students), but it might be better to pay them a Citizen's Income than to exclude them by creating a tangle of regulations or a playground for discretion.

---

[534] Jordan, Bill (1989) *The common good. citizenship, morality and self-interest*, Oxford: Basil Blackwell, p 124

[535] There might well be groups of people not currently on the electoral register who ought to receive a Citizen's Income. Members of the House of Lords and those whose refugee status is still undetermined would be two such groups.

[536] Whether there is a civil liberties dimension to be debated is an open question. At present it is possible to choose not to be on the electoral register, and that decision has no implications for one's income. However, there would be no compulsion to receive a Citizen's Income or to be on the register, and some citizens might make this choice.

If all of those in receipt of Citizen's Income were permitted to seek employment, then the tax paid on earnings would in most cases repay the Citizen's Income.

These two approaches: the link to the electoral register, and the parallel with current Child Benefit regulations, could be considered either separately or together; and one way of combining them would be to determine eligibility for a Citizen's Income via a set of simple rules and then use receipt of a Citizen's Income as the gateway both to voter registration and to Child Benefit for one's children.

The effects of a Citizen's Income on citizenship

The definition of the citizen

A 'Citizen's Income' is an unconditional income paid by the state to every man, woman and child as a right of citizenship, which means that it is no surprise that Maurice Roche follows his call for a reformulation of social citizenship with the suggestion that a Citizen's Income might provide a new basis for social citizenship. A Citizen's Income 'would ... institutionalise citizenship principles and the social rights of citizenship,'[537] those principles being universality, equality, and participation. But whatever civil, political, social or economic definition we give to 'citizenship', a Citizen's Income of any amount would cohere with such a definition, for it would provide an economic foundation for individual liberty and for contracts between individuals, it would encourage political participation because it would create a measure of social solidarity, and it would provide a context for other social rights (such as education) and duties (for it would alleviate the poverty and unemployment traps and thus encourage people to seek employment).

Whatever set of regulations is eventually chosen to determine who should receive a Citizen's Income, the establishment of a Citizen's Income would create a clearer boundary for the citizenry. Citizenship is, according to Goodin, 'a social creation, constituted out of symbols of one sort or another,'[538] so a welfare entitlement *creates* citizenship, both because it is an economic right of citizenship, and because it is a

---

[537] Roche, Maurice (1992) *Rethinking citizenship: Welfare ideology and change in modern society*, Cambridge: Polity Press, p 185
[538] Goodin, Robert E. (1988) *Reasons for welfare: The political theory of the welfare state*, Princeton: Princeton University Press, p 85

set of symbols.[539] This would be particularly the case with a universal and unconditional income, for it would create a new social solidarity, even if the amount of the Citizen's Income were initially quite small.

In an article written in 1974, Ralf Dahrendorf worried about the possibility that citizenship rights, by granting greater autonomy to the individual, might destroy the fabric of society needed to underpin those rights.[540] A Citizen's Income would *not* have this effect. Because it would be a universal and unconditional income, it would deliver social solidarity and thus contribute positively to the necessary foundation for other civil, political, social and economic rights.

Citizenship duties

As well as making citizenship rights more diverse and more secure, a Citizen's Income might also offer a realistic prospect that citizenship duties that are now difficult to fulfil would become easier to fulfil. By ameliorating to some extent the poverty and unemployment traps, a Citizen's Income would encourage people to take employment, and particularly self- and part-time employment. This would enable them to fulfil their obligations to their families[541] and to their community, as well as the obligation to work for a living. With a Citizen's Income, the duty to work could mean less paid employment and more unpaid work: work in the family and in the community; and a Citizen's Income, by recognising the importance of unpaid work, might encourage people to do it. In particular, by increasing someone's ability to accept part-time employment rather than full-time employment, a Citizen's Income would make it easier for both women and men to fulfil their parental duties towards their children.

Far from discouraging the fulfilment of citizenship obligations, a Citizen's Income would encourage their fulfilment; and it would encourage the fulfilment of an obligation to participate in society by making possible a more diverse definition of work and by making it

---

[539] On the sense of economic citizenship created by the non-means-tested Invalid Care Allowance, see McLaughlin, Eithne (1990) *Social security and community care: The case of the Invalid Care Allowance*, Department of Social Security, Research Report no 4, London: Stationery Office, pp 47–8

[540] Dahrendorf, Ralf (1974) 'Citizenship and beyond: the social dynamics of an idea,' *Social Research*, vol 41, no 4, p 684

[541] See Novak, Michael (1987) *The new consensus on family and welfare*, Washington DC: American Enterprise Institute for Public Policy Research. Novak recommends workfare (p 111). A Citizen's Income would have the same beneficial effects as workfare and none of the drawbacks.

more possible to *do* more kinds of work. Just as importantly, a Citizen's Income would give status and self-respect to those who are for various reasons excluded from the paid labour market, but who are able to take on unpaid work and to make a contribution to society.

Citizenship rights

The Irish Conference of Major Religious Superiors' definition of citizenship 'is not simply about political rights such as the right to vote, to equality before the law, to possession of a passport. It is also about social rights such as the right to adequate income, to meaningful work, to participation in society.'[542] They recognise that in the past these rights were mainly delivered via full employment, but that that is now unlikely to be the case, and that a Citizen's Income might now provide a certain amount of economic security in order to combat the social exclusion that will inevitably follow from the permanent loss of full employment. They also believe that a Citizen's Income, by somewhat uncoupling a full-time job from income, would contribute to a redefinition of 'work' as 'anything one does that contributes to the development of one's self, one's community or the wider society.'[543] Thus a Citizen's Income would create rights both to income and to work.

The labour market will remain one means of providing an income, of providing useful work, and of achieving social participation, but it will no longer be a vehicle for *rights* to these social necessities: which is why Fred Twine believes that 'the concept of social interdependence ... provides a powerful rationale for a [Citizen's] Income as a means of sharing in industrial societies where people are dependent upon selling their labour power as a means to life but where this cannot be guaranteed.'[544] Similarly, a Citizen's Income would integrate those members of society who are permanently without paid work (because

---

[542] Reynolds, Brigid, SM, and Healy, Sean, SMA (eds) (1993) *New frontiers for full citizenship*, Dublin: Conference of Major Religious Superiors of Ireland, p 8

[543] Reynolds, Brigid, SM, and Healy, Sean, SMA (eds) (1993) *New frontiers for full citizenship*, Dublin: Conference of Major Religious Superiors of Ireland, p 69. cf. Vilrokx, Jacques (1993) 'Basic Income, Citizenship and Solidarity: Towards a Dynamic for Social Renewal', pp 205–214 in Coenen, Harry and Leisink, Peter (eds) *Work and citizenship in the New Europe*, London: Edward Elgar. Vilrokx takes the extreme position that full citizenship is only possible when citizenship's link with the labour market is completely severed. This is unnecessary. It is quite sufficient to loosen the link so that the labour market becomes one component of the right to income, the right to work, and the right to social participation.

[544] Twine, Fred (1994) *Citizenship and social rights: The interdependence of self and society*, Beverly Hills: Sage, p 167

they have a severe disability or are caring for someone who has, because they are over retirement age, or because they are caring for the young or the old) with those who permanently or occasionally gain their livelihood and other social necessities through the labour market. At present there is little in the tax and benefits structure that unites these two sections of society. A Citizen's Income of any size would be a means to social integration for those necessarily permanently without paid work, as well as for those without paid work because they cannot find any. A Citizen's Income would thus contribute to the social solidarity we need if we are to balance the pursuit of individual freedom with the pursuit of community.

Whether a Citizen's Income would have an adverse effect on the right to receive a fair economic reward for labour is a complex issue, but clearly an important one. Like 'Tax Credits', a Citizen's Income could act as a subsidy to low wages, and it is possible that wage rates would fall if employers no longer had to cover the whole of someone's subsistence income. It is also possible that an increase in part-time employment and in low-paid employment would reduce the skills base, reduce the development of innovative technologies, and reduce employment rights generally. This would matter because economic efficiency requires a high-skill and high-wage economy. Employment rights legislation and the National Minimum Wage are two of the roots of such a scenario, and we would need to keep these legislative provisions.[545] When a National Minimum Wage was established, we heard plenty of predictions that it would cause unemployment to rise and employment rates to fall. The opposite has happened.[546] Similarly, we might find that, far from reducing the natural level of wages, a Citizen's Income would increase it, because a wage would no longer be someone's only economic resource. Someone currently faced with unpleasant and poorly paid full-time employment as their only realistic livelihood option would, with a Citizen's Income, find themselves with more options, including part-time employment and self-employment. The wage paid for intrinsically unpleasant paid work might therefore have to increase in order to attract workers; and because those who chose to take on necessary but unpleasant tasks would no longer be supplicants for a subsistence income, but would instead be relatively free

---

[545] Parker, Hermione and Sutherland, Holly (1996) 'Earnings top-up or Basic Income and a minimum wage', *Citizen's Income Bulletin*, no 21, February, pp 5–8, p 8

[546] Dolton, Peter, Bondibene, Chiara Rosazza and Wadsworth, Jonathan (2010) 'The UK National Minimum Wage in retrospect', *Fiscal Studies*, vol 31, no 4, pp 510–32

individuals choosing to undertake socially necessary activity, they might be ascribed the moral worth that undertaking such activity deserves.

As well as providing more of an exit option for workers in low-paid and unpleasant full-time employment, a Citizen's Income would also provide an exit option in relation to means-tested benefits.[547] A worker's Citizen's Income would provide them with an income floor[548] on which they could build with a variety of part-time employments and self employments, making it possible to leave behind undesirable full-time employment if that is what they wished to do. For the first time every citizen would have exit options in relation to both the means-tested benefits system and low-paid full-time employment.

A Citizen's Income would confer rights to an income, it would confer rights to better paid employment, and to more choice over employment options, and it would deliver increased rights to paid employment because it would make it easier to pursue full-time employment, part-time employment, or self-employment, or to seek further education or training. By giving workers more options, by alleviating to some extent the poverty and unemployment traps, and by making the labour market more flexible, a Citizen's Income would make its own contribution to the efficient and just economy that we need. A Citizen's Income, by revitalising citizens' social rights, might also thereby create a new sense of social identity.[549]

A variety of citizenships

The introduction to the 'Dahrendorf Report' is as good a statement as any of the kind of citizenship to which we might aspire:

> 'Wealth' summarises what people value in their social lives. The wealth of nations is therefore an objective which transcends the boundaries of economics in the narrow sense. Wealth must be socially sustainable. This is where *social cohesion* comes in to describe a society which offers opportunities to all its members within a framework of accepted values and institutions. Such a society is therefore

---

[547] Handler, Joel F. (2005) 'Myth and ceremony in welfare: rights, contracts, and client satisfaction', *The Journal of Socioeconomics*, vol 34, no 1, pp 101–124, p 120

[548] Spicker, Paul (2011) *How Social Security Works: An introduction to benefits in Britain,* Bristol: Policy Press, pp 15, 123–4

[549] See Purdy, David (1990) 'Citizenship, Basic Income and democracy', in *BIRG Bulletin*, no 10, Autumn/Winter, p 13, on the ways in which a Citizen's Income might change the citizenship rights agenda.

one of inclusion. People belong: they are not allowed to be excluded. They show *commitment* to values and institutions. The result is a *stakeholder society* in which companies, organisations and communities are linked to common purposes. Its members enjoy the rights and accept the obligations of citizenship.[550]

Such a citizenship will encompass civil, political, and social rights and duties; it will be founded on economic rights and obligations;[551] and it will reverse the trend towards loss of social citizenship for people in vulnerable financial situations.[552] As Barrientos and Pellissery put it: 'Citizenship is commonly understood to be associated with the exercise of civil and political rights at the national level, most notably at elections. At a deeper level, citizenship signifies that the wellbeing of individuals, their households, and communities, are valuable.'[553] In a changing world, that means a universal financial security and so ideally a Citizen's Income.[554]

If lessons learnt from the Namibian and Indian pilot projects inform the social security institutions that will emerge there and elsewhere, then the resulting Citizen's Income will promote a new kind of citizenship. We have already discussed citizenship as a layered reality, and the possibility of a Citizen's Income being established at a variety of levels (– and there is surely no reason why a Citizen's Income should not be established for more than one level, say at both national and European levels). A further way of understanding citizenship as a layered reality is to see ourselves as a diversity of communities, thus transforming the idea of citizenship into that of an inherently diverse reality. Iris Young worries about the homogenising effect of the citizenship idea, as that idea is usually understood. Her kind of citizenship is diverse,

---

[550] Dahrendorf, R., Field, F., and Hayman, C. (1995) *Report on wealth creation and social cohesion in a free society* (the Dahrendorf Report) London: Commission on Wealth Creation and Social Cohesion, p vii

[551] Lister, Ruth (1996) 'One step nearer to genuine citizenship: reflections on the Commission on Social Justice Report', *Soundings,* Issue 2, pp 193–201

[552] McKeever, Gráinne (2012) 'Social citizenship and social security fraud in the UK and Australia', *Social Policy and Administration*, vol 46, no 4, pp 465–82

[553] Barrientos, Armando and Pellissery, Sony (2011) 'The road to global citizenship?' pp 6–14 in Barrientos, Armando, Davy, Benjamin, Davy, Ulrike, Dean, Hartley, Jacobs, Harvey M., Leisering, Lutz and Pellissery, Sony, *A road to global social citizenship? Financial Assistance, Land Policy, and Global Social Rights* Working Paper no 10, www.tinyurl.com/3n9jh5h, p 6

[554] Dahrendorf, Ralf (1991) 'Can it happen?', an interview with Susan Raven, *BIRG Bulletin*, no 13, August, pp 12–13

and includes 'pride in group specificity against ideals of assimilation.'[555] It is precisely this kind of citizenship that a Citizen's Income would encourage, because, unlike prescribed public education or healthcare, the content of what is purchased with an income is not prescribed. A Citizen's Income, by increasing an individual's liberty, would contribute both to social solidarity and to cultural diversity; and because it would impose no cultural norms (as means-tested benefits regulations do by assuming the financial dependence of one member of a couple on the other), a Citizen's Income would create a society in which different cultures and lifestyles could relate to one another on a more equal basis. We have already discovered that a Citizen's Income would contribute to social cohesion. We can now see that at the same time it would contribute to social diversity. For a social policy to achieve both would be enormously helpful as our society both globalises and diversifies.

The Dahrendorf Report's verdict on a Citizen's Income is that it 'has obvious attraction … it would allow a consolidation of benefits for all, link them explicitly to people's status as citizens, and thus promote social cohesion.'[556] This chapter has not solved the problems related to the concept of citizenship, or those related to who should and who should not receive a Citizen's Income: but it has made some suggestions for further study, particularly in relation to the electoral register and to the kind of residence criteria that currently grant entitlement to Child Benefit. In the end, whether we are going to remain subjects of a monarch or become citizens will be a political decision. Our citizenship rights and duties will remain political decisions, and whether a Citizen's Income is to be implemented will be a political decision. But one question of which we should remain aware during future discussion of these issues is this: Are we going to define citizenship and then include citizens on the electoral register and give them a Citizen's Income, or are we going to decide who goes on the electoral register and who gets a Citizen's Income (and these might or might not be the same people) and then allow such decisions to determine the boundaries of a national citizenry? The British constitutional tradition has tended to

---

[555] Young, Iris Marion (1989) 'Polity and group differences: a critique of the ideal of universal citizenship', *Ethics,* vol 99, no 2, p 251

[556] Dahrendorf, R., Field, F., and Hayman, C. (1995) *Report on wealth creation and social cohesion in a free society* (the Dahrendorf Report) London: Commission on Wealth Creation and Social Cohesion, p 86

follow the latter path,[557] and it will probably continue to do so, which makes the decision as to who should and who should not receive a Citizen's Income a particularly important one.

'Citizenship' is a multifaceted concept, involving civil, political, social and economic rights and duties, and involving rights and duties in relation to cultural, local, national, regional and global levels. A Citizen's Income would provide a good foundation for the exercise of all of these rights and duties, it would itself contribute to the definition of citizenship, and it would move us towards changed rights and responsibilities more in tune with a world of rapid economic and social change.

---

[557] See The Speaker's Commission on Citizenship (1990) *Encouraging citizenship*, London: Stationery Office, Appendix D, p 63, by J.P. Gardner, on legislation relating to questions of citizenship. The author charts an evolutionary process of some complexity, particularly in relation to commonwealth citizenship. He identifies a general problem relating to obscurely drafted legislation. A Citizen's Income would be relatively simple to legislate, and would encourage a more general simplification of legislation relating to who is and who is not a citizen.

CHAPTER 13

Is a Citizen's Income politically feasible?[558]

In Chapter 3 we reached the conclusion that a Citizen's Income would be difficult to implement because it might reduce the number of civil servants. Civil servants construct the reports and statistics that ministers read, and it is not difficult to write a report that proves that a Citizen's Income is an unrealistic proposition.

Civil servants are examples of what De Wispelaere and Noguera term as 'readily identifiable actors with distinctive interests, roles, capacities, and intentions'.[559] Other such 'identifiable actors' are members of parliament and government ministers, and they might be considering the following questions in relation to a proposal for a Citizen's Income: 1. Does it fit with our party's political convictions about the kind of society and the kind of economy that we want to build? 2. Does it fit with our current policy directions? 3. Are there any serious objections to it? And possibly: 4. Might the policy gain all party support? If a government were able to answer 'Yes', 'yes', 'no', and 'yes' to these questions, then we could say that a Citizen's Income was politically feasible and therefore that it could happen.

In this chapter we shall ask whether a Citizen's Income would be coherent with a variety of the UK's political ideologies, whether those same ideologies generate objections to a Citizen's Income, and whether a Citizen's Income might cohere with today's policy directions.

The New Right

This ideology sets out from the position that we are self-interested individuals. Our relationships are economic and contractual, and are for mutual benefit. The public sector is inefficient, so as much

---

558 A more detailed dissertation on the arguments generated by political ideologies both for and against a Citizen's Income can be found among the website appendices at www.citizensincome.org

559 De Wispelaere, Jürgen and Noguera, José Antonio (2012) 'On the political feasibility of universal Basic Income: an analytic framework', pp 17–38 in Caputo, Richard K. (ed.) *Basic Income guarantee and politics: International experiences and perspectives on the viability of income guarantee,* New York: Palgrave Macmillan

economic activity as possible needs to be in the private sector; and this economic activity might include such public services as healthcare and education.[560] It is a mistake to call the New Right 'conservative'. It is not. It is quite happy to dispense with time-honoured institutions. It is in many ways a radical version of classical liberalism, with an added dose of moral prescription.

> There is no such thing as society. There is a living tapestry of men and women and people and the beauty of that tapestry and the quality of our lives will depend upon how much each of us is prepared to take responsibility for ourselves and each of us is prepared to turn round and help by our own efforts those who are unfortunate. (Margaret Thatcher)[561]

As for the economy: free markets deliver wealth for all, and attempts to equalise wealth have the inevitable effect of making people poor and keeping them that way. There are both practical and more theoretical positions here. The more theoretical position is that redistribution is theft from the wealthy. The more practical argument is that redistribution requires progressive taxation and/or means-testing, and that such methods are a 'deterrent to hard work … It is only a modest degree of redistribution that can be justified in the name of relieving poverty.'[562]

New Right politicians and thinkers might support a Citizen's Income because it would facilitate a free market in labour because earned income would no longer need to provide for the whole of someone's household's subsistence.[563] Working age adults have an obligation to provide for themselves and for their families as best they can in the context of a free market economy. This is not the state's role. There should therefore be as few disincentives as possible in the way of people seeking and keeping employment, and of them improving their skills, so that they can as easily as possible improve their ability to earn an income. Means-tested benefits impose disincentives because they are

---

[560] Giddens, Anthony (1998) *The third way: The renewal of social democracy*, Cambridge: Polity Press, pp 8, 13

[561] Thatcher, Margaret (1987) Interview for *Woman's Own*, 31 October, www.margaretthatcher.org/document/106689

[562] Joseph, Keith and Sumption, Jonathan (1979) *Equality*, London: John Murray, pp 19, 23–4, 27

[563] Fitzpatrick, Tony (1999) *Freedom and security: An introduction to the Basic Income debate*, Basingstoke: Macmillan, p 84. This properly raises the question as to whether a National Minimum Wage will continue to be needed.

withdrawn as earned income rises, and at the same time they generate 'welfare dependency'.[564] As Charles Murray puts it in relation to welfare provision in the US in the 1960s and '70s: we 'tried to provide more for the poor and produced more poor instead. We tried to remove the barriers to escape poverty, and inadvertently built a trap.'[565] Rising unemployment, single-parenthood, and welfare dependency, became 'rational responses to changes in the rules of the game of surviving and getting ahead'.[566] Universal benefits create neither disincentives nor dependency. Instead, they enable individuals to derive the maximum possible benefit from low levels of earned income.[567] Above all, and in the longer term, a Citizen's Income would provide people with autonomy, and with the ability to provide for their own welfare, and so would remove much of the government interference that many people assume is just the way life is.

It would thus appear that a Citizen's Income would provide everything for which a New Right politician might be looking: a free market in labour, personal autonomy, financial reward for hard work, and the worker's ability to provide for their dependents.[568]

However, some on the New Right might find a Citizen's Income more difficult to support. This is because they might think that 'something for nothing' could discourage labour market activity, and also because individuals should take responsibility for themselves and their families, so the state's only responsibility is to provide a last resort safety net. If someone falls on hard times then it is up to them, their families, their friends and their neighbours to provide for them.

During the Conservative Party conference in 2010, after the Chancellor of the Exchequer had announced that a household containing a higher rate taxpayer would be deprived of its Child Benefit, televised members of the audience suggested that 'They don't need it' and 'the money should be targeted on the poor'.

---

564   Mead, Lawrence (1992) *The new politics of poverty: The non-working poor in America*, New York: Harper Collins, p ix
565   Murray, Charles (1984) *Losing ground: American social policy, 1950–1980*, New York: Basic Books, p 9
566   Murray, Charles (1984) *Losing ground: American social policy, 1950–1980*, New York: Basic Books, p 155
567   Murray, Charles (2008) 'Guaranteed income as a replacement for the welfare state', *Basic Income Studies*, vol 3, no 2, pp 1–12
568   Murray, Matthew C. (2012) 'Conclusion: a new day', pp 250–62 in Murray, Matthew C. and Pateman, Carole (eds) *Basic Income worldwide: Horizons of reform*, New York: Palgrave Macmillan, p 257

Socialism

'Socialism' has a wide variety of meanings. It can mean an ideal society in which all contribute according to their ability, and all consume according to their need,[569] in perfect harmony and without coercion; a democratically elected government nationalising major industries in order to provide subsidized public services; an oligopoly controlling the means of production on behalf of a population; local control of the means of production, or a network of cooperative enterprises; workers managing industries; a government providing universal public services and redistributing wealth and income from rich to poor; or any combination of these. Underlying all of these approaches is the conviction that we are all members of the human race and so share a fundamental human equality that needs to be given effect in social and economic relations.

A Citizen's Income represents social provision for universal needs, and therefore ought to be an attractive policy option for any socialist. Just as the franchise has evolved towards universality (almost), so welfare provision has to some extent travelled the same road, and a Citizen's Income could be seen as an important new step in this socialist direction.[570] It would be an 'emblem of full citizenship' and provide the security and means to enjoy other social rights.[571]

A Citizen's Income also represents a socialist concern for greater equality. Alex Callinicos, in his *Equality*, advocates a Citizen's Income as *the* answer to inequality;[572] and in his *Anti-capitalist manifesto* he seeks steps on the way to socialism, and again recommends a Citizen's Income:

> A basic income would radically alter the bargaining power
> between labour and capital, since potential workers would
> now be in a position, if they chose, to pursue alternatives
> to paid employment. Moreover, because all citizens would
> receive the same basic income (perhaps with adjustments for

[569] Marx, Karl (1938) *Critique of the Gotha Programme*, London: Lawrence and Wishart (first published in Russian in 1891), p 14

[570] Brown, G.J. (1981) 'The end of the welfare state?' pp 408–423 in W. J. Mommsen, *The emergence of the welfare state in Britain and Germany, 1850–1950*, London: Croom Helm, p 421; Hill, Michael (1990) *Social security policy in Britain*, Aldershot: Edward Elgar, p 165

[571] Pateman, Carole (2005) 'Another way forward: welfare, social reproduction, and a Basic Income', pp 34–64 in Mead, Lawrence and Beem, Christopher (eds) *Welfare reform and political theory*, New York: Russell Sage Foundation, pp 37, 50

[572] Callinicos, Alex (2000) *Equality*, Cambridge: Polity Press, pp 114–18

economic handicaps such as age, disability, and dependent children), its introduction would be an important step towards establishing equality of access to advantage.[573]

Breitenbach et al argue that a Citizen's Income would end what they call the 'dull compulsion to labour' and

> would allow individuals to choose whether or not to work. Initially, basic income would need to be set at a level low enough just to allow a bare existence without income from work for those who wished to live in this way. It seems to us unlikely that many people would actually choose this as a mode of life except for short periods, but the fact that it would be possible to live in this fashion would considerably reduce the monitoring, surveillance and enforcement of regulations on the duty to work that would otherwise be necessary.[574]

For socialists such as Callinicos,

> the basis of capital's power lies ... in its control of production, not in the financial markets. One of the attractions of the idea that every citizen be granted as of right a basic income set, say, at a level that would allow them to meet their socially recognized subsistence needs, is that it could help to emancipate workers from the dictatorship of capital.[575]

While universality and equality are important socialist concerns, so also is the ability of the worker to reap the rewards of their production: and it is in this respect that some socialists have anxieties about a move towards additional universal benefits. During the transition to socialism, a Citizen's Income might depress wages, meaning that capitalist profits might rise and workers' share of the product of their labour might be reduced; and, by providing a stable contribution to a household's subsistence income, a Citizen's Income might reduce the significance of earned income and thus reduce trade unions' bargaining power. Many members of trade unions are among the higher paid, and they

---

[573] Callinicos, Alex (2003) *An anti-capitalist manifesto*, Cambridge: Polity Press, p 134

[574] Breitenbach, Hans, Burden, Tom and Coates, David (1990) *Features of a viable socialism*, Hemel Hempstead: Harvester Wheatsheaf, pp 31–2, 33

[575] Callinicos, Alex (2003) *An anti-capitalist manifesto*, Cambridge: Polity Press, p 134

might therefore be less likely to understand the benefits that a Citizen's Income could offer; and in countries in which trade unions manage unemployment provision (such as Belgium), they are unlikely to be in favour of a universal benefit that might reduce the scope of their own schemes.[576]

Bill Jordan offers a different perspective on socialism's concern with the industrial workforce and its wage levels: The industrial workforce is declining, so the working class is now divided into an organised working class with full-time employment and a marginalised, casualised and insecure working class (the 'precariat'[577]). By recognising the meeting of need as a citizenship issue, a Citizen's Income could reconcile these two working classes without compromising trade unions' goal of maximising their members' access to the fruits of production. A Citizen's Income could conceivably increase trade unions' bargaining power because there would now be another stable element to subsistence income, meaning that it would be more possible for workers to decline undesirable employment.[578] For the sake of their members, there is every reason for trade unions to be seriously discussing a Citizen's Income,[579] as they have done in some countries for some time.[580]

One nation conservatism

Our evolved social structures are stable and valuable, and our differentiated meritocracy works to the benefit of all in society. Society is a complex structure, within which everyone has a place: and those with better life chances have obligations towards those without them. Similarly, the economy is a complex structure within which we all have a place; and that economy is now global and European, so the UK belongs in Europe. This position is genuinely 'conservative', always conserving what it can of our evolved social structure and its institutions. Thus free trade is the norm, as is the individual's earning of a living so that they can support their family: but those who suffer

---

[576] Vanderborght, Yannick (2006) 'Why trade unions oppose Basic Income', *Basic Income Studies*, vol 1, no 1, pp 1–20

[577] Standing, Guy (2011) *The precariat: The new dangerous class*, London: Bloomsbury

[578] Jordan, Bill (1987) *Rethinking welfare*, Oxford, 1987: Basil Blackwell, p 161

[579] Sherman, Barrie and Judkins, Phil (1996) 'Labour market effects of CI: A trade union standpoint', *Citizen's Income Bulletin*, no 21, February, pp 2–4

[580] Lubbi, Greetje (1991) 'Towards a full BI', *BIRG Bulletin*, no 12, February, pp 15–16; van Berkel, Rik (1994) 'Basic Income as trade union policy', *Citizen's Income Bulletin*, no 17, January, pp 18–21

free trade's ill effects need to be protected by the welfare institutions that have evolved to do that.

A Citizen's Income would signify that we all have a place in society, it would reduce government interference in people's lives,[581] and it would make it easier for families to earn their own way out of poverty. As David Howell puts it:

> The more you relate benefits to some measure of means (and also, the lower down the income scale you take income taxation), the greater the deterrent to benefit recipients to lift their earnings. ... Here, in the impenetrably complex brew of benefits, thresholds, tax allowances, penalties and disregards, we have the makings of that strange paradox whereby unemployment and labour shortage coexist, where saving makes you poorer, where a subculture of benefit dependency flourishes. [The solution is] a partial basic income payment for all.[582]

The Tax Credits scheme proposed by the Conservative government in 1972, and Brandon Rhys Williams' scheme for a Citizen's Income, came out of the One Nation Conservative tradition. Brandon Rhys Williams saw a Citizen's Income

> as the basis of a Europe-wide process of reform, underpinning the growth of the great Single Market. ... as a *translucent* process that people would genuinely understand, as against the murky pattern of today. ... Extreme administrative simplicity is ... an objective in its own right.[583]

A Citizen's Income would encourage 'thrift, saving and small-scale capital ownership to spread and deepen, so as to create a genuine

---

[581] Atkinson, A.B. (1989) *Basic Income schemes and the lessons from public economics,* Tax, Incentives and the Distribution of Income paper no 136, London: LSE, p 3, summarising Rhys Williams, Brandon (1989) *Stepping stones to independence* (edited by Parker, Hermione) Aberdeen: Aberdeen University Press, for the One Nation Group of Conservative MPs

[582] Howells, David, MP, in the Foreword to Rhys Williams, Brandon (1989) *Stepping stones to independence* (edited by Hermione Parker) Aberdeen: Aberdeen University Press, for the One Nation Group of Conservative MPs, pp vii–viii

[583] Rhys Williams, Brandon, House of Commons, 1/3/1985, quoted in Rhys Williams, Brandon (1989) *Stepping stones to independence* (edited by Hermione Parker) Aberdeen: Aberdeen University Press, for the One Nation Group of Conservative MPs, p 22

capital-owning democracy' (David Howells).[584] Economic liberty is as important to One Nation Conservatives as it is to Liberals, and, according to Brandon Rhys Williams, a Citizen's Income would set people free:

> We need liberation for the millions held in dependency on state benefits to take work without committing a crime; liberation for savers to accumulate fortunes and put them to work fruitfully, without the risk of confiscatory taxation; liberation of women, so that they become wholly equal citizens whether single or married; and liberation for employers from needless, costly paperwork. ... Even a very small Citizen's Income would give people more choices than they have now.
>
> There is no reason to suppose that people on low incomes react differently to increased economic incentives than people who are rich, and to improve incentives at the bottom of the earnings range is more important than preserving them at the top, because 'more people are involved at the bottom.'[585]

Brandon Rhys Williams' model is Child Benefit:

> It is one of the easiest benefits to administer and take-up is almost 100 per cent. ... Child benefit helps all families equally. My answer to those who attack it on the grounds that rich families do not need it, is to say that child benefit does not belong either to the father or to the mother, but is the start of a life-long relationship of obligation and entitlement between the child as junior citizen and the community.[586]

---

[584] Howells, David, MP, in the Foreword to Rhys Williams, Brandon (1989) *Stepping stones to independence* (edited by Hermione Parker) Aberdeen: Aberdeen University Press, for the One Nation Group of Conservative MPs, pp viii

[585] Rhys Williams, Brandon, House of Commons, 1/3/1985, quoted in Rhys Williams, Brandon (1989) *Stepping stones to independence* (edited by Hermione Parker) Aberdeen: Aberdeen University Press, for the One Nation Group of Conservative MPs, pp 22, 41

[586] Rhys Williams, Brandon, House of Commons, 1/3/1985, quoted in Rhys Williams, Brandon (1989) *Stepping stones to independence* (edited by Hermione Parker) Aberdeen: Aberdeen University Press, for the One Nation Group of Conservative MPs, pp 35–6, 28

I have not been able to find any One Nation Conservatives arguing against the implementation of a Citizen's Income, and the only possible arguments that might emerge from this political ideology are that a Citizen's Income would mean that we might no longer merit our success, and that a Citizen's Income might encourage arguments for further equality of outcome.

Liberalism

Individual freedom is the highest human aspiration, and together we can create the conditions for that. As Samuel Brittan puts it: 'It is individuals who feel, exult, despair and rejoice. And statements about group welfare are a shorthand way of referring to such individual effects.'[587] Society is a society of free individuals, together maintaining the conditions for individual liberty so that free trade between individuals can be the heart of a national economy (– though whether an economy increasingly dominated by transnational companies at the expense of small businesses constitutes such a network of free trade between individuals is an interesting question[588]). Similarly, free trade between nations is at the heart of the global economy. Regulation is required, but only to optimise the economy in order to foster the greatest possible individual liberty. The state is an instrument for promoting individual freedom whenever it controls aspects of society or of the economy that conflict with individual autonomy.[589]

For individuals to experience 'real freedom'[590] they need to be able to realise the value of their labour in a free market. The problem at the moment is that the poverty and unemployment traps make the 'ladder of opportunity' rather shaky. A Citizen's Income would ameliorate these traps and thus encourage people to seek out new economic opportunities. 'It is positively desirable that people should have a means of subsistence independent of needs' because this would 'separate the libertarian, free choice aspects of capitalism from the puritan work ethic.'[591] Samuel Brittan sees a Citizen's Income 'not as a handout, but as

---

[587] Brittan, Samuel (1998) *Towards a humane individualism*, London: John Stuart Mill Institute, p 11

[588] Alperovitz, Gar, 'On liberty', pp 106–10 in Cohen, Joshua and Rogers, Joel, *What's wrong with a free lunch?* Boston: Beacon Press

[589] Brittan, Samuel and Webb, Steven (1990) *Beyond the welfare state: An examination of Basic Incomes in a market economy*, Aberdeen: Aberdeen University Press, p 5

[590] Van Parijs, Philippe (1995) *Real freedom for all: What (if anything) can justify capitalism?* Oxford: Clarendon Press, pp 1, 33

[591] Brittan, Samuel and Webb, Steven (1990) *Beyond the welfare state: An examination of Basic Incomes in a market economy*, Aberdeen: Aberdeen University Press, p 2

a property right', as a 'return on the national capital',[592] and as 'a device for tackling a weakness in market capitalism'.[593] A Citizen's Income is

> a superior alternative to the minimum wage ... Minimum wages represent just that kind of interference with markets which does most harm. ...Those most likely to suffer are just the people whom the proponents of minimum wages say they most want to help. They include those on the fringes of the labour market or on the borderline of disablement or other incapacity ... and all the others who face a choice between low pay and no pay. Minimum wages are a denial of the human right to sell one's labour to a willing buyer and to make one's own decision about whether or not to take paid work at going rates.[594, 595]

A Citizen's Income is also preferable to means-tested systems because their intrusive nature is destructive of personal liberty: so while the taxation necessary to pay for a Citizen's Income might compromise the liberty of taxpayers, they ought to want to see it spent on a liberty-enhancing Citizen's Income rather than on non-liberating means-tested systems.[596]

The only argument against a Citizen's Income from a liberal perspective that I have been able to discover is from Johannes Richardt: that a Citizen's Income is 'underpinned by a negative image of humankind as weak, vulnerable and isolated. The basic thrust of this sentiment is that people cannot cope within the harsh environment of

---

[592] Brittan, Samuel and Webb, Steven (1990) *Beyond the welfare state: An examination of Basic Incomes in a market economy*, Aberdeen: Aberdeen University Press, p 3

[593] Brittan, Samuel (2005) 'Review of *Promoting income security as a right: Europe and North America*, edited by Guy Standing, Anthem Press [2004]', *Citizen's Income Newsletter*, issue 2, pp 8–9, p 9

[594] Brittan, Samuel and Webb, Steven (1990) *Beyond the welfare state: An examination of Basic Incomes in a market economy*, Aberdeen: Aberdeen University Press, p 7

[595] An exchange in Parliament, 17 June 2011, between Philip Davies MP and Edward Leigh MP, raised precisely this issue in relation to people with disabilities who could not find employment at the National Minimum Wage but might be able to do so for a lower wage.

[596] Munger, Michael (2011) 'Basic Income is not an obligation, but it might be a legitimate choice', *Basic Income Studies*, vol 6, no 2, pp 1–13; Liebermann, Sascha (2012) 'Germany: far, though close – problems and prospects of BI in Germany', pp 83–106 in Caputo, Richard (ed.) *Basic Income guarantee and politics: International experiences and perspectives on the viability of Income Guarantee*, New York: Palgrave Macmillan, pp 95–6

globalised capitalism without state assistance.'[597] He adds that a Citizen's Income would be too expensive.

Social democracy

Equality, liberty, solidarity and autonomy are all important ideals, and in a just society every citizen should experience all of them to some extent, so social democracy is a 'synthesis of economic prosperity, political participation, social justice and cultural maturity' (Tony Fitzpatrick).[598] The state is the instrument through which different needs are balanced and met, and through which different rights are guaranteed, all in the service of the most just society possible under the circumstances.[599] Social democracy is realistic in the sense that it recognises that a balancing act is required between an efficient economy and such ideals as equality and freedom.

The balanced position underlying the report of the Labour Party's Commission on Social Justice locates it in the world of social democracy. The introduction states that the UK 'can be both fairer and more successful: indeed, that it must be both fairer and more successful if it is to be either.'

The report's argument for a Citizen's Income is worth quoting at length:

> The case for Citizen's Income is partly moral and partly economic. The moral case rests on the principle of social citizenship ... civil and political rights must go hand in hand with economic and social rights. And just as civil and political rights belong unconditionally to all citizens as individuals, irrespective of need or desert, so all citizens have a right to a share in the social and national product sufficient to make it possible for them to participate fully in the common life of society ... the state is no more entitled to say which citizens have a right to a sufficient share in the common stock to participate fully in the life of the

---

[597] Richardt, Johannes (2011) 'Basic Income, low aspiration', *The Sp!ked Review of Books*, issue 41, January. www.spiked-online.com/index.php/site/reviewofbooks_article/10136/

[598] Fitzpatrick, Tony (2003) *After the new social democracy: Social welfare for the twenty-first century*, Manchester: Manchester University Press, pp 2, 5

[599] Page, Robert (2008) 'Social democracy', pp 77–83 in Alcock, Peter, May, Margaret and Rowlingson, Karen, *The student's companion to social policy*, 3rd edn, Oxford: Blackwell, p 77

society than to say which citizens have a right to vote or to a fair trial. And in modern conditions that principle can be realised more simply and more completely by a Citizen's Income than by any other mechanism. The economic case rests upon the falling demand for unskilled labour. ... a Citizen's Income ... enables those without saleable skills to take low-paid or casual jobs of some kind, while at the same time receiving an income large enough to enfranchise them, without the stigma of a means test.[600]

If social democracy can be defined as the desire to integrate socialism's equality with liberalism's personal autonomy, then Bill Jordan's argument for a Citizen's Income as 'the best cornerstone of ... equal autonomy in an advanced economy'[601] describes the essence of social democracy's argument for a Citizen's Income.

As well as offering arguments for a Citizen's Income, the Labour Party's Commission on Social Justice also suggests three

severe difficulties: 1. A change of this magnitude would have to be backed by a broad-based consensus, of which there is, as yet, no sign. In a society with a strong work ethic many people would oppose, as giving 'something for nothing', a scheme deliberately designed to offer unconditional benefits to all ... 2. although Citizen's Income is intended to be a means of social inclusion, it could just as easily become a means of social exclusion ... 3. ... the tax rates that would be required for funding, and their possible effects.

However,

it would be unwise ... to rule out a move towards Citizen's Income in future: if it turns out to be the case that earnings simply cannot provide a stable income for a growing proportion of people, then the notion of some guaranteed income, outside the labour market, could become increasingly attractive. Work incentives might matter less and those who happened to be in employment, knowing that they probably would not remain so throughout their

---

[600] Commission on Social Justice (1994) *Social justice: Strategies for national renewal*, London: Vintage, pp 261–2

[601] Jordan, Bill (1987) *Rethinking welfare*, Oxford: Basil Blackwell, p 159

'working' lives, might be more willing to finance an unconditional payment. Our measures would not preclude a move to Citizen's Income in the future.[602]

New Labour ('the Third Way', 'the new social democracy', and possibly 'compassionate conservatism')

We live in a global free market economy, and we cannot change that. Those who can work should support themselves and their dependents. The state will support those who cannot do that.

> The overall aim of third way politics should be to help citizens pilot their way through the major revolutions of our time: globalization, transformations in personal life, and our relationship to nature [by promoting] an active civil society, the democratic family, the new mixed economy, equality as inclusion, positive welfare, the social investment state, the cosmopolitan nation, cosmopolitan democracy. (Anthony Giddens)[603]

The New Social Democracy is a 'third way' between two paths *not* taken: old-style social democracy (with too much faith in the state) and neoliberalism (with too much faith in unregulated markets):[604] it is a recognition that global capitalism is inevitable and that we must mitigate its worst effects.[605]

In relation to the welfare state, advocates of the Third Way write of 'positive welfare', which replaces the 'welfare state' with the 'investment state': for instance, by replacing a fixed retirement age with more flexible arrangements. Benefits systems should be reformed where they induce moral hazard, and a more active risk-taking attitude should be encouraged, wherever possible through incentives, but where necessary by legal obligations.[606]

---

[602] Commission on Social Justice (1994) *Social justice: Strategies for national renewal*, London: Vintage, pp 262–3, 263–4

[603] Giddens, Anthony (1998) *The third way: The renewal of social democracy*, Cambridge: Polity Press, pp 66, 64, 70

[604] Callinicos, Alex (2001) *Against the third way: An anti-capitalist criticism*, Cambridge: Polity Press, p 2

[605] Fitzpatrick, Tony (2003) *After the new social democracy: Social welfare for the twenty-first century*, Manchester: Manchester University Press, pp 3–4

[606] Giddens, Anthony (1998) *The third way: The renewal of social democracy*, Cambridge: Polity Press, pp 117, 124, 122

> The restructuring of welfare systems should have several
> ends in view ... reacting to new social and economic
> conditions and coping with the perverse outcomes to which
> the welfare state has given rise.[607]

For advocates of the 'Third Way', a Citizen's Income would reduce
disincentives and would therefore encourage good behaviour in the
labour market; it would support the incomes of the virtuous; it would
be employment-friendly and savings-friendly; it would offer equality
of opportunity; it would target those in need (because the wealthy
already pay more tax than the poor); and it would offer 'universal
equal autonomy'. It would be at a level 'which allows the labour power
supplied to be efficiently used for socially necessary purposes'.[608]

I could not find any New Labour or Third Way adherents offering
arguments against a Citizen's Income, but one conceivable argument
would be that those not behaving well in the labour market would still
receive a Citizen's Income, and perhaps they should not.

Green perspectives

The biggest issues facing humankind in the longer term are global
warming and resource depletion: concerns represented by Green
Parties and to differing extents within parties focused on other political
ideologies. So the question that we must ask is this: Would a Citizen's
Income help or hinder the protection of the environment and the
reduction of global warming? – though, as we have seen before, the
better question to ask might be this: Would a Citizen's Income be better
for the planet than the current benefits system?

At the heart of the problem are two relationships: the relationship
between overwork, over-consumption, and lack of leisure, for those
in employment;[609] and the relationship between underwork, under-
consumption, and too much leisure, for those without employment.
These relationships look as if they are cemented in place by the way
in which the current system links employment to subsistence income,
thus encouraging employment, which in turn correlates with Gross
Domestic Product. It therefore looks as if breaking the link between
income and employment might reduce employment and thus reduce

---

[607] Giddens, Anthony (2000) *The third way and its critics*, Cambridge: Polity Press, pp
112, 121

[608] Jordan, Bill (1998) *The new politics of welfare*, London: Sage, pp 174–5, 178–9

[609] Robinson, Tim (2006) *Work, leisure and the environment*, London: Edward Elgar, p ix

economic growth measured in terms of Gross Domestic Product.[610] This is the approach recommended by Devine, Pearmain and Purdy, in their search for 'a sustainable post-capitalist world', that takes the danger of climate change seriously, and is characterised by a combination of 'social equality and human solidarity' and by 'positive freedom and democratic self-government'.[611] They recommend a Citizen's Income as the means of breaking the link between work and income; and similarly, Van Parijs shows how a Citizen's Income would tackle unemployment by fostering a more flexible labour market which would in turn 'tackle unemployment without relying on faster growth'.[612]

But the real question is surely one of causality. It is the demand for products and services that fuels economic growth, and demand depends on net incomes. If a Citizen's Income were to redistribute net incomes towards the poor, then they would consume more, thus increasing consumption, resource depletion, and global warming. Such consumption might not be particularly discriminating. As Casassas and González Bailón suggest, a Citizen's Income 'would not necessarily lead to more conscientious consumers;'[613] and, in general, a Citizen's Income 'guarantees a minimum income for all and challenges the employment ethic, but it also seems to depend upon the ecologically very damaging activities to which Greens object'.[614] A Citizen's Income could mean greater human equality and solidarity, and thus increasing concern for the environment, and it could mean more hours spent in community activity and less in manufacturing; but it could also mean more secure incomes and thus increasing consumption.[615] These influences could work in opposite directions, and it is difficult to know which would

---

[610] Fitzpatrick, Tony (1999) *Freedom and security: An introduction to the Basic Income debate*, Basingstoke: Macmillan, p 186

[611] Devine, Pat, Pearmain, Andrew and Purdy, David (eds) (2009) *Feelbad Britain: How to make it better*, London: Lawrence and Wishart, pp 65–6. See also Nissen, Sylke (1992) 'The jobs dilemma: ecological versus economic issues', *BIRG Bulletin*, no 14, pp 9–11

[612] Van Parijs, Philippe (2001) 'A Basic Income for all', pp 3–26 in Cohen, Joshua and Rogers, Joel, *What's wrong with a free lunch?* Boston: Beacon Press, p 21

[613] Casassas, David and Bailón, Sandra González (2007) 'Corporate Watch, Consumer Responsibility, and Economic Democracy: Forms of political action in the orbit of a Citizen's Income', *Citizen's Income Newsletter*, issue 3, pp 8–12, p 9

[614] Fitzpatrick, Tony (2002) 'With no strings attached? Basic Income and the greening of security', pp 138–54 in Fitzpatrick, Tony and Cahill, Michael (eds) *Environment and welfare: Towards a green social policy*, Basingstoke: Palgrave Macmillan, p 150

[615] Lord, Clive (2012) 'Reconciling old conflicts', pp 136–53 in Lord, Clive, Kennet, Miriam and Felton, Judith (eds) *Citizen's Income and green economics*, Reading: The Green Economics Institute, p 149

be the strongest. So why is it so often the same people who advocate 'green' social policies and a Citizen's Income? Van Parijs suggests that post-industrial society makes space for an 'autonomous sphere', separate from both the market and the state, and that in this autonomous sphere we find both sustainability and Citizen's Income, and people who advocate both of them.[616] Here the same personality type wants to see less consumption in order to save the planet, will themselves wish to consume less, will want more time for community and political activity, and will therefore value the freedom that a Citizen's Income would give to them to create 'social goods'.[617] Maybe he is right; and maybe it will be the shift in values that a Citizen's Income would inspire that will bring environmental benefits, rather than any direct effect on consumption. [618] Another possible link between concern for sustainability and advocacy for a Citizen's Income is suggested by the UK's Green Party: that 'we cannot expect people still stuck in the poverty trap to think of [saving the planet] as a priority. Creating a fairer society and saving the planet go hand-in-hand.'[619] No direct ideological link between a Citizen's Income and an ecological mindset is either present or required.

We have already discussed the fact that the effects of the implementation of a Citizen's Income on a variety of aspects of our economic and social life will be more to do with the way in which the existing tax and benefits structure relates to them than with the way in which a Citizen's Income would do so. The same is true here. If a Citizen's Income were to be funded by reducing tax allowances and most contributory and means-tested benefits, then we might see little change in resource depletion or global warming; but if it were to be funded by taxing fossil fuels then we could see less fossil fuel use and less global warming.[620] For this reason, Fitzpatrick recognises that 'a Green policy package should include not only BI [Citizen's

---

[616] Van Parijs, Philippe (2009) 'Political ecology: from autonomous sphere to Basic Income', *Basic Income Studies*, vol 4, no 2, pp 1–9
[617] Van Parijs, Philippe (1992) 'Competing justifications of Basic Income', pp 3–43 in Van Parijs, Philippe (ed.) *Arguing for Basic Income*, London: Verso, pp 26–8; Fitzpatrick, Tony (2009) 'Basic Income, post-productivism and liberalism', *Basic Income Studies*, vol 4, no 2, pp 1–11
[618] Boulanger, Paul-Marie (2009) 'Basic Income and sustainable consumption strategies', *Basic Income Studies*, vol 4, no 2, pp 1–11
[619] Green Party (2008) 'Policy: Citizen's Income: an end to the poverty trap', leaflet, London: Green Party
[620] Birnbaum, Simon (2009) 'Introduction: Basic Income, sustainability and post-productivism', *Basic Income Studies*, vol 4, no 2, pp 1–7

Income] but also land and energy taxes, working-time reductions and the expansion of informal exchanges in the third sector', with the Citizen's Income seen not so much as one of a number of ingredients, but as 'the instrument by which that package is constructed in the first place'.[621] As Jan Otto Andersson suggests, there is no reason why we should not use a Citizen's Income with carbon taxes to manage the transition to a sustainable economy in wealthier countries, and a Citizen's Income to promote additional production and consumption in poorer societies.[622] Here the Iranian experience discussed in Chapter 5 is instructive. Subsidised fuel was causing overconsumption of oil and increasing pollution of the environment. The government removed subsidies and, largely by accident, implemented a Citizen's Income to protect incomes. Because of the higher prices, less oil-based fuel is consumed, and the environment is less damaged. Carbon taxes used to fund a Citizen's Income would have the same effect: less resource depletion, less environmental damage, and incomes protected:[623] and the fact that carbon tax revenue would be distributed to the entire population would generate the necessary democratic pressure to ensure that such taxes would rise rather than be reduced.

So perhaps we can now be a little more confident that a Green perspective and a Citizen's Income really do belong together. A package containing both a Citizen's Income and carbon taxes is just what we need to kickstart sufficient care for the planet to arrest both global warming and resource depletion. It is on arguments such as these, as well as on the argument that 'we cannot expect people still stuck in the poverty trap to think of [saving the planet] as a priority',[624] that Green Parties should base their advocacy of a Citizen's Income.

---

[621] Fitzpatrick, Tony (1999) *Freedom and security: An introduction to the Basic Income debate*, Basingstoke: Macmillan, p 201. Cato, Molly Scott (2010) *Green economics: An introduction to theory, policy and practice*, Abingdon: Earthscan, also places a Citizen's Income at the heart of a green economics.

[622] Andersson, Jan Otto (2009) 'Basic Income From an Ecological Perspective', *Basic Income Studies*, vol 4, no 2, pp 1–8

[623] Van Parijs, Philippe (2012), remarks delivered at closing session, 16 September, 14th BIEN Congress, Munich; Tabatabai, Hamid (2012) 'Iran: a bumpy road toward Basic Income', pp 285–300 in Caputo, Richard (ed.) *Basic Income guarantee and Politics: International experiences and perspectives on the viability of Income Guarantee,* New York: Palgrave Macmillan; Tabatabai, Hamid (2012), contribution to a panel on Caputo, Richard (ed.) *Basic Income guarantee and politics*, 15 September, 14th BIEN Congress, Munich

[624] Green Party (2008) 'Policy: Citizen's Income: an end to the poverty trap', leaflet, London: Green Party

Tentative conclusions

All of the political ideologies studied in this chapter generate arguments for a Citizen's Income. These arguments are generally positive and robust, and are closely related to the ideologies concerned. They tend not to be negative arguments related to the perceived shortcomings of the current benefits system. The fact that a Citizen's Income can garner support from within such a wide range of political ideologies is surely significant,[625] and encourages us to believe that it would be possible for a Citizen's Income to gather all party support and find its way onto the UK's statute book. Other countries' political spectra will be different from that of the UK, but a similar range of ideologies will be evident. This suggests that in no country would political agreement be impossible.

Arguments against a Citizen's Income are not so closely related to the ideologies from within which they have been offered, similar arguments are found across the field, and they can all be answered:

- *A Citizen's Income would be too expensive.* That surely depends on the particular scheme. It would of course be perfectly possible to propose a scheme that saved the Exchequer money.
- *We should not pay people to do nothing.* We are already doing that, and the way in which we do it now discourages people from increasing their earned income.
- *Rich people do not need it.* Rich people pay more in tax than they would receive in Citizen's Income, and the low administrative costs of universal benefits mean that it is more efficient to give the Citizen's Income to everyone.
- *A Citizen's Income would discourage people from seeking employment.* Precisely the opposite is true. It is today's system that discourages people from seeking employment. A Citizen's Income would deliver lower marginal deduction rates and so would provide a greater employment incentive than people experience today; and it would reduce the budgetary chaos that households experience when someone's labour market status changes, and so would enable households to rearrange their employment patterns if that was what their own and the labour market's needs required. This means that with a Citizen's Income people would be more likely to seek employment, not less.

---

[625] Fitzpatrick, Tony (1999) *Freedom and security: An introduction to the Basic Income debate*, Basingstoke: Macmillan, p 5

These four objections have deep roots in our collective conscious and subconscious minds, which means that to propose a Citizen's Income might meet with public resistance. This ought not to deflect policy makers towards less 'demanding' policies.[626] If a government has good reasons for implementing a change in policy, then even if the change does not *at the time* resonate with public opinion, it can both lead and change it.[627] A classic case is equalities legislation, which has generally been ahead of public opinion and has helped to form it; and another more recent case, in a variety of European countries, is the banning of smoking in public places. The proposed policy has to possess the capacity to garner public support after implementation. In the UK, Family Allowances achieved this quickly, and a new Single-tier State Pension will easily do the same. If a Citizen's Income were to be implemented, then its advantages would quickly become clear, and public acceptance and then approval would be rapid.

Because universal benefits find ideological support within such a wide variety of political positions – a fact interesting in itself, and suggestive of a new political current with which people of a variety of current persuasions could identify[628] – it will be no problem that the UK currently has a coalition government and that we might see further coalition governments both here and elsewhere in the future. Ministers of different parties will be able to argue for increased use of universal benefits from within their own ideologies, they will be able to agree on pragmatic arguments, and they will be able to answer objections from people in their own parties.

Would the ideology of the party in government affect the effects of a Citizen's Income implemented by that government? The answer is: Citizen's Incomes of different amounts would of course have different effects, and different means of paying for the Citizen's Income would have different labour market and social implications: but otherwise the answer is 'no'. Any difference would be caused by interactions

---

[626] Midtgaard, Søren F. (2008) 'Rawlsian stability and Basic Income', *Basic Income Studies*, vol 3, no 2, pp 1–17

[627] In terms of the conceptual structure employed in De Wispelaere, Jürgen, and Noguera, José Antonio (2012) 'On the political feasibility of universal Basic Income: an analytic framework', pp 17–38 in Caputo, Richard (ed.) *Basic Income guarantee: International experiences and perspectives on the viability of income guarantee*, New York: Palgrave Macmillan: 'Psychological feasibility' can belong in the retrospective ('viability') constraints category rather than in the prospective ('achievability') constraints category: see www.bien2012.de/sites/default/files/ppt_033_en.pdf

[628] Purdy, David (1998) 'Towards a BI democracy', *BIRG Bulletin*, no 8, Autumn, pp 10–12

between the Citizen's Income and the government's other social policies: and because the character of those interactions would relate almost entirely to the complexities of other policies, and hardly at all to the radical simplicity of the Citizen's Income, it is the government's other policies that would determine different social and economic outcomes. Similarly, at the point of implementation, it would be changes to interactions between existing policies that would create different social and economic consequences. Those changes would depend on how existing benefits and allowances were reduced, and on how those reductions interacted with other social policies, and not on the characteristics of the Citizen's Income itself. So yes, implementation of a Citizen's Income would create different effects in different political contexts, but the cause of those different effects would not be the Citizen's Income.

It is true, though, as Tony Atkinson has suggested, that 'in a rational world, the Partial [Citizen's] Income may have a lot to recommend it, but political decisions are not made in that way'.[629] This is not to believe that 'given the unpredictability of historical development it is illusory to suppose that a political state can steer an economy to "deliver" welfare';[630] but it is to say that 'account has to be taken of the background of shifting political objectives and support, and programmes for reform have to be designed with a view to the political processes necessary for their introduction' (Atkinson and Sutherland).[631]

Politics is relationships and values in institutional form,[632] and politics is how society makes its decisions.[633] The argument of this chapter suggests that there is no reason to suppose that it would be impossible for the political processes in a wide variety of countries to deliver Citizens' Incomes.

---

[629] Atkinson, A.B. (1985) *Income maintenance and social insurance: A survey*, Welfare State Programme, paper no 5, London: LSE, p 102

[630] O'Brien, Martin and Penna, Sue (1998) *Theorising welfare: Enlightenment and modern society*, London: Sage, p 104

[631] Atkinson, A.B. and Sutherland, Holly (1988a) *Integrating incomes taxation and social security: Analysis of a partial Basic Income*, Tax, Incentives and the Distribution of Income paper no 123, London: LSE, p 18

[632] Parker, Hermione (1989) *Instead of the dole: An enquiry into integration of the tax and benefit systems*, London: Routledge, pp 6–7; cf. Farnsworth, Kevin (2011) 'From economic crisis to a new age of austerity: the UK', pp 251–70 in *Social Policy in Challenging Times: Economic crisis and welfare systems*, Bristol: Policy Press, pp 267–8

[633] Fitzpatrick, Tony (2011) *Welfare theory: An introduction to the theoretical debates in social policy*, 2nd edn, Basingstoke: Palgrave Macmillan, p 211

Policy directions of our time

In previous chapters we explored a number of criteria for an ideal benefits system and measured both our current system and a Citizen's Income against them. We have now studied the broad outlines of a variety of political ideologies and asked whether they might translate into support for a Citizen's Income. Equally important is to study current political trends and ask whether a reform proposal might cohere with them, because such trends might or might not all be coherent with a single political ideology, or indeed with any recognisable political ideologies. While maybe it ought not to concern us whether a Citizen's Income fits with the concerns of today's politicians, our ability to advocate a Citizen's Income will undoubtedly be affected by the scheme's characteristics and effects, and by the ways in which those characteristics and effects might or might not be consistent with today's immediate political concerns.

We might characterise the UK government's current policy directions as follows: a) the encouragement of enterprise in a free market context, b) the extension of choice, c) equality between women and men, d) active and equal citizenship, and e) 'we're in it together' … .[634] Readers in other countries might wish to characterise their own government's current concerns, and then test a Citizen's Income against them.

a) The encouragement of enterprise in a free market context

In the absence of any benefits system, workers have to demand at least a subsistence income, whatever the economic benefit of their labour; and the employer or customer has to pay that subsistence income. With a means-tested benefits system, a worker might price their labour at a certain value per hour, but because benefits are withdrawn as earnings rise, the worker might need to demand more than that price in order

---

[634] Cf. The Four Propositions on Social Justice in The Social Justice Commission (1994) *Social justice: Strategies for national renewal*, the report of the Social Justice Commission, London: Vintage, pp 20f: '1. We must transform the welfare state from a safety net in times of trouble to a springboard for economic opportunity. Paid work for a fair wage is the most secure and sustainable way out of poverty … 2. We must radically improve access to education and training, and invest in the talent of all our people … 3. We must promote real choices across the life-cycle in the balance of employment, family, education, leisure and retirement … 4. We must reconstruct the social wealth of our country. Social institutions, from the family to local government, must be nurtured to provide a dependable social environment in which people can lead their lives. Renewal must come from the bottom up as well as from the top down.'

to achieve that net value. In either case the market is skewed. So with our current benefits system we simply cannot operate a free market in labour. Only by reducing withdrawal rates, preferably to zero, would we have anything like one.[635]

The current system does little to promote enterprise. If you are on means-tested benefits then starting a business is hardly worth thinking about. Either the new business will end up in the informal economy, or it will never be attempted. After all, why start a business, or seek additional earnings, or seek training so that you can be promoted, if you keep only a few pence in every additional pound earned ? And in particular: why risk the chaos that results from declaring fluctuating self-employed earnings?

Eithne McLaughlin offers a useful agenda:

> Reforms should encourage and enable all those whose potential earnings are low to take any form of paid work – full-time, part-time (whether long or short hours), casual, fixed term or own-account ... Reforms should ensure that both men and women, two parent and lone parent families, can improve their incomes in the short-term by engaging in more employment or self-employment ... Reforms should ensure that both men and women, two-parent and lone-parent families, can secure financial well-being in the long term, including after retirement.[636]

As we have seen in Chapters 9 and 10, one means to this end would be a Citizen's Income.

b) The extension of choice

The current system makes it difficult for parents to share the care of children or elderly relatives between them. If two members of a couple both decide to work part-time, rather than one working full-time and the other taking on the caring role, then a difficult relationship with the tax and benefits systems can become an impossible one. It is so much simpler for one member of the couple to work full-time and the other not to be employed (or perhaps to take occasional employment of a

---

[635] Vobruba, Georg (1991) 'Basic Income, democracy and the labour market', *BIRG Bulletin*, no 13, August, pp 18–19

[636] McLaughlin, Eithne (1994) *Flexibility in work and benefits*, London: IPPR/ Commission on Social Justice, p 4

few hours here and there): so that is normally what happens, even if it would be better for the family to do it differently. The current system offers no rewards to people who care for children or choose to care for elderly or disabled relatives. They end up without an independent income (except where specifically disability related or attendance benefits are being paid), even though they are contributing to society by providing for the welfare of the next generation or the previous one.

As we have seen in Chapter 7, a Citizen's Income would make things a lot easier.

c) Equality between women and men

The current system still assumes that in a couple the man is the breadwinner and the woman is dependent on him; and even where it is possible for either party to make the claim for benefits, it will generally be the man that makes it, and it is the household-based system that makes this possible. We would not put up with this in any other social sphere. The problem is that recipients of means-tested benefits have little voice, though why 'Tax Credits' claimants are not a bit more audible is rather difficult to fathom. It looks as if 'Universal Credit' will be administered in the same way, perpetuating the disadvantage of women in the domestic economy.

d) Active and equal citizenship

The current system fosters a divided society, with some people paying tax and some suffering a very different means test. Taxpayers are treated as responsible individuals, whereas many 'Tax Credit' recipients – those whose spouses receive the household's entitlements – are not. This is far from the active and equal citizenship that we might wish to see; and it looks as if it will not change under 'Universal Credit'.

Chapter 12 contains an extended discussion of citizenship and its relationship to a Citizen's Income.

e) 'We're in it together'

The UK's current system relieves the poorest at the expense of the not quite so poor by extracting from the not quite so poor a high proportion of their means-tested benefits when their earned income rises. It is this withdrawal of additional earnings that pays the lion's share of the means-tested benefits paid to the poorest, not the relatively minor tax incursions experienced by the wealthy. Many UK benefits recipients experience tax rates of 95 per cent, and many more of 85 per cent. Under 'Universal Credit' it will be 65 per cent for those below the tax threshold, and 76 per cent for those above it.[637] This is an improvement. However, the highest earners tell us that an Income Tax rate of 50 per cent would choke off enterprise and encourage them to leave the country. The government takes notice of this argument, but fails to see the connection with discussion of marginal withdrawal rates for poorer households.

With Child Benefit, however, we really are 'all in it together'. Child Benefit binds every child, and every family with children, into a single society;[638] and it rightly declares children to be members of both present and future society, and not simply their parents' consumption choice. Not only does Child Benefit provide every family with a secure income floor on which to build, but, because it is genuinely universal, it recognises, symbolises, and reinforces the unity of our society. It is unfortunate that Child Benefit is the only part of our benefits system that recognises that we all belong in a single society. Everything else divides us up into categories: employed and unemployed, married and single, recipients of National Insurance benefits and claimants of means-tested benefits, taxpayers and benefits recipients.[639]

We live in a society more diverse than ever. Not only are we now a multiracial, multifaith and multicultural society, but we now have highly diverse experiences of household arrangements, family relationships, and relationships to the economy and the labour market. Social cohesion is an increasingly urgent need, and an increasingly difficult one to fulfil: but whose responsibility is it to provide for social cohesion? While there might be legitimate debate about the precise extent to which the government is responsible for social cohesion, it is clearly essential that certain minimum levels of solidarity and community safety are required, and that the government must provide for them if nobody else is doing so.[640] We assume that the government has some responsibility for providing for a variety of individuals' needs, so there is no reason for not assuming that it also bears some responsibility for satisfying a variety of social needs. It must also be true that if there are

637 DWP (2011) *Universal Credit: welfare that works*, Cm 7957, London: The Stationery Office, p 50, www.dwp.gov.uk/policy/welfare-reform/legislation-and-key-documents/universal-credit/

638 Smith, Roger (1997) 'Children, families and Citizen's Income', *Citizen's Income Bulletin*, no 23, February, pp 2–3

639 Brown, Joan (1988) *Child Benefit: Investing in the future*, London: Child Poverty Action Group, pp 35, xiii, 25

640 Spicker, Paul (2000) *The welfare state: A general theory*, London: Sage, p 138

two ways of spending public money, one of which contributes positively towards social cohesion, and one of which damages it, then it is the former that must be government policy. As Carol Walker has pointed out, 'universal benefits show solidarity between the rich and the poor; between the sick and the well; between the old and the young; between families with children and those without.'[641] A Citizen's Income would therefore contribute to social cohesion, and means-tested benefits damage it: so if the replacement of means-tested benefits by a Citizen's Income would cost no additional public expenditure, then it is surely the government's responsibility to establish a Citizen's Income.

It also seems reasonable to assume that the government's responsibility is to ensure the high quality of public services. As Richard Titmuss has rightly suggested, 'poor quality selective services for poor people were the product of a society that saw "welfare" as a residual, as a public burden.'[642] Universal benefits, on the other hand, go to everyone and so are more likely to remain of high quality;[643] and because they benefit everyone, they make 'welfare' into something that we share, something that we ensure that everyone experiences, and something to which everyone contributes according to their means. When Paul Spicker surveys the evidence he discovers that

> the schemes which do best, like provision for older people in Sweden, are the ones which provide for people regardless of need. Schemes which offer a 'safety net' do not do so well in securing a minimum income. If a system is based on support for everyone, poor people will also be helped. If it supports only the poor, some are likely to be excluded.[644]

In particular, universal benefits promote one of the societal attributes most necessary to social cohesion: trust. A Norwegian research project has found that being on means-tested benefits reduces levels of interpersonal trust, but that universal benefits increase them. The promotion of trust in society is a proper responsibility for government,

---

[641] Walker, Carol (2011) 'For universalism and against the means test', pp 133–152 in Walker, Alan, Sinfield, Adrian and Walker, Carol (eds) *Fighting poverty, inequality and injustice: A manifesto inspired by Peter Townsend*, Cambridge: Polity Press, pp 149–50

[642] Titmuss, Richard (1968) *Commitment to welfare*, London: George Allen & Unwin, p 134

[643] Walker, Carol (2011) 'For universalism and against the means test', pp 133–152 in Walker, Alan, Sinfield, Adrian and Walker, Carol (eds) *Fighting poverty, inequality and injustice: A manifesto inspired by Peter Townsend*, Cambridge: Polity Press, pp 149–50

[644] Spicker, Paul (2007) *The idea of poverty*, Bristol: Policy Press, p 136

because contracts require an adequate level of trust within society, and because only if there is a certain level of trust between individuals, institutions and the government will citizens pay their taxes. Because the government is responsible for maintaining the level of trust within society, it is surely also responsible for ensuring the maximum number of universal benefits. Trust is an asset; the maintenance of social assets is a government responsibility; so a welfare state structure that maximises the levels of social trust should be a primary concern for governments.[645]

Because a Citizen's Income would go to every individual, it would immediately create a whole new sense of social cohesion, and lay the foundation for a 'social citizenship' based on trust, inclusion, and reciprocity.[646] No longer would we be divided into workers (subject to tax regulations) and non-workers (subject to benefits regulations): a division central to the European Union's 'Social Charter',[647] which is about workers and not citizens, and which therefore bears little relation to today's social or labour market realities. If we wish to maintain social cohesion, then both the Social Charter and our income maintenance policies need to be about 'citizens'.

There would still, of course, be considerable differences in treatment between different categories of people in other parts of the benefits and tax systems. A means-tested safety net might still be needed for a while, and this would pay out different amounts to different people; the tax system will always treat different people in different ways, according to their financial circumstances; and people with disabilities will always have additional needs that will require individually tailored benefits provisions. But a Citizen's Income would go to the wealthiest person in the country and to the poorest, and in the same amounts to the married and the single; to the employed, the self-employed and the unemployed; and to the person suffering disability and the person not. Citizen's Incomes for older people and for the young might be of different amounts, but those amounts would be entirely determined by the person's age, and not by any other circumstances: so every seventy

---

[645] Hyggen, Christer (2006) 'Risks and resources: social capital among social assistance recipients in Norway', *Social Policy and Administration*, vol 40, no 5, pp 493–508, p 507

[646] Taylor-Gooby, Peter (2009) *Reframing social citizenship*, Oxford: Oxford University Press

[647] The Social Charter is not a 'social chapter' of the Maastricht Treaty because the UK government insisted on not implementing it. The following Labour government failed to implement the social charter, presumably because the Labour Party is largely financed by trade unions, and thus by workers, and mainly full-time ones. (Gray, Anne (2004) *Unsocial Europe: Social protection or flexploitation*, London: Pluto Press, pp 153–4)

year old would be treated in the same way, and every five year old would be treated in the same way, whatever their health, wealth, income, housing, or family relationships. The owner of the burnt down shop would receive a Citizen's Income, and the arsonist who burnt it down would receive one too – and in order to express the hope that people in prison will return to society as valued and responsible members of it, it might be important for prisoners to receive their Citizen's Incomes while they are inside.

It is difficult to predict some of a Citizen's Income's effects, in relation to the labour market, the economy, family relationships, and household structure. It is also difficult to predict exactly the effect that a Citizen's Income might have on social cohesion: but it does not take much of a stretch of the imagination to believe that it cannot fail to be a positive one.

Political feasibility

We have discussed the political feasibility of a Citizen's Income in terms of the effect of the proposal on the civil service, and in terms of how politicians' ideological commitments might lead them to react. Equally important is to know precisely which political actors are in favour of a Citizen's Income. For a political party marginal in electoral terms to espouse a Citizen's Income could lead other parties with more political power to react against it. Only by persuading mainstream parties, with large numbers of seats in national parliaments, that universal benefits are coherent with their political ideologies, will a Citizen's Income be the result. However, how such 'readily identifiable actors' might relate to a proposal for a Citizen's Income is only one factor in assessing whether a Citizen's Income might be politically feasible. De Wispelaere and Noguera distinguish between 'readily identifiable actors' and 'an amorphous set of actors': that is, the general public, or sections of it. How this collective reality chooses to relate to a Citizen's Income proposal could be just as important to its implementation as how identifiable actors might relate to it, because identifiable actors might be substantially influenced by the views of the 'amorphous set of actors'. For a Citizen's Income to be achieved, the proposal needs to be 'strategically feasible' (that is, identifiable actors need to be persuaded to act), and it needs to be 'psychologically feasible' (that is, the 'amorphous set of actors' need to be persuaded: or at least need to be persuaded not to resist the proposal). But that is not the end of the story, either. For a Citizen's Income to thrive, it needs to be 'institutionally feasible': that is, the Citizen's Income, as implemented, needs to produce the effects promised: and that will to some extent depend on the institutional environment in which it is implemented. For instance, if simplicity of administration is not in fact achieved (for instance, in the UK context, if just as many individuals as before find themselves on means-tested benefits), then the 'identifiable actors' will react against a Citizen's Income and it will not thrive. Similarly, if a Citizen's Income does not produce the expected effects for individuals (for instance, in terms of more predictable net incomes, fewer administrative burdens, additional employment choices, and a growth in labour market activity and efficiency), then 'behavioural feasibility' would not be achieved, and again the Citizen's Income would not thrive.[648]

The arguments that we have offered in Chapters 6 to 9 suggest that neither institutional nor behavioural feasibility should be impossible to achieve once a Citizen's Income is implemented. The arguments offered in this chapter suggest that strategic feasibility should also be possible. The more difficult imponderable is whether psychological feasibility is possible. As I have suggested in relation to equalities legislation, strategic feasibility can engender psychological feasibility. This suggests that persuading identifiable political actors of the benefits of a Citizen's Income is the main task ahead of us.

Given that a Citizen's Income, once implemented, would need to garner psychological, institutional and behavioural feasibility in order to thrive, we need to revisit the question discussed in Chapter 4 as to which might be the best way to implement a Citizen's Income. Because it might be difficult for a very small Citizen's Income to generate the psychological, institutional and behavioural feasibilities to enable it to thrive and grow, it might be better to implement a Citizen's Income one demographic group at a time. The Citizen's Income for each group would then be able to prove itself, providing both strategic and psychological feasibilities that would between them promote implementation for additional demographic groups.

Conclusion

In the preface to a volume of essays for and against the establishment of a Citizen's Income in the United States, the editors point out that none of the authors condemn the proposal on the grounds of cost.

---

[648] De Wispelaere, Jürgen and Noguera, José Antonio (2012) 'On the political feasibility of universal Basic Income: an analytic framework', pp 17–38 in Caputo, Richard K. (ed.) *Basic Income guarantee and politics: International experiences and perspectives on the viability of income guarantee,* New York: Palgrave Macmillan

> The main hurdles to establishing a UBI in the United States are honest disagreements of political morality ... [Citizen's Income] could be done. The question is whether we want to achieve it'[649]

This suggests that the content of our next chapter, on affordability, might be rather less important than the content of this one.

In relation to the crucial issue for humankind – whether we shall still have a viable planet to inhabit – differences in political outlook pale into insignificance; and perhaps the crucial debate to be had has little to do with a changing labour market, changing family structures, social cohesion, or differing political ideologies, and much more to do with the effects on our environment of a change from means-tested to universal benefits. Given the multiple complex factors involved in the relationship between the tax and benefits systems and the sustainability of the environment, only a sizeable Citizen's Income pilot project can provide the necessary evidence: a possibility that we have already raised in relation to discovering a Citizen's Income's effects on the employment market.

---

[649] Cohen, Joshua and Rogers, Joel (2001) *What's wrong with a free lunch?*, Boston: Beacon Press, Preface, pp xvii–xviii, p xviii

CHAPTER 14

Can we afford a Citizen's Income?

There are two parts to this question: In order to know what we are funding, we shall need to know precisely how large a Citizen's Income we are attempting to fund. We shall also need to know how to calculate the costs of a Citizen's Income. Once these questions have been answered, we shall need to study the funding options.

How large should a Citizen's Income be?

There are several ways of answering this question:

- **Ease of implementation:** Turning existing tax allowances into a Citizen's Income, and reducing means-tested and most contributory benefits by an amount equal to the Citizen's Income, would be the easiest way to establish a universal benefit. The amount of Citizen's Income paid to every citizen would therefore be determined by the current levels of tax allowances and benefits. This is the approach taken by Hermione Parker: see the next section.
- **Political testing:** One way of testing the political sustainability of a Citizen's Income would be to start with a small one and let it grow, while testing public opinion along the way. The level reached after several years would thus be democratically controlled.
- **A needs-based approach:** We could argue that all members of society have certain subsistence needs in common, and that all other needs and desires are subsidiary.[650, 651] This suggests that an assessment of common subsistence needs is required – though whether we should take a normative approach to this, based on some extrinsic notion of what human beings need, or whether opinion sampling should determine the basket of basic needs, is of course an ideological question. (London Weekend Television was a pioneer of the opinion-sounding approach in 1983,[652] and useful

---

[650] Cribb, Jonathan, Joyce, Robert, and Phillips, David (2012) *Living standards, poverty and inequality in the UK: 2012*, London: Institute for Fiscal Studies, pp 95–117

[651] Fitzpatrick, Tony (2011) *Welfare theory: An introduction to the theoretical debates in social policy*, 2nd edn, Basingstoke: Palgrave Macmillan, pp 7–8, 24–5, 108

[652] Lansley, Stewart and Mack, Joanna (1983) *Breadline Britain*, London: London Weekend Television

work has been done more recently by the Family Budget Unit,[653] government statisticians, and the Institute for Fiscal Studies.) Once a decision is made as to how much money an individual needs in order to satisfy basic subsistence needs, the Citizen's Income could be set at that level[654] (though see Chapter 16 on the problem posed by differential housing costs). Such a needs-based approach would match an equal Citizen's Income to equal subsistence needs, and a variety of variable sources of income to variable subsidiary needs and desires.[655]

Calculating costs

Calculating the cost of a change in tax or benefits is far from easy.[656] First of all, the data on which any costing estimate needs to be based is subject to error. The relatively small size of samples for income surveys means that calculating statistics for regions, and for the country as a whole, is an inexact science, and surveys generally underestimate self-employed earnings.[657] The figures for earnings in the national accounts include an estimate for self-employed earnings, and that is all it can be: an estimate.[658] While a survey of incomes might indicate what the tax base ought to be, the income on which tax is in fact collected will be

---

[653] Bradshaw, Jonathan (1991) 'How much is enough?' *BIRG Bulletin*, no 12, February, pp 13–14; Nelson, Michael and Mayer, Anne-Marie (1992) 'Modest-but-adequate food budgets', *BIRG Bulletin*, no 14, February, pp 11–14; Yu, Autumn C.S. (1994) 'Citizen's Income and family budgets', *Citizen's Income Bulletin*, no 17, January, pp 21–24; www.york.ac.uk/res/fbu. The Family Budget Unit was wound up in 2011, and its intellectual property transferred to the Minimum Income Standards Project, www.minimumincomestandard.org at the University of Loughborough.

[654] Miller, Anne (2009) 'Minimum Income Standards: A challenge for Citizen's Income', *Citizen's Income Newsletter*, issue 3, pp 6–14

[655] For an argument against a Citizen's Income rising above subsistence level see Barry, Brian (2001) 'UBI and the work ethic', pp 60–69 in Cohen, Joshua and Rogers, Joel, *What's wrong with a free lunch?* Boston: Beacon Press

[656] Atkinson, A.B. (1984) *The costs of social dividend and tax credit schemes*, Tax, Incentives and the Distribution of Income paper no 63, London: LSE; Parker, Hermione (1985) 'The debate about costings', *BIRG Bulletin*, no 4, Autumn, pp 5–8; Parker, Hermione (1989) *Instead of the dole: An enquiry into integration of the tax and benefit systems*, London: Routledge, pp 385–400

[657] www.hmrc.gov.uk/stats/income_distribution/inc-distribution-note.pdf; www.ons.gov.uk/ons/rel/ashe/annual-survey-of-hours-and-earnings/ashe-results-2011/ashe-statistical-bulletin-2011.html#tab-background-notes

[658] Atkinson, A.B. and Sutherland, Holly (1988a) *Integrating incomes taxation and social security: Analysis of a partial Basic Income*, Tax, Incentives and the Distribution of Income paper no 123, London: LSE, p 5

a smaller amount. Atkinson therefore suggests working from the tax base currently experienced by Her Majesty's Revenue and Customs, and calculating how it might change if changes were made to the tax and benefits systems, rather than relying on income survey figures or national accounts.[659]

Further complications arise: If tax allowances are lowered, then Income Tax will need to be collected on smaller earnings, and this might prove problematic. Also, any change to the tax and benefits structure will cause changes to labour market behaviour and therefore to earned incomes.[660] Such feedback mechanisms are notoriously difficult to include in costings calculations, and this can easily result in pessimism about a proposed reform option. Atkinson counsels against such pessimism because it 'may be premature, reflecting the limitations of the tools of analysis as much as of the proposals themselves.'[661]

If for the moment we leave these problems to one side, and assume that we are going to fund a Citizen's Income by reducing tax allowances and most means-tested and contributory benefits, then we still have decisions to make, and particularly over the levels of the Citizen's Income and of the Income Tax rates (though these will of course be linked if revenue neutrality is the aim).

In 1988, Atkinson and Sutherland published research on a Citizen's Income of £10 per week per working age adult (1988 figure: so today's figure would be approximately £22), paid for by reducing tax allowances to (almost) zero and reducing means tested and most other benefits. Atkinson and Sutherland calculated that one earner couples would generally have gained from their proposal, that two earner couples would have suffered generally small losses, and that higher rate taxpayers would have suffered small losses too. By employing

---

[659] Atkinson, A.B. (1984) *The costs of social dividend and tax credit schemes*, Tax, Incentives and the Distribution of Income paper no 63, London: LSE, p 22

[660] Atkinson, A.B. (1984) *The costs of social dividend and tax credit schemes*, Tax, Incentives and the Distribution of Income paper no 63, London: LSE, p 29. cf. Atkinson, A.B., Gomulka, J., Micklewright, J. and Rau, N. (1982) *Unemployment Benefit, duration, and incentives in Britain: How robust is the evidence?* Tax, Incentives and the Distribution of Income paper no 43, London: LSE, pp 36–7: 'There is considerable variation in the estimated elasticity when we consider alternative benefit variables, different specifications of the replacement rate, different time periods, and the inclusion/exclusion of family circumstances.' Elasticity varies between 0 [duration of unemployment doesn't change when the level of Unemployment Benefit changes] to 0.6 [duration does change with level of Unemployment Benefit]. 'There are limits to our knowledge.'

[661] Atkinson, A.B. (1989) *Basic Income schemes and the lessons from public economics*, Tax, Incentives and the Distribution of Income paper no 136, London: LSE, p 19

microsimulation software, they calculated that the scheme would be revenue neutral if the personal tax allowance fell to £16.60 per week.[662]

The microsimulation software employed by Atkinson and Sutherland (a successor of which this author has been privileged to be able to use) employs Family Expenditure Survey data (now termed Family Resources Survey data). 57,276 individuals complete annual questionnaires about income and expenditure, and because the sample is a full 0.1 per cent of the population, the anonymised data gives something like a true picture of the UK's population as a whole. But as Atkinson and Sutherland point out, even this large dataset has its problems. Households without children are underreported, simply because they are less likely to be at home when the interviewer calls; and estimating the way in which the data should be adjusted to take into account such underreporting is a fraught business.[663] But survey data is our only means of estimating proposed tax and benefit changes' effects on households' net incomes, and in relation to Hermione Parker's Citizen's Income proposal , a simulation showed that 'a fifth of all losers are in the bottom half of the [earnings] distribution'.[664] Is this a problem? No, not if the new labour market behaviour that the changed system makes viable can lift the household's earned income sufficiently to compensate for the immediate net loss, and can then continue to lift it.

Atkinson and Sutherland conclude that a partial Citizen's Income is 'a definite and practicable scheme', easily introduced, and with few distributional consequences. Their additional calculations showed that 'if the Income Tax rate became 40% for all, with National Insurance

---

[662] Atkinson, A.B. and Sutherland, Holly (1988a) *Integrating incomes taxation and social security: Analysis of a partial Basic Income*, Tax, Incentives and the Distribution of Income paper no 123, London: LSE, pp 10–11. On Parker's and Sutherland's similar research, see House of Commons Treasury and Civil Service Committee Sub-Committee (1982) *The structure of personal income taxation and Income Support: Minutes of evidence*, HC 331–ix, London: Stationery Office, pp 424–53; Parker, Hermione (1985) 'Costing Basic Incomes', *BIRG Bulletin*, no 3, pp 4–15; Parker, Hermione (1989) *Instead of the dole: An enquiry into integration of the tax and benefit systems*, London: Routledge, pp 121–37, 224–53, 333–80

[663] Atkinson, A.B. and Sutherland, Holly (1988a) *Integrating incomes taxation and social security: Analysis of a partial Basic Income*, Tax, Incentives and the Distribution of Income paper no 123, London: LSE, p 13. See also Atkinson, A.B. (1995) *Public economics in action: The Basic Income/flat tax proposal*, Oxford: Clarendon Press, pp 128–9

[664] Atkinson, A.B. and Sutherland, Holly (1988a) *Integrating incomes taxation and social security: Analysis of a partial Basic Income*, Tax, Incentives and the Distribution of Income paper no 123, London: LSE, p 15

Contributions being abolished, it would be possible to nearly double the [Citizen's] Income', making it more redistributive from rich to poor.[665]

From the costings point of view, it is difficult to fault a Citizen's Income: though, as we have noted several times already, however sensible a scheme might look on paper, if the politics or the machinery of government are against it then it is unlikely to happen. Such political factors will influence the apparently objective assessment of a reform option as much as they will influence decisions about whether or not to implement the scheme. As Atkinson suggests,

> The analysis of government policy is an exercise in applied theory and can be no more firmly based than the theory on which it draws ... The formulation of objectives, and the treatment of constraints, depends on improved understanding of ethical principles and of political behaviour.[666]

Funding options

Having asked about the size of the Citizen's Income that we are attempting to fund, and about some of the difficulties that we might encounter as we attempt to calculate the cost of a Citizen's Income, we turn now to a discussion of a number of possible funding methods.

Funding a Citizen's Income from within the existing Income Tax and benefits structure

A government will always find additional money for a policy if it wants it to happen, whether that be the second Iraq war, bailing out the banks, or a Citizen's Income. But let us suppose, for the sake of argument, that the government does not wish to add to public sector borrowing in order to fund a Citizen's Income. It will therefore need either a revenue neutral scheme (i.e., reductions in tax allowances and most existing benefits will pay for the Citizen's Income), or it will need to raise additional tax revenue.

Taking revenue neutral schemes first: that is, schemes that pay for a Citizen's Income by reducing tax allowances and most means-tested and

---

[665] Atkinson, A.B. and Sutherland, Holly (1988a) *Integrating incomes taxation and social security: Analysis of a partial Basic Income*, Tax, Incentives and the Distribution of Income paper no 123, London: LSE, pp 17–18

[666] Atkinson, A.B. (1982) *The theory of the design of income taxation: Review and prospects*, Tax, Incentives and the Distribution of Income paper no 38, London: LSE, pp 55–6

other benefits, and possibly by raising the Income Tax rate. As Atkinson shows, as the Income Tax rate rises, the amount of tax collected rises at first, but then the rate of increase of revenue falls, and eventually revenue plateaus and then falls (because some people, if faced with a higher tax rate, would prefer additional free time to working the same number of hours for a lower net income). At the limit, a 100 per cent Income Tax rate would mean no hours worked, no tax collected, and no Citizen's Income. Only a narrow range of Income Tax rates is in practice available to the government, and this will limit the range of possible Citizen's Income schemes. Political considerations might well define the feasible tax rate range even more narrowly than does the range of tax rates within which tax revenue plateaus.[667]

A further question to ask is this: We currently apply higher Income Tax rates to higher earners. A flat tax – that is, the same tax rate on all income – would simplify the system considerably, particularly if tax allowances were turned into Citizen's Incomes. A flat tax would enable all tax to be collected at source (on earnings, investments, capital disposal and so on), and the taxpayer would need to make no returns, and the government no calculations.[668] We have higher rates for higher earners for distributional reasons, so the political question is whether redistribution should be traded for simplicity: but this is an entirely separate question, and a Citizen's Income, or, indeed, any benefits system,[669] could be funded equally well by a progressive Income Tax or by a flat Income Tax.

It is possible to construct a revenue neutral Citizen's Income scheme that redistributes from rich to poor, with small gains going to the

---

[667] Atkinson, A.B. (1995) *Public economics in action: The Basic Income/flat tax proposal*, Oxford: Clarendon Press, pp 5–9, 87

[668] Atkinson, A.B. (1995) *Public economics in action: The Basic Income/flat tax proposal*, Oxford: Clarendon Press, pp 24–46. For a sustained argument that a flat tax is always a good second best option, and therefore that in an imperfect world it might be the best option, see Epstein, Richard A. (2002) 'Can anyone beat the flat tax?' pp 140–71 in Paul, Ellen Frankel, Miller, Fred D. Jr., and Paul, Jeffrey, *Should differences in income and wealth matter?* Cambridge: Cambridge University Press

[669] Hirsch, Donald (2006) *Flatter taxes: Rich giveaway or a new deal for the poor?* York: Joseph Rowntree Foundation. Hirsch finds that if 'Tax Credits' were to become non-withdrawable and a single Income Tax rate were to be applied to earned income then 'the main gainers from such a system would be families with children on modest to middle incomes, while the main losers would be the highest earners without children' (p 3). If National Insurance Contributions were to retain their current structure then under 2006 regulations the flat tax rate would have been 35 per cent. If National Insurance Contributions were also flattened then the flat tax rate would have been 33 per cent and the total withdrawal rate 46 per cent.

lowest paid and small losses for higher earners: which means that the proportional increases experienced by the low earners will be much higher than the proportional losses among high earners.[670] At the extreme ends of the spectrum, the lowest decile (the lowest ten per cent of incomes) will on average experience large proportional gains, and the highest decile (the ten per cent of highest incomes) will experience low proportional losses. However, within the average gains and losses for different earned income deciles, there will be low earning households suffering losses, and higher earning households experiencing gains. The tax and benefits systems are complex, and people's circumstances are complex, which means that gains and losses can only be predicted on a case by case basis, taking into account all of the relevant detailed characteristics of the existing tax and benefits systems, all of the household's characteristics, all of the household's incomes and expenditures, and all of the effects of any change to the system. Microsimulation software can reveal gains and losses for individual households in the Family Resources Survey data, and can therefore calculate how many individuals would suffer gains or losses of a particular level.[671] While the establishment of a Citizen's Income would be the establishment of a simple system, the complexity of the current system will inevitably cause gains to some higher earners and losses to some low earners. To reiterate: This will not be an effect of the Citizen's Income, which is inherently simple and has completely predictable effects on household income. It will be an effect of the current tax and benefits rules that interact with personal and household circumstances to create a variety of redistributional patterns.

A Citizen's Income funded by turning tax allowances into the Citizen's Income, and by reducing most existing benefits by the amount of the Citizen's Income, would generate relatively few gains and losses. If everyone were an individual living alone, then there would be almost no gains or losses. The gains and losses occur mainly because current benefits (in-work means-tested benefits as well as out of work benefits) have the household as the claimant unit. Current benefits rates for couples are less than twice the benefits rates for individuals, whereas with a Citizen's Income a couple would receive between them twice as much as an individual. Therefore couples become better off, which means that individuals living alone will be worse off if no additional funding is made available.

---

[670] See the website www.citizensincome.org for this minimally redistributive scheme.

[671] See the website www.citizensincome.org for a microsimulation showing the number of individuals suffering particular gains and losses

In Chapter 7 we discussed the benefits to couples of a Citizen's Income because it would enable them to reap the benefits of economies of scale generated by two people sharing one home and its related costs rather than two homes and their costs. Here we simply recognise that on the implementation of a Citizen's Income people living alone will lose out initially, and that that will mean lone parents losing out. One solution to that problem would be to increase Child Benefit. In a revenue neutral scheme, which would need to fund the Child Benefit increase by decreasing the adult Citizen's Income, an increased Child Benefit would increase the loss suffered by individuals without children, and might wipe out the increase experienced by adults living together.

The longer term solution to these problems is of course provided by the changed labour market activity that a Citizen's Income would generate. Because a Citizen's Income would not be withdrawn as earnings rose, lone parents would be more likely to seek part-time employment, and they would therefore find it relatively easy to make up any small loss of benefit. A further long term change would be that individuals on means-tested benefits would no longer find their net income reduced when they moved in with someone else, because a Citizen's Income would not be reduced by their partner's earnings.

The transition from our current complicated system to one based on a Citizen's Income would, of course, be considerably eased for many households if there were to be additional funding available at the beginning of the transition, so that the Citizen's Income received by people living alone could match their current benefits, and couples could benefit from the economies of scale generated by people living together. If argued for on that basis – that is, on the basis that the change would support families, and encourage the parents of children to live together – then such transitional additional funding, and the consequent rise in Income Tax rates, should not be too difficult to achieve politically.

Taxing appropriation of common resources ('the commons')

As James Robertson points out, gainful employment is a contribution to society, so to tax it seems rather strange, as taxing an activity can discourage it. It would surely be better to tax those things that we wish to discourage, such as fossil fuel usage. Another problem with taxing paid employment is that supply and demand are elastic: that is, to tax paid employment might reduce both demand for it (because it becomes more expensive to hire labour) and the supply of it (because the monetary reward for labour goes down, so we might prefer to use more of our time for other activities). So the result of taxing paid employment is likely to reduce the amount of paid employment, meaning that there will be less of it to tax. Far better, surely, to tax things that do not change in quantity when they are taxed, such as land. It does not matter how much tax is applied to land, there will always be the same amount of it. Taxation of land might reduce land's desirability as an investment option, and all taxation needs to be sufficiently intelligent not to compromise the ability to tax (so land should never be taxed at a level that means that landowners are unable to pay the tax), but the principle remains true: it is better to tax things that do not reduce in quantity if they are taxed.

Land and carbon are common resources. In principle they belong to all of us. Certain people and organisations have acquired greater rights than others over such resources, and that is why we tax them: to return some of their value to the population as a whole. This suggests that the revenue raised should be applied in this way, and should provide benefits to all equally. To pay a Citizen's Income out of taxation raised on common resources would therefore be a most appropriate use of the revenue.

James Robertson looks for a society

- which rewards people – rather than taxing them – for the useful work that they and their organisations do, for the value they add, for what they contribute to the common good;
- in which the amounts that people and organisations are required to pay to the public revenue reflect the value that they subtract by the use of 'common' resources;
- in which all citizens are equally entitled to share in the annual revenue so raised, partly by way of services provided at public expense and partly by way of a citizen's income.[672]

A Financial Transaction Tax

If I buy a holiday then I pay a consumption tax (Value Added Tax in Europe), but if I buy currency to take on holiday then I will pay a commission to the vendor but I will pay no tax. The fact that currency

---

[672] Robertson, James (1996) 'Towards a new social compact: Citizen's Income and radical tax reform', *The Political Quarterly*, vol 67, no 1, pp 54–8, p 57

transactions are costless in this sense has been blamed for the volume of currency transactions undertaken for purely speculative purposes: that is, currencies bought and sold on the expectation of making a profit if the currency bought increases in value relative to the currency used to pay for it. Currency transactions undertaken to facilitate the import or export of goods or services can be of value to the economy and to society, but it can be argued that purely speculative transactions are not. For this reason James Tobin recommended a Financial Transaction Tax (a 'Tobin Tax'), to slow the markets down: as he put it, to 'throw sand into the wheels of the economy'. There are two ways in which such a tax could make economies more rather than less efficient: they would stabilise exchange rates and therefore could make it easier for exporters and importers to plan ahead; and, because economies are already far from efficient, a tax on currency transactions could make them more efficient.

One problem with such a tax is that it would not discriminate between currency transactions which benefit economies and those that damage them. For this reason the recent Mirrlees Review commission recommended a financial activity tax on banks and other financial institutions, which would behave rather like Value Added Tax. A further possible objection to a Financial Transaction Tax is that if one country were to implement it then transactions might move abroad, which they easily could. Only a global tax would prevent this from happening. This objection can be answered. A tax that was low enough would not have this effect because there are plenty of good reasons for enacting transactions in the UK. The UK already taxes purchases of shares in UK companies at 0.5 per cent, and New York levies a similar tax on its stock exchange: but there are still plenty of share transactions in the UK and in New York. If a Financial Transaction Tax were low enough then it would not drive business abroad.

Most of the debate about Financial Transaction Taxes has centred on currency exchange transactions. There is of course no reason why a tax should not be levied on other kinds of financial transactions as well.[673]

A national Financial Transaction Tax, or a similar financial activity tax, could be used to fund a national Citizen's Income; a European tax could fund a European Citizen's Income; and, in the longer term, a global Financial Transaction Tax could fund a global Citizen's Income. A Financial Transaction Tax could therefore create a Citizen's Income,

---

[673] Adam, Stuart, et al (2011) *Tax by design: The Mirrlees Review*, Oxford: Oxford University Press, pp 151–3, 195–215

with all of its benefits, and at the same time slow down currency speculation and therefore make the economy more efficient.

Consumption taxes

Consumption taxes are regressive because poorer people spend a higher proportion of their incomes on taxed goods than do wealthier people.[674] However, this is only true if we study consumption taxes on their own. A collection of essays on the funding of Citizen's Income in a variety of European countries finds that in many countries consumption taxes would be a viable funding method, and that the total package of Citizen's Income and consumption taxes could redistribute from rich to poor. This means that funding a Citizen's Income using consumption taxes could be both financially and socially feasible.[675]

While at the moment this method of funding a Citizen's Income might not seem particularly significant as an option, it is possible that the ways in which the labour market is changing might make consumption taxes more significant in the future. One of the benefits to industry and commerce of a Citizen's Income would be that the labour market would behave more like a classical market. In some industries this might mean additional employment at low wage rates; but in other industries it might mean unpleasant jobs being declined at their current wage rates. Some of these jobs could be mechanised rather than offered at higher wage rates.[676] We cannot know the extent to which mechanisation will replace unpleasant jobs, nor the extent of additional employment; and neither can we know to what extent mechanisation will in any case replace human labour in the years ahead. If this happens to any great extent then labour will take a smaller proportion of the value of production, and capital investment and company profits will take larger shares. This suggests that, whether or not a Citizen's Income is implemented, the tax burden might need to shift from personal income to company profits or to the products now being produced more efficiently and therefore more cheaply.

---

[674] Irvin, George, Byrne, Dave, Murphy, Richard, Reed, Howard and Ruane, Sally (2009) *In place of cuts: Tax reform to build a fairer society*, London: Compass, p 15

[675] Dommen-Meade, Bridget (ed.) (2010) *Le financement d'un revenu de base inconditionnel*, Zürich: Seismo, for BIEN-Suisse; Werner, Götz W. and Goehler, Adrienne (2010) *1.000 Euro für jeden*, Berlin: Econ, Ullstein Buchverlage, pp 241–50

[676] Liebermann, Sascha (2012) 'Germany: Far, though Close – Problems and prospects of BI in Germany', pp 83–106 in Caputo, Richard (ed.) *Basic Income guarantee and politics: International experiences and perspectives on the viability of income guarantee*, New York: Palgrave Macmillan, pp 93–4

Company profits are increasingly difficult to tax, which suggests that production will need to be taxed directly as consumption taxes, rather than indirectly through wage taxation.

Dividends from capital funds

In Chapter 5 we discussed the Alaskan dividend payments: an annual rather than a weekly or monthly Citizen's Income. This is funded from a permanent fund, and the payment is a genuine dividend: a payment out of the profits of the fund. A similar proposal has been made for Colombia: a fund that would be built up over twenty years and would then pay universal benefits out of its dividends.[677] An interesting question is why other countries' sovereign wealth funds do not pay out dividends to those countries' populations. Angela Cummine draws the fairly obvious conclusion that those controlling the funds would rather control the capital and the revenue than pay dividends to others and thus attract demands for greater accountability in relation to management of the funds.[678]

And ...

Numerous other funding mechanisms have been proposed: the taxation of lifetime gifts to fund a Citizen's Income thought of as a 'social inheritance';[679] tax on rare natural resources (which, as Sullivan and Wetzel point out, is a variant of a land tax);[680] energy taxes (that would directly reduce the use of fossil fuels);[681] and a megabyte tax[682] (internet traffic continues to expand exponentially, so such a tax at a very low rate could provide a valuable source of revenue).

---

[677] Hernández, Diego (2005) 'Universal Basic Income as a preferential social dividend, a proposal for the Colombian case', *The Journal of Socioeconomics*, vol 34, no 1, pp 27–38

[678] Cummine, Angela (2011) 'Overcoming dividend skepticism: why the world's sovereign wealth funds are not paying Basic Income dividends', *Basic Income Studies*, vol 6, no 1, pp 1–18, pp 16–17

[679] O'Neill, Martin (2007) 'Death and taxes', *Renewal*, vol 15, no 4, p 70

[680] Sullivan, Dan and Wetzel, Dave (2007) 'Let's use natural wealth to pay for a citizen's income', *Citizen's Income Newsletter*, issue 2, p 16

[681] Fitzpatrick, Tony (1999) *Freedom and security: An introduction to the Basic Income debate*, Basingstoke: Macmillan, p 201; Cato, Molly Scott (2010) *Green economics: An introduction to theory, policy and practice*, Abingdon: Earthscan, also places a Citizen's Income at the heart of a green economics.

[682] Claus Offe (2012) Presentation, 14 September, 14th BIEN Congress, Munich

Conclusion

While this chapter leaves numerous questions unanswered, none of the evidence cited, and none of the arguments discussed, suggest that a Citizen's Income would not be feasible. This is most encouraging. In the last chapter we found that from within every political ideology we can argue for a Citizen's Income, and that any arguments against it are less connected with the ideology and are easily answered. We have now found that there is a variety of possible funding methods, and that the method on which there has been most research – funding a Citizen's Income by reducing tax allowances and most means-tested and contributory benefits – could fund a Citizen's Income that would redistribute slightly from rich to poor and would not create too many individual gains or losses.

Given the clear economic and social advantages of establishing a Citizen's Income, it is difficult to think of an argument (apart from lethargy) for not putting the political effort into doing so.

CHAPTER 15

Alternatives to a Citizen's Income

In this chapter we study three proposals for reform with characteristics similar to those of a Citizens' Income: a Negative Income Tax, genuine Tax Credits, and a participation income. (Additional alternative schemes can be found in a website appendix, www.citizensincome.org).

Tax Credits

In Chapter 3 I described a Tax Credits scheme proposed by the UK's Conservative government in 1972. This was close to a genuine Tax Credits scheme because it allocated a credit that was paid out if there were no earnings, and was withdrawn as earnings rose, up to a break-even point, after which Income Tax was deducted. We noted some disadvantages to this particular scheme: for instance, that workers earning below a threshold wage were not included in the scheme, and non-earners were not included either. There is no reason why an alternative Tax Credits scheme should not include every citizen from the date of its implementation, so the particular problems did not relate to the idea of a Tax Credit.

Some disadvantages of the Heath scheme, though, would be experienced by any Tax Credit scheme. For someone employed, the Tax Credit is reduced as earnings rise, so either the Credit has to be administered by an employer (which causes problems as workers move from one employer to another, and also means that the employer needs to know the worker's personal circumstances in order to work out their entitlement), or the Tax Credit has to be paid by a separate government agency which will then need to know the worker's earnings and every change in those earnings (as the Department for Work and Pensions will for 'Universal Credit'). Neither solution would make for easy administration. If the former method were to be employed, then if someone experienced a period of unemployment between two employments, the administration of their Tax Credits would pass from the employer to the government agency and then back again. This is not a good recipe for seamless administration.

It rather looks as if Tax Credits are designed for a world of long-term full-time employment. The Heath scheme was also designed for a world of stable families. The level of the Tax Credit depended on whether someone was married, so changes in personal circumstances would not only have affected the level of the Tax Credit, but would also have been known to someone's employer. An individual-based Tax Credit scheme would of course be perfectly feasible, and would avoid such problems.

A too little noted problem with Tax Credits is the restriction imposed on tax rates by the fact that they are managed via a noncumulative tax system. Our current Income Tax system is a cumulative one. Each earner is allocated an annual tax allowance, so there is an annual amount of income that is not taxed. Each week, or each month, the employer has to work out how much tax to deduct so that by the end of the year the correct amount of tax has been paid, at the correct rates, on the correct amounts of taxable pay (i.e., on earned income minus the tax allowance, and taking into account the thresholds between the different tax rates). Tables are published, and software is available, based on a system of tax codes related to earners' circumstances; and if at the end of the year the correct amount of tax has not been paid, then an adjustment takes place: a tax refund, a tax demand, or next year's tax code amended so as to recoup unpaid tax during the following year. One of the advantages of a Tax Credit scheme is its noncumulative tax system. Each week, or each month, the employer can work out tax due, or Tax Credit to be paid out, simply from the Tax Credit withdrawal rate, the tax rate, and the earner's circumstances (e.g., whether married or single, and whether they have dependent children). Only those paying higher rate tax would have required either an end of year adjustment, or a cumulative scheme designed just for them (so that the higher tax could be collected throughout the year rather than all together at the end). The Heath government's Tax Credit scheme envisaged the vast majority of earners experiencing a 30 per cent tax rate and a 30 per cent Tax Credit withdrawal rate.

The problem is that, while a noncumulative tax system enables a relatively simple Tax Credit scheme to operate, it restricts a government's ability to redistribute income. Atkinson's conclusion is 'that the solution to the problem of providing adequate income support lies not in the merger of the tax and social security systems but rather in their coordination and development'.[683] As an alternative to the Heath Tax Credits scheme he recommended that Child Benefit should replace Family Allowance, Family Income Supplement, and Child Tax

---

[683] Atkinson, A.B. (1973) *The Tax Credit scheme and the redistribution of income*, London: Institute for Fiscal Studies, p 70

Allowances, and that Income Tax should be progressive, i.e., higher earners should pay higher rates of tax.[684]

Atkinson recognised that a sizeable and universal Child Benefit, alongside a progressive Income Tax system, would give to governments the greatest possible ability to redistribute (or not) as they saw fit. There are ways in which genuine Tax Credits would be an improvement on the current system (– for instance, Tax Allowances benefit higher rate taxpayers more than they benefit those not paying the higher rate, whereas Tax Credits do not suffer from such poor-to-rich redistribution[685]): but a Citizen's Income, which would replace tax allowances, but would not itself be part of the tax system, would give to governments all of the advantages of Tax Credits and none of the disadvantages. A Citizen's Income would also offer the greatest possible control over redistribution policy because it would leave the government entirely free to design the Income Tax system of its choice.

Negative Income Tax

The term 'Negative Income Tax' suggests that below the tax threshold money is paid out to the employee rather than taken from them: so, in essence, a Negative Income Tax scheme is the same as a Tax Credit scheme. Often it is merely the specification that differs. To specify a Tax Credit scheme, the amount to be paid out if there are no earnings is specified along with a withdrawal rate as earnings rise. For a Negative Income Tax scheme, the threshold is specified along with a tax rate. For earnings below the threshold, the same amount is paid out for earnings of £x below the threshold as would be collected in tax on earnings of £x above the threshold. Negative Income Tax schemes have been suggested with different rates above and below the threshold, just as there are Income Tax schemes with different tax rates for different levels of earnings. The advantage of a low rate of withdrawal below the threshold is that the low paid end up with higher net earnings without the break-even point being too high.[686]

As the system is essentially the same as a Tax Credit scheme, all of the same problems would apply.

---

[684] Atkinson, A.B. (1973) *The Tax Credit scheme and the redistribution of income*, London: Institute for Fiscal Studies, pp 76–8, 80

[685] Batchelder, Lily L. and Goldberg, Fred T., Jr, (2007) 'Reforming tax incentives into uniform refundable tax credits', *Basic Income Studies*, vol 2, no 2, pp 1–11

[686] Atkinson, A.B. (1985) *Income maintenance and social insurance: A survey*, Welfare State Programme, paper no 5, London: LSE, p 51

An additional 'problem' arose during a Negative Income Tax experiment in the United States. The particular scheme tested in the US treated the household as the tax unit, and the tax deducted or payments made depended on the combined incomes of married couples.[687] Women tend to earn less than men, so they benefited more than men from the new system, particularly if they left the marriage and established a new claimant unit (because although their previous tax allowance had been useless to them if they earned below the tax threshold, the Negative Income Tax paid out money if their earnings were below the threshold, so their net income was now higher than their earned income). Greater financial independence gave to some women the ability to leave their husbands, whereas their previous financial dependence had prevented them from doing so. Whether we would now regard as a problem the greater freedom that an increase in net income had given to these women I rather doubt. If it is only financial dependence that is holding together a marriage then perhaps it *ought* to end. It also needs to be said, of course, that if the individual is taken as the tax unit then it makes no difference financially whether a couple stay together, except that separating will result in having to maintain two homes rather than one, so the couple is more likely to stay together. There can be no clearer example of the necessity of predicting the consequences of scheme design, and in particular of studying the effects of different claimant units.

In some respects, though, the Negative Income Tax experiments were unambiguously helpful. Even though marginal deduction rates fell and net incomes rose, the experiments found no evidence of labour market withdrawal, and no evidence that labour supply falls if marginal deduction rates fall. Some particularly interesting results were that there was some labour market withdrawal among women with children, suggesting that for some families it had become possible for a parent to spend more time with their children; and that some men took longer than before to accept a new job if they became unemployed, suggesting that they were now more able to seek the right job rather than simply any job. The results suggest that a Citizen's Income would not stop people from wanting to earn an income, and that there would be sufficient tax base to enable the payment of a Citizen's Income. A particular conclusion drawn from the experiments is that a Citizen's Income at 150 per cent of the poverty line would be 'well within the bounds of financial feasibility'.

---

[687] Parker, Hermione (1989) *Instead of the dole: An enquiry into integration of the tax and benefit systems*, London: Routledge, pp 153–5

As in the Namibian Citizen's Income pilot project, there were some other interesting outcomes. School attendance and performance rose, nutritional adequacy increased, there was less low birth weight, and home ownership rose. A recent examination of data collected during a similar Negative Income Tax experiment in Canada during the mid-1970s has produced some equally interesting results. Engagement in education beyond the age of 16 rose substantially, as much among members of those households whose net incomes did not rise during the experiment as among those whose incomes did; and a variety of health indicators improved. As with the United States experiments, no primary earner labour market withdrawal occurred, and some secondary earner withdrawal did.[688] This all rather suggests that security of net income is at least as important as the level of net income.

These are all positive and significant results with clear implications for the current debate on the Citizen's Income approach to tax and benefits reform.

As we have seen, a problem faced both by Tax Credit and Negative Income Tax schemes is that they are themselves complex, and that they are complex to administer because they take the household as the tax unit, and because they require the constant adjustment of amounts paid out as circumstances change.[689] This means that if they did not enable the abolition of all other benefits then they would add considerably to the complexity of the tax and benefits systems. As we saw with the Heath government's Tax Credit scheme, a substantial number of people would have been left out of the scheme, and the only

---

[688] Widerquist, Karl (2005) 'A failure to communicate: what (if anything) can we learn from the Negative Income Tax experiments', *The Journal of Socioeconomics*, vol 34, no 1, pp 49–81, pp 57, 60, 68; Pasma, Chandra (2010) 'Working through the work disincentive', *Basic Income Studies*, vol 5, no 2, pp 1–20, pp 3–4; Widerquist, Karl, and Sheahan, Allan (2012), 'The United States: the Basic Income guarantee – past experience, current proposals', pp 11–32 in Murray, Matthew C. and Pateman, Carole (eds) *Basic Income worldwide: Horizons of reform*, New York: Palgrave Macmillan, pp 18–22; Forget, Evelyn L. (2012), 'Canada: the case for Basic Income', pp 81–101 in Murray, Matthew C. and Pateman, Carole (eds) *Basic Income worldwide: Horizons of reform*, New York: Palgrave Macmillan, pp 90–96

[689] Spicker, Paul (2011) *How social security works: An introduction to benefits in Britain*, Bristol: Policy Press, p 122. For a detailed discussion of the administrative and other complexities of Negative Income Tax, see Parker, Hermione (1989) *Instead of the dole: An enquiry into integration of the tax and benefit systems*, London: Routledge, pp 138–55. See Block, Fred (2001) 'Why pay Bill Gates?' pp 85–9 in Cohen, Joshua and Rogers, Joel, *What's wrong with a free lunch?* Boston: Beacon Press. Block argues that a Negative Income Tax is preferable to a Citizen's Income but unfortunately does not discuss their very different administrative arrangements.

benefit to be replaced would have been Family Income Supplement, the in-work means-tested benefit that preceded Family Credit and New Labour's 'Tax Credits'. It is not surprising that a minority on the Parliamentary Select Committee had hesitations about putting employers and employees through a major change that would not have reduced complexity and might have increased it.[690]

A Citizen's Income would, of course, achieve everything that either a Negative Income Tax or genuine Tax Credits would achieve, and it would do all of it in a far simpler way and at reduced administrative cost.[691] Administrative differences are bound to result in behavioural differences, and Pech shows that for maximum acceptability a Citizen's Income needs a more progressive tax system and a Negative Income Tax a flatter system,[692] but these effects will be small in relation to the more important aspects of the administrative differences outlined, and in particular the simplicity of a Citizen's Income and the administrative complexity of a Negative Income Tax.

The simplicity of the Citizen's Income is the result of the universal payment being entirely separate from the tax system, enabling the universal payment to remain as simple as possible, and leaving the tax system to deal with revenue collection and the fine detail of income redistribution. A simpler and more efficient system simply is not possible.[693]

Graphical representations of a Citizen's Income and of Tax Credits / Negative Income Tax

Figure 15.1 shows a Citizen's Income's effects on net earnings. Figure 15.2 shows the effect of a Tax Credits scheme or a Negative Income Tax.

---

[690] Spicker, Paul (2011) *How social security works: An introduction to benefits in Britain,* Bristol: Policy Press, p 122

[691] Harvey, Philip (2006) 'The relative costs of a universal Basic Income and a Negative Income Tax', *Basic Income Studies,* vol 1, no 2, pp 1–24 compares the costs of a Citizen's Income and a Negative Income Tax in the US and finds the Citizen's Income twice as expensive. This is because the Negative Income Tax assumes a household claimant unit and the Citizen's Income an individual claimant unit. As Harvey rightly points out, the additional costs of a Citizen's Income relate to additional money going to non-earning family members.

[692] Pech, Wesley (2010) 'Behavioral economics and the basic income guarantee', *Basic Income Studies,* vol 5, no 2, pp 1–17, p 14

[693] Cf. Kesselman, J.R. and Garfinkel, I. (1978) 'Professor Friedman meet Lady Rhys-Williams: NIT v. CI', *Journal of Public Economics,* vol 10, pp 179–216, p 211: 'Contrary to the conventional wisdom, the universal payment, flat-marginal-rate form, may be more efficient than the income-tested form.'

Figure 15.1: Graphical representation of a Citizen's Income

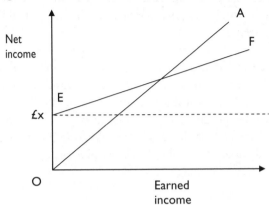

Figure 15.2 Graphical representation of a Negative Income Tax or Tax Credits

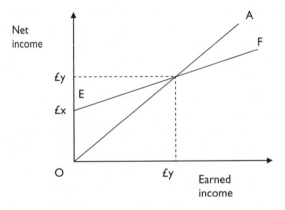

For Tax Credits, if the individual or household has no earnings, then a Tax Credit of £x is paid. As earned income rises, less Tax Credit is paid, until at earned income £y no Tax Credit is received. At this earnings level Income Tax begins to be paid. The line EF shows net income rising as earned income rises. The slope of the line represents both the tax rate and the rate at which Tax Credits are withdrawn. If the rates are different then the slopes of EF will be different either side of £y of earned income. The graph looks the same for a Negative Income Tax, the only difference between Tax Credits and Negative Income Tax being a matter of administrative mechanism.

As we can see, if the rate of withdrawal of Tax Credits is the same as the Income Tax rate, then Tax Credits have the same effects on net income as a Citizen's Income would have. The difference is one of administration. (There might also be differences created by giving additional Tax Credits to such categories as married men, as in the Heath government's scheme.)

If, as we can see, Tax Credits or Negative Income Tax have the same income effects as a Citizen's Income, and if, as we can see, costs related to income levels will be the same, then the only difference is administrative. The administration of Tax Credits and of Negative Income Tax would be more complex than the administration of a Citizen's Income. The only potential advantage of Tax Credits or Negative Income Tax over a Citizen's Income would come from higher levels of public acceptability. There could be no inherent advantage.

A Participation Income

Tony Atkinson has recognised, as we have done, that 'it will be difficult to secure political support for a Citizen's Income while it remains unconditional on labour market or other activity'. He suggests that a compromise is required, whereby some kind of participation in society would be required from those who were to receive what would otherwise be an unconditional and non-withdrawable income, although such 'participation' would be assumed if people would be participating if they were not prevented from doing so by such contingencies as sickness, old age, or lack of employment opportunity. The list of possible 'participation' conditions would therefore include employment or self-employment, retirement, absence from work because of sickness or injury, inability to work because of disability, and approved forms of voluntary activity. Students, trainees, those caring for the young, for older people, or for disabled dependents, and those unemployed but available for work, would also be counted as 'participating'.[694, 695]

It is no surprise that Stuart White thinks that a Participation Income, alongside continuing contingency benefits, would be a useful step;[696] and that Tony Fitzpatrick can see how social democracy, along with social liberalism and social conservatism, might see a Participation Income as an attractive first step, and would then be content for it

---

[694] Atkinson, Tony (1993) 'Participation Income', *Citizen's Income Bulletin*, no 16, July, pp 7–11; Atkinson, A.B. (1996) 'The case for a participation income', *The Political Quarterly*, vol 67, no 1, pp 67–70

[695] See the website www.citizensincome.org for an appendix on the small number of people who would not receive a Participation Income under these conditions.

[696] White, Stuart (2003) *The civic minimum: On the rights and obligations of economic citizenship*, Oxford: Oxford University Press, pp 170–5

to become a Citizen's Income.[697] A Citizen's Income would *invite* reciprocation in terms of paid and unpaid contributions to society's welfare, but a Participation Income would *require* it. White is able to recommend *both* a Citizen's Income *and* a Participation Income, because both, in their different ways, would promote both the civic minimum and civic labour: both citizenship rights and citizenship obligations. What he does not sufficiently recognise is that a Participation Income would be complex to administer, would require a casework approach, and would hand to junior civil servants the kind of discretion that contributes to means-tested benefits being so demeaning.[698]

Jürgen De Wispelaere and Lindsay Stirton suggest that 'Participation Income might not be such a great idea after all', because all three of these questions will require an answer:

- What sort of activities qualify as participation?
- How will the system identify those engaging in these activities?
- How do we ensure compliance with such a broad set of requirements?

Any answers to these questions inevitably raise further questions, particularly in relation to the third question. A Participation Income would generate a variety of behavioural responses. Some claimants would seek just enough voluntary labour to enable them to claim the Participation Income; organisations would offer this bare minimum; and administrators would develop their own rules of thumb to enable them to grant the Participation Income whenever possible. De Wispelaere and Stirton call this 'creative compliance',[699] and it would quickly compromise any public acceptability of Participation Income posited on the idea that only genuine participation in society entitles someone to the benefit. Perhaps more importantly, a Participation Income would compromise the justice of the reciprocity experienced by claimants – for they *would* be *claimants*, and not citizens receiving a civic minimum.

Would arguing for a Participation Income make it more or less likely that we would one day see a Citizen's Income? A Participation Income would not be a Citizen's Income, but it could soon become one, because relatively few people would not receive the Participation Income, and

---

697 Fitzpatrick, Tony (1999) *Freedom and security: An introduction to the Basic Income debate*, Basingstoke: Macmillan, pp 101, 111–22

698 It is not unusual for academics not to factor in the administrative questions that come naturally to those of us who have administered the benefits system, however long ago our experience of doing so might be.

699 De Wispelaere, Jurgen and Stirton, Lindsay (2008) 'Why Participation Income might not be such a great idea after all', *Citizen's Income Newsletter*, issue 3, pp 3–8

because the administrative burden involved in evaluating who was and who was not participating in society would soon lead the government to abolish the participation conditions and establish a true Citizen's Income. We might therefore see a Participation Income as a politically acceptable way to establish a Citizen's Income. Alternatively, we might find that the difficulties of establishing and managing a Participation Income were so onerous (as the implementation of the much more restricted *revenu minimum d'insertion* in France proved to be[700]) that a difficult experience of something like a Citizen's Income could make it much more difficult to argue for a true Citizen's Income. As Hermione Parker has suggested, 'a major public education exercise is necessary before voters are likely to adjust their value systems to the problems of post-industrial societies. Fudging the issues could delay this process'.[701]

---

[700] Euzéby, Chantal (1994) 'From "insertion" income to "existence" income', *Citizen's Income Bulletin*, no 17, January, pp 14–18
[701] Parker, Hermione (1994) 'Citizen's Income', *Citizen's Income Bulletin*, no 17, January, pp 4–12, p 9

CHAPTER 16

What can a Citizen's Income *not* cope with?

> [A Citizen's Income] is the fairest way of sharing out rights, roles, obligations and access in our present situation, but it would not give rise to a just society without an equally determined policy commitment to communal resources for sharing in a good quality of national and local life. (Bill Jordan)[702]

A universal benefit is precisely that: the same for everyone. As we have seen, there are some very good reasons for universalising benefits as much as possible. The higher the proportion of benefits that are universal, the more we shall increase choices in the labour market, the more efficient will be our economy, the more choices people will have over relationships, over household structure, and over how their household organises its income-generating activity, and the more we shall know ourselves to be members of a single society.

But there will always be some aspects of household budgets that cannot be dealt with by universal benefits. Housing costs are different in different parts of the country, and can be different from one side of the road to the other; and because a number of factors are involved when people decide where to live (and particularly where they are employed and where other family members live), the labour market and universal benefits between them are unlikely to provide sufficient funds for housing costs for every household in every place. A family living in a northern town might well be able to afford to rent or buy housing of sufficient size for a family if both partners are earning and they receive Citizen's Incomes, while a family living in an inner London borough, because that is where they are employed, and because that is where other family members provide childcare, might well need additional funds in order to rent or buy accommodation of sufficient size.

Fuel costs pose problems similar to those posed by housing costs; and someone with a disability that means that they are unable to earn

---

702 Jordan, Bill (1992) 'Basic Income and the common good', pp 155–177 in Van Parijs, Philippe, *Arguing for Basic Income*, London: Verso, p 173

a living might have housing and care needs that a universal benefit would never be able to cover. A particularly difficult issue is child care costs. If a child's parents are both employed full-time, then child care will have to be provided by someone other than the parents. Either relatives will care for the child while the parents are working, or the parents will have to pay an individual or an organiSation, such as a nursery. The number of hours of child care required will vary, and costs will vary depending on how child care is provided. Transport costs pose issues similar to child care costs. They are costs that fall on a household because someone is employed, and they vary between different people because people's journeys to work can be very different.

This suggests that any Citizen's Income scheme will need to be supplemented by other benefits. The question then arises: on what basis should those benefits be paid? In this chapter I shall choose three of the cases that we have outlined because they present somewhat different issues. We have no control over whether we have a disability; we have some control over how much we spend on heating our homes; and we have some choice over the location and quality of the accommodation that we occupy. This means that it is simpler to solve the income needs of people with disabilities than it is to solve the problems of housing or fuel costs. Someone's housing costs (and the related fuel costs) are a moving target affected to some extent by our choices, whereas the care and living costs of someone with a disability are not subject to personal choice in the same way.

I shall also look at 'passported benefits': benefits that someone receives because they receive other benefits. Here the question at issue is how to choose who should receive such benefits as free prescriptions. The decision is generally made with reference to someone's position in relation to the means-tested benefits system. A Citizen's Income would change that system. The 'passport' mechanism therefore needs to be discussed.

Disability

People with physical or mental disabilities would, of course, receive a Citizen's Income along with everybody else; but whereas a Citizen's Income would provide additional choices for people in the labour market, or able to enter it, such additional choices might not be available to disabled people simply because of their disabilities. In addition, many disabled people have care needs beyond those experienced by people without disabilities.

As things stand, social care needs are assessed by local authorities, the contributory or means-tested Employment and Support Allowance is paid to provide a subsistence income to people who cannot earn one; the non-means-tested Disability Living Allowance (for under 65s) or Attendance Allowance (for people over 65) is paid to help to fund the care that disabled people need; someone caring for a disabled person can claim means-tested Carer's Allowance; and disabled people are increasingly given a local authority budget to enable them to pay for the care that they need. It would make sense to maintain local provision for payment for care, and to roll Attendance Allowance and Disabled Living Allowance into it. One immediate benefit of a Citizen's Income is that it would for the first time provide an unconditional income for relatives who choose to care for people with disabilities: an income that should continue to be topped up by payment from the local authority budget allocated to the disabled person for whom they care.[703] But this still leaves unsolved the problem that many disabled people cannot earn a living, so they will need to receive a higher Citizen's Income, an additional unconditional benefit, or an additional conditional benefit.[704] There will be arguments for and against all three of these options, but it would probably be best not to complicate the administration of the Citizen's Income itself. It would be preferable to pay either an additional unconditional and non-withdrawable benefit, or to pay a means-tested benefit – the latter not being such a problem as means-tested benefits in other contexts, because the disabled person will already be suffering from labour market disincentives of a different kind, and any related to a means-tested disability benefit would be likely to be small by comparison.

Whatever route is chosen to provide for the care and subsistence needs of people with disabilities,

> the goal is clear. Those adults requiring care should have an unconditional and adequate income that enables them to make the kind of choices that the rest of us take for granted. Both they and their carers should be able to relate to each

---

[703] Leaper, R.A.B. (1986) 'Cash and caring', *BIRG Bulletin*, no 5, Spring, pp 20–22

[704] 'Implications of Basic Income for people with disabilities', *BIRG Bulletin*, no 7, Spring 1988, pp 10–19; Howard, Marilyn and Lawrence, Tim (1996) 'Private provision – public concern: Meeting the needs of people with disabilities', *Citizen's Income Bulletin*, no 22, July, pp 9–11

other and the outside world with dignity. Basic income would play a part in bringing this about. (Tony Walter)[705]

Housing costs[706]

The UK has traditionally focused on four ways of providing housing support: the provision of social housing at affordable, below-market rents; the regulation of private sector rents; means-tested Housing Benefit; and tax benefits for owner-occupiers.

Housing Benefit is means-tested, is withdrawn at a rate of 65 per cent as earnings rise, and is therefore a major cause of the poverty and unemployment traps into which those with low earnings potential will frequently fall. While Housing Benefit is available to those in work and to those out of work, and so in theory should not prove a disincentive to seeking employment, the high marginal deduction rate to which it contributes will certainly be a disincentive to taking employment if there is no certainty that net income will rise sufficiently to make the transition financially worthwhile. In his report on the future of social housing, John Hills offers the example of a couple with two children, paying a rent of £120 per week. In this case, the household would gain only £23 a week from an increase in earnings from £100 to £400 per week.[707] This will remain largely true when Housing Benefit is integrated with 'Universal Credit': for although a household's housing element will not push the marginal deduction rate above 65 per cent at any particular earnings level, it will impose that marginal deduction rate across a much wider earnings range.

This is one of the reasons for questioning the way in which Housing Benefit is calculated and administered. The other is that Housing Benefit pays up to 100 per cent of unregulated private market rents, and this creates an incentive for landlords to maximise rental return from Housing Benefit claimants, and a lack of incentive for Housing Benefit claimants to seek cheaper accommodation. (As Stuart Lowe has pointed out, social housing rents are often little different from private rents.[708]) A household not on Housing Benefit will balance affordability against housing need, thus creating a genuine market in

---

[705] Walter, Tony (1989) *Basic Income: Freedom from poverty, freedom to work*, London: Marion Boyars, p 131

[706] Eliot, Jake (2011) 'Where does housing fit in?' *Citizen's Income Newsletter*, issue 2, pp 14–16

[707] Hills, John (2007) *Ends and means: the future roles of social housing in England*, London: CASE, LSE

[708] Lowe, Stuart (2011) *The housing debate*, Bristol: Policy Press, p 236

rented accommodation in which price is the link between demand and supply. If their children grow up and move out then a couple might seek somewhere smaller, thus freeing larger accommodation for households in more need of it. Such market mechanisms work with nothing like the same efficiency for Housing Benefit applicants[709]. This is apart from the fact that expenditure on Housing Benefit is projected to rise to £24 billion by 2014/15:[710] hence the government's restricting of total benefit levels, and the establishment of the Local Housing Allowance: a specification of the amounts of rent that will be covered by Housing Benefit, calculated for each housing area. Since the budget in June 2010, tenants can only claim 100 per cent of the rent for the cheapest 30 per cent of properties in the local area, and the government has changed from 25 to 35 the age below which single people can only claim Housing Benefit for a room in a shared house rather than for self-contained accommodation.

Due to the inefficiencies and structural problems within the UK housing market, dedicated support for housing costs will be needed for the foreseeable future. In expensive areas it is simply not possible for many households to afford rent or mortgage payments for the size of accommodation that they need. So how should housing costs be met if, in the future, our benefits system is based on a Citizen's Income, which by definition is the same for everyone and is *not* adjusted for housing costs? In the end, the only solution is to reduce the cost of housing. This will only happen if far more of it is built, and if households have both the opportunity and the incentive to move out of accommodation that is now larger than they need. In the meantime, we are left with a choice between different kinds of housing benefit: the current means–tested variety, or a flat rate, individualised housing benefit, adjusted for the level of housing costs in an area. The logic of the latter suggestion is the same as that for a Citizen's Income: that it would be simple to administer, that it would not create market distortions, and that, although the rich might be able to pay for housing without it, it would be no problem for them to receive it because they would be paying more in tax than they would be receiving in universal housing benefit.[711]

---

[709] (From 2013 if a family in social housing has more bedrooms than it is deemed to need, then its Housing Benefit will be restricted: a rather draconian attempt to create an incentive to move to smaller accommodation)

[710] Smith, The Rt Hon. Iain Duncan, Secretary of State for Work and Pensions (2010) Speech to Institute for Public Policy Research, Tuesday 7 December

[711] Torry, Malcolm (2002) 'A contribution to debate: The reform of Housing Benefit', *Citizen's Income Newsletter*, issue no 1, pp 10–11

In the absence of such a radical solution to the problem of housing costs, we must look for ways of improving the situation for hard-pressed tenants. As Lowe has pointed out, rental and house purchase markets are now important factors in the provision of welfare, broadly understood; and the social division between households in rented accommodation and owner occupied households is at least as important as any division caused by differences in earned income.[712] A Citizen's Income cannot on its own solve the problem of housing costs, but two things it can do: because its marginal deduction rate would be zero, for many households it would leave a residual means-tested housing benefit as the only means-testing that they would suffer, providing an incentive to move to cheaper accommodation and to increase earned income in order to escape from means-testing; and in a situation in which inequalities are multiplying, and in which sources of social cohesion are hard to find, a Citizen's Income can bind us together as a society – a not inconsiderable advantage. However different people's earned incomes might be, or however different their relationships, household structures, assets, and housing tenures, every individual would receive a Citizen's Income. That has got to be good for individuals, for households, and for society.

Fuel poverty

Another problem that a Citizen's Income would not solve is fuel poverty. Poorer people often live in accommodation of poor quality. Insulation might not be adequate, heating systems might not be efficient, and, on larger estates, tenants might have little control over the type, level, and cost of heating, and in particular might only have electricity available for heating, and this tends to be more expensive than gas. If householders have a coin or key meter then they might not have available to them the cheaper direct debit tariffs. Either fuel bills will be higher than they can afford, or they will turn the heating down or off, meaning that their homes will not be sufficiently warm, and health problems will be the result. A recent report estimates that five million individuals are currently affected by fuel poverty.[713]

The only long-term solution is to improve the quality of the entire housing stock: but, in the meantime, ensuring that households can afford

---

[712] Lowe, Stuart (2011) *The Housing debate*, Bristol: Policy Press, pp 199–223, 237; cf. Matsaganis, Manos and Flevotomou, Maria (2007) 'A Basic Income for housing? Simulating a universal housing transfer in the Netherlands and Sweden', *Basic Income Studies*, vol 2, no 2, pp 1–25

[713] Hills, John (2011) *Fuel poverty: The problem and its measurement*, interim report of the Fuel Poverty Review, London: CASE, LSE, p 22

sufficient heating to enable them to keep warm must be a priority. A Citizen's Income would not solve this problem, but it would do for fuel poverty what it would do for housing costs: it would give to many households a larger number of options. Households in which no-one was employed might seek employment because with a Citizen's Income it would be more worthwhile to do so. Sufficient warmth would therefore become more affordable. Or people already employed might seek higher earnings because it would be more worthwhile to do so; and more people would start their own businesses, because the Citizen's Income would give them sufficient financial security to take the risk of coming off means-tested benefits and relying on their own skills and motivation. As we have seen, because a Citizen's Income would provide such additional options, it would be easier for people to move to new accommodation, and this might be better insulated and more efficiently heated.

A Citizen's Income would not, on its own, solve the problem of fuel poverty, just as it would not solve the problem of expensive, inadequate, or absent housing: but it would begin to make a difference to the options available to thousands, and perhaps millions, of households, and it would therefore make a contribution to the solution to fuel poverty.

Passported benefits

By 'passported benefits' we mean those benefits to which working-age claimants of certain means-tested benefits are automatically entitled: for example, free school meals, free prescriptions, and free dental treatment.[714]

This definition was occasioned by the UK government's Social Security Advisory Committee's review of passported benefits in the light of the impending transition from 'Tax Credits' and Jobseeker's Allowance to 'Universal Credit'. If a Citizen's Income were to be implemented, then an even more thorough review would clearly be required. The transition to 'Universal Credit' might result in a few households not in receipt of passported benefits receiving them, and some in receipt not receiving them; but a Citizen's Income would automatically remove large numbers of households from means-tested benefits (and would make it advantageous, and therefore likely, for other households to abandon means-tested benefits in favour of employment or self-employment), which would mean that far fewer households

[714] Social Security Advisory Committee (2011) 'Public consultation: passported benefits under Universal Credit – review and advice', press release, 15 June

would be entitled to current passported benefits if the regulations relating to them remained as they are.

A small Citizen's Income would require a continuing means-tested safety net, particularly for housing costs, so there would still be a mechanism for testing some of the poorer households for passported benefits, if such benefits were regarded as beneficial in their current form:[715] but another approach would be to make the current passported benefits universal. So, for instance, school meals could be free for every child. This would be no more of a problem than Child Benefit is now: that is, it would not be a problem, because wealthier families would be paying far more in Income Tax than they would be receiving in the value of school meals. The benefits of universal school meals could be considerable. No longer would a school's families be divided into those receiving free school meals and those not; and universal provision of nutritious school meals would improve child health and thus the health of the whole population in the future.

Further problems would arise, of course. Schools receive additional funding for children receiving free school meals. Thus a passported benefit has itself become a passport to other benefits. It would not be difficult to find another way to allocate additional resources to schools facing particular challenges.

Conclusions

There is a case for contingency benefits – benefits related to particular needs, such as disability – and there might be a case for means-testing them. There is a case for financial help with actual housing costs, and for a structure of payments to allow for individual choice over the type of accommodation that someone occupies: though care would need to be taken not to disincentivise employment or to incentivise the occupation of expensive or over-large accommodation. There is a similar case, though not an identical one, to be made in relation to fuel costs, child care costs, and transport costs: and similar caveats to be offered. If means-testing of some variety were to be retained alongside a Citizen's Income, then currently passported benefits would either have to be made universal (for instance, school meals for every child) or access would need to be controlled by a household's relationship to remaining means-tested benefits such as Housing Benefit.

---

[715] Miller, Anne (2012) 'Passported benefits and a Citizen's Income', *Citizen's Income Newsletter*, issue 1, pp 1–4

The important thing is to allocate benefit types on the basis of rational argument. Housing costs vary, and we have some choice over the housing we occupy, so it makes sense to tailor income to actual housing costs and to a family's ability to pay them, and also to construct a system that incentivises a family to achieve housing costs that they can manage on a combination of earnings and universal benefits. But subsistence costs are much less amenable to personal choice, and everybody's subsistence costs are similar. It therefore makes sense to pay a universal benefit that makes a substantial contribution to subsistence costs, and to expect people to be able to earn the rest of the income they need in a labour market which, in the context of a new benefits structure, would offer them the hours of employment, or the self-employment opportunities, that they require.

The ideal situation would be a Citizen's Income on which could be constructed additional benefits for contingencies such as disability and housing costs. As Richard Titmuss has put it: 'In all the main spheres of need, some structure of universalism is an essential prerequisite to selective positive discrimination:' the universal foundation providing a 'sense of community' and providing the basis for a 'welfare society' rather than just a 'welfare state'.[716]

This chapter has been about the things that a Citizen's Income cannot do: but it is important to remember that the rest of the book has been about what a Citizen's Income *can* do. It *can* make the employment market, and therefore the economy, more efficient; it *can* create a more cohesive society; it *can* make it more worthwhile for all of us to seek paid employment, to seek self-employment, to seek new skills, and to increase our earned income; and it *can* give to every individual and household more freedom to decide how to organise their activity and their time.

There is so much that a Citizen's Income *can* do that it is surely essential for the government to test a Citizen's Income through a pilot project. The pilot project's designers would need to decide what to do about passported benefits: so while it would be possible to leave to one side questions relating to disability, fuel, and housing costs, questions relating to passported benefits would need to be answered before embarking on the pilot project.

---

[716] Titmuss, Richard (1968) *Commitment to welfare*, London: George Allen & Unwin, p 135

CHAPTER 17

A brief summary[717]

What is a Citizen's Income?

A Citizen's Income is an unconditional, automatic and non-withdrawable payment to each individual as a right of citizenship.

A Citizen's Income is sometimes called a Basic Income, a Universal Grant, or a Universal Benefit.

A Citizen's Income scheme would phase out as many tax allowances and as many existing state financed cash benefits as possible, and replace them with a Citizen's Income paid automatically to every man, woman and child.

The Citizen's Income attack on poverty is three pronged. Such a scheme would

- ameliorate the poverty and unemployment traps, hence boosting employment;
- provide a safety net from which no citizen would be excluded;
- create a platform on which all citizens are free to build.

A Citizen's Income scheme would encourage individual freedom and responsibility and would help to

- bring about social cohesion. Everybody is entitled to a Citizen's Income and everybody pays tax on all other income;
- end perverse incentives that discourage work and savings.

A Citizen's Income would be simple and efficient and would be:

- affordable within current revenue and expenditure constraints;
- easy to understand. It would be a universal entitlement based on citizenship that is non-contributory, non-means-tested and non-taxable;
- cheap to administer and to automate.

---

[717] This summary is drawn from an introductory booklet published by the Citizen's Income Trust in 2007. The complete text, along with calculations for a revenue-neutral Citizen's Income scheme, can be found on the website www.citizensincome.org

How would it work?

A Citizen's Income scheme would coordinate the Income Tax and benefits systems. A single government agency would credit the Citizen's Incomes automatically, and would recoup the cost via Income Tax levied on *all* income, rather than running separate systems of means testing, benefit withdrawal, and taxation. Instead of different rules for claimants and taxpayers, everybody would be treated alike.

Automatic payments. Each week or each month, every legal resident would automatically be credited with the Citizen's Income appropriate to his or her age. For most adults this could be done through the banking system, and for children it could be done through the bank accounts of their parents. For adults without bank accounts special provisions would be necessary. Citizen's Income supplements would be paid to older people and to those with chronic disabilities, but there would be no differences on account of gender or marital status, nor on account of work status, contribution record, or living arrangements.

Tax-free and without means test. The Citizen's Incomes would be tax-free and without a means test, but tax would be payable on all, or almost all, other income. This is necessary in order to finance the scheme. The rate of tax would depend on the Citizen's Income amounts. The higher the Citizen's Income, the higher the tax rate

There would be various ways of funding a Citizen's Income. The most commonly discussed method is to fund it by removing tax allowances and reducing means-tested and most contributory benefits, but a Citizen's Income could also be funded by a land value tax, a carbon tax, or any one of a variety of consumption taxes.

Six fundamental changes

- **Citizenship becomes the basis of entitlement**, subject to a minimum period of legal residency. Every citizen would have a small independent income, whether or not they are in paid employment.
- **The individual would be the tax/benefit unit.** The Citizen's Income would be paid to individuals, not couples, families or households. Unlike the existing benefits system, a Citizen's Income would be symmetrical between men and women. Marriage, civil partnership and cohabitation would be neither subsidised nor penalised.
- **The Citizen's Income would not be withdrawn as earnings and other income rises**, nor would it be reduced by owning assets. It would be a base on which to build without having to report to

officials every minor change in earnings or household composition. Benefits fraud would be reduced significantly. Work and savings of all types would be encouraged.

- **Availability-for-work rules would be abolished**. Under many current systems, young people in education or training, unemployed people who study or train for more than a few hours a week, or who undertake occasional casual employment, forfeit benefits. With a Citizen's Income this would not happen. School attendance, further and higher education, voluntary work, vocational training and retraining would all be facilitated.
- **Access to a Citizen's Income would be easy and unconditional**. Instead of the current maze of regulations experienced by claimants in most developed countries, often resulting in perverse incentives, everybody would know their entitlement and their obligations. Take-up, as with the UK's Child Benefit, would be nearly 100 per cent.
- **Benefit levels could be indexed to earnings or to GDP per capita rather than to prices**. To index the Citizen's Income lower than this would merely store up problems for the future. While all citizens would benefit from a more generous payment, there would be an equal and opposite pressure against Income Tax rises to fund it. So two basic variables – the Citizen's Income level and the Income Tax rate required to fund it – would be inherently linked and stable.

Three frequently asked questions

Would people still work if they received a Citizen's Income?

Under the current system, in spite of sizeable benefit withdrawal rates, the vast majority of working age adults choose to seek employment. With a Citizen's Income the withdrawal rates would fall, making it even more likely that working age adults would seek employment.

At the moment, parents and other carers find that employment for a few hours a week brings only small financial gains – again, because of the benefit withdrawal rates. A Citizen's Income would reduce this problem, so those working age carers who cannot or do not wish to seek full-time employment would be more likely to seek and to accept part-time employment.

Is it fair to ask people in employment to pay for everyone to receive a Citizen's Income?

As a society we have chosen to fund payments to those not in paid work out of general taxation. At the moment, those in employment pay for the benefits received by people who are not. With a Citizen's Income scheme both those currently receiving means tested benefits, and those not currently receiving them, would receive a Citizen's Income. This is fairer than the current system.

Isn't guaranteeing a right to work a better way to prevent poverty?

The best way to prevent poverty is through well-paid employment; and the best way to ensure the widespread availability of such employment is to make the labour market as free and as flexible as possible, and to ensure that people in employment keep as much as possible of any additional income that they earn. A Citizen's Income achieves this. It would therefore prevent poverty in ways in which a means-tested system cannot.

Figure 17.1 shows what a Citizen's Income looks like.

Figure 17.1: Graphical representation of a Citizen's Income

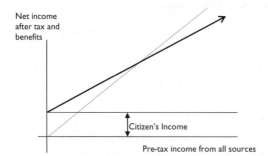

——— This line, at 45°, shows what net income would be if there were no benefits and no taxation

——— This line shows what net income would be with a Citizen's Income and a flat rate Income Tax

AFTERWORD

Hermione Parker concludes her *Instead of the dole* with some words of Barbara Wootton:

> The limits of the possible constantly shift, and those who ignore them are apt to win in the end. Again and again, I have had the satisfaction of seeing the laughable idealism of one generation evolve into the accepted common-place of the next.[718]

In the UK during the 1920s, family allowances were 'seen as an issue for cranks and utopians', and the 1930s were a time of recession and rising unemployment; but by 1946 every family with more than one child was in receipt of family allowances.[719]

As this book has shown, a Citizen's Income is no longer an issue for cranks and utopians. Given the significant benefits that a Citizen's Income would offer to society and to the economy, it is an issue that every policy maker needs to address. It is high time for a substantial pilot project, and, after that, for implementation.

---

[718] Wootton, Barbara (1967) *In a world I never made*, London: George Allen & Unwin, p 279, quoted in Parker, Hermione (1989) *Instead of the dole: An enquiry into integration of the tax and benefit systems*, London: Routledge, p 384

[719] Levitas, Ruth (2012) 'Utopia calling: eradicating child poverty in the United Kingdom and beyond', pp 449–73 in Minujin, Alberto and Nandy, Shailen (eds) *Global child poverty and well-being: Measurement, concepts, policy and action*, Bristol: Policy Press, p 450

SELECT BIBLIOGRAPHY

A complete bibliography can be found at **www.citizensincome.org**
The main journals referenced are:

BIRG Bulletin

CIRG Bulletin

CI Bulletin

Citizen's Income Newsletter (The *BIRG Bulletin* and the *Citizen's Income Bulletin* are numbered successively in a single series. They were followed by the *Citizen's Income Newsletter*, which is numbered separately within each year. All of them are published by the Citizen's Income Trust (previously the Basic Income Research Group), London.)

Basic Income Studies (Basic Income Studies is an internet journal and every article is paginated 1–.)

Atkinson, A. B. (1995) *Public economics in action: The Basic Income/flat tax proposal*, Oxford: Clarendon Press

Birnbaum, Simon (2012) *Basic Income reconsidered: Social justice, liberalism, and the demands of equality*, New York: Palgrave Macmillan

Brittan, Samuel and Webb, Steven (1990) *Beyond the welfare state: An examination of Basic Incomes in a market economy*, Aberdeen: Aberdeen University Press

Caputo, Richard (ed.) (2012) *Basic Income guarantee and politics: International experiences and perspectives on the viability of income guarantee*, New York: Palgrave Macmillan

Cunliffe, John and Erreygers, Guido (eds) (2004) *The origins of universal grants: An anthology of historical writings on basic capital and Basic Income*, Basingstoke: Palgrave Macmillan

Fitzpatrick, Tony (1999) *Freedom and security: An introduction to the Basic Income debate*, Basingstoke: Macmillan

Groot, Loek (2004) *Basic Income, unemployment and compensatory justice*, Dordrecht: Kluwer Academic Publishers

Huws, Ursula (1997) *Flexibility and security: Towards a new European balance*, London: Citizen's Income Trust

Jordan, Bill (1987) *Rethinking welfare*, Oxford: Basil Blackwell

Jordan, Bill, Agulnik, Phil, Burbidge, Duncan and Duffin, Stuart (2000) *Stumbling towards Basic Incomes: The prospects for tax-benefit integration*, London: Citizen's Income Trust

Murray, Matthew C. and Pateman, Carole (eds) (2012) *Basic Income worldwide: Horizons of reform*, New York: Palgrave Macmillan

Parker, Hermione (1989) *Instead of the dole: An enquiry into integration of the tax and benefit systems*, London: Routledge

Parker, Hermione (ed.) (1993) *Citizen's Income and women*, London: Citizen's Income Trust

Parker, Hermione (1995) *Taxes, benefits and family life: The seven deadly traps*, London: Institute of Economic Affairs

Rhys Williams, Brandon (1989) *Stepping stones to independence* (edited by Parker, Hermione), Aberdeen: Aberdeen University Press, for the One Nation Group of Conservative MPs

Standing, Guy (2005) *Promoting income security as a right: Europe and North America*, London: Anthem Press

Van Parijs, Philippe (ed.) (1992) *Arguing for Basic Income: Ethical foundations for a radical reform*, London: Verso

Van Parijs, Philippe (1995) *Real freedom for all: What (if anything) can justify capitalism?* Oxford: Clarendon Press

Walter, Tony (1989) *Basic Income: Freedom from poverty, freedom to work*, London: Marion Boyars

Widerquist, Karl and Howard, Michael W. (eds) (2012) *Alaska's Permanent Fund dividend*, New York: Palgrave Macmillan

Widerquist, Karl, Lewis, Michael Anthony, and Pressman, Steven (2005) *The ethics and economics of the Basic Income guarantee*, Aldershot: Ashgate

Names index

n denotes an entry in a footnote and is followed by the number of the note.

Subject index

n denotes an entry in a footnote and is followed by the number of the note.